EXPLORING THE
WORSHIP SPECTRUM

Books in the Counterpoints Series

Church Life

Exploring Theology

EXPLORING THE WORSHIP SPECTRUM

6 VIEWS

- **Paul Zahl**
- **Harold Best**
- **Joe Horness**
- **Don Williams**
- **Robert Webber**
- **Sally Morgenthaler**

- **Paul E. Engle** *series editor*
- **Paul A. Basden** *general editor*

GRAND RAPIDS, MICHIGAN 49530 USA

Exploring the Worship Spectrum
Copyright © 2004 by Paul A. Basden

Requests for information should be addressed to:

Zondervan, *Grand Rapids, Michigan 49530*

Library of Congress Cataloging-in-Publication Data

Exploring the worship spectrum : six views / contributors, Paul F. M. Zahl . . .
    [et al.] ; Paul A. Basden, general editor.—1st ed.
        p. cm.—(Counterpoints)
    Includes bibliographical references and index.
    ISBN 0-310-24759-4
    1. Public worship.   I. Zahl, Paul F. M.   II. Basden, Paul, 1955–.
III. Counterpoints (Grand Rapids, Mich.)
BV15.E93 2004
264—dc22   2003024153

Printed in the United States of America

04 05 06 07 08 09 10 /❖ DC/ 10 9 8 7 6 5 4 3 2

Dedicated to Robert Brandon,

worship leader,

lead worshiper,

servant of the Word and Spirit in music.

I thank God for your friendship

and collaboration over the years.

I am happily in your debt.

CONTENTS

BIBLE TRANSLATIONS

Paul Zahl: *Revised Standard Version*

Harold Best: Various versions

Joe Horness: *New American Standard Bible*

Don Williams: Various versions

Robert Webber, Sally Morgenthaler, Paul A. Basden: *New International Version*

Other versions:

INTRODUCTION

Paul A. Basden

Worship is once again hitting the big time, getting its due, coming into its own. Whether or not that is a good thing, you will have to decide for yourself. But it certainly is not a new thing.

Throughout Christian history, public worship has attracted attention, stimulated discussion, and even provoked contention. Christ-followers have debated controversial issues—when and whom to baptize, how to observe Holy Communion, how often and how long to preach—only to watch those debates degenerate into rancorous fights and full-blown schisms. For example, Eastern and Western churchmen fought over the role of icons in worship, eventually dividing Christendom; Calvinists killed Anabaptists over the baptism question; Luther split with Zwingli over the meaning of the Lord's Supper; Puritans separated from Anglicans over the priority of the preached Word.

Worship wars have been ugly before. Will history repeat itself?

Today's worship debates center mostly on these overlapping questions:

- Should adoration of the one true God express itself in one true way of worship?
- Since God is one and longs for his people to be one, should our public worship be more unified than diverse?
- Does the freedom of worshipers compromise the integrity of the One we worship?
- Does worship preference reflect our legitimate freedom in Christ or our selfish sinful nature?

- Simply put, does God want all people to offer public worship to him in more or less the same way? Or does God affirm and bless all of our approaches that seek to give him glory and honor? And if he blesses some and not others, what are his criteria for rejecting those approaches that do not make the grade? (And while we are at it, why has he not been clearer about communicating the grading scale?)

No one in his or her right mind wants to fight over worship. Keeping debates civil requires clarity and humility. Both of these qualities can be enhanced if we will look at worship through the eyes of theology, the Bible, and church history.

THROUGH THE EYES OF THEOLOGY

Worship is inherently theological. It is primarily about God. Specifically, it is about how Christ-followers offer to God their love, gratitude, and praise. Several theologians have served us well by defining public worship in ways we can understand. For example:

- "True worship is that exercise of the human spirit that confronts us with the mystery and marvel of God in whose presence the most appropriate and salutary response is adoring love."[1]
- "Christian worship is the glad response of Christians to the holy, redemptive love of God made known in Jesus Christ."[2]
- "Worship, in all its grades and kinds, is the response of the creature to the Eternal."[3]
- "The [Trinitarian] view of worship is that it is the gift of participating through the Spirit in the incarnate Son's communion with the Father."[4]
- "Worship is ...
  - To quicken the conscience by the holiness of God,
  - To feed the mind with the truth of God,
  - To purge the imagination by the beauty of God,
  - To open the heart to the love of God,
  - To devote the will to the purpose of God."[5]

Notice the underlying commonality: Worship is our response to God's holy nature and redemptive acts. God's love evokes our love. But having agreed on that core conviction, we find that these definitions of worship begin to diverge. Some emphasize God's mystery, others his revelation; some stress God's holiness, others his loving-kindness; some are monotheistic, others Christocentric, still others Trinitarian.

The conclusion? There is no ideal definition of worship. No one has defined worship so completely as to plumb the depths of this divine-human encounter. To make matters more interesting, ancient creeds and modern confessions of faith have not settled on a single orthodox understanding of and approach to worship that has won the approval of Christians worldwide. There is no Chalcedonian formula for corporate worship.

Many believers say, "If you will just read your Bible, you will see how God wants his people to worship. (And it's usually the way I worship!)" What exactly does the Bible say about worship?

THROUGH THE EYES OF THE BIBLE[6]

A brief glance at worship in the Bible provides significant clues about how we should understand and practice it. Abraham built altars and offered sacrifices to God as a way of thanking him for making and keeping promises that one day Abraham would be a blessing to all nations. During the Exodus, Moses continued to build altars and offer animal sacrifices, but he introduced new elements as well: singing, festival days, reading God's covenant, sprinkling worshipers with the "blood of the covenant," receiving offerings, and building a tabernacle.

King David revolutionized Israelite worship. It all began when he located the long-lost Ark of the Covenant and brought it to Jerusalem, leading the joyous procession by dancing in such an undignified manner that it ultimately cost him his marriage. That "honest to God" mind-set led him to write songs for corporate and individual worship that have lasted for centuries as the Psalms. He organized Israel's worship by assigning the priests and Levites to be ministers of temple worship, appointing them as gatekeepers, musicians, and treasurers.

As Israel's worship matured and evolved, idolatry and immorality were lurking in the shadows. The people preferred to worship false gods of their own making—which they could see and manipulate—rather than worship the one true God whom they could not control. So God sent prophets to judge his people and to call them to heartfelt worship and righteous living. Persistent disobedience led to permanent judgment as God sent pagan nations to defeat both Israel and Judah, destroy the city of Jerusalem and Solomon's temple, and thrust many of the survivors into exile.

During the next five and a half centuries (587 B.C.–4 B.C.), worship changed dramatically. Sacrifice and music all but disappeared. In their place emerged three practices: reading the Torah, saying prayers, and reciting psalms. Keeping the Torah in all its detail became the goal of worship. Upon returning to the Promised Land, the Israelites formed houses of instruction and worship called synagogues. The synagogue service included a call to worship, extended prayers, recitation of the *shema* (Deuteronomy 6:4), Scripture readings, and a sermon. It also became the transition from Old Testament worship to New Testament worship.

To the chagrin of many Christians, nowhere in the New Testament can we find a full description, detailed order, or divinely ordained style of worship. Instead what we find are pointed reminders to gather together as believers in order to engage in several practices that summarize worship: praying, singing, reading and preaching and teaching Scripture, collecting offerings, baptizing, and observing the Lord's Supper. But no prescribed approach is sanctioned as God's favorite. Instead we see diversity early on.

- When we read about the early church in Acts, we discover that the first believers in Jerusalem gave priority to the apostles' teaching, Holy Communion, prayers, and communal living;
- When we turn to Paul's earlier letters, we find him correcting—not rejecting—the charismatic impulses of Corinthian worshipers, encouraging them to speak in tongues, interpret tongues, sing in the Spirit, and perform miracles;
- When we look at Paul's prison letters, we notice that worship in the Asia Minor churches of Ephesus and Colossae consisted primarily of singing, teaching, and thanksgiving.

Whoever looks to the New Testament for liturgical uniformity meets just the opposite. Within thirty-five years of Jesus' death and resurrection we can discern at least these three distinct patterns of worship in the early church.

To summarize: The Old Testament reveals varying emphases in worship in different periods in Israel's history, while the New Testament unveils varying approaches to worship based on different locations and cultures. If we turn from the Bible to church history, I wonder what we will find.

THROUGH THE EYES OF HISTORY[7]

The spontaneous praise and preaching of the New Testament house church evolved into structured two-part worship by the second century: the service of the Word and the service of the Table. This represented a fusion of the synagogue service and the Upper Room meal. It also introduced a formal approach to worship foreign to the New Testament. Once Christianity was legalized and legitimized early in the fourth century, public worship moved from simple homes and assembly halls to elaborate cathedrals and sanctuaries. Worship increasingly began to reflect secular culture.

During the next millennium (A.D. 500–1500), worship changed dramatically. Clergy became actors, laity became audience, and priests performed the worship: reading the Scriptures, offering prayers, handling the elements of the Mass. The Eucharist assumed exclusive priority, overshadowing all other acts of worship commended by the Bible. In essence, "God had become unapproachable; Christ's death had become unintelligible; the Spirit's power had become unavailable."[8] Few similarities remained between the simple, heartfelt, participatory worship of the New Testament and the formal, lifeless, priest-led service of the Mass in the medieval church.

Several church leaders stepped forward in the sixteenth century to reform worship and reground it in the Bible. Chief among the reformers was Martin Luther. Luther abhorred the sacramentalism of his own Roman Catholic faith and sought to return the church to Word-centered worship. He replaced the standard seven sacraments with just two: baptism and Eucharist, both interpreted Christologically. He also stressed the importance of biblical preaching as a sign that the church was to be captivated by Holy Scripture alone.

Luther's friend, Ulrich Zwingli, was more radical in his approach to change. Believing that nothing in our sinful world could truly communicate the beauty of God's spiritual world, Zwingli rejected music and musical instruments (especially organs!). He dramatically parted ways with Luther over the Mass, convinced that the words of institution—"This is my body"—must be interpreted figuratively since the earthy elements of bread and wine could not be vehicles of divine grace.

Several years later, a new reformer, John Calvin, offered a moderating approach to their two extreme views. While he despised the empty, unbiblical ritualism of Roman worship, he wanted to avoid the excesses of Zwingli. He is best remembered for regarding the Mass as communion with the Lord, whose presence was dynamically active at the Supper; preferring divinely authored psalms to humanly written hymns; and stressing weekly exegetical preaching of the Bible.

While Calvin and Luther thought Zwingli went too far, some did not think he went far enough. A group of radical reformers emerged in central and northern Europe, known disparagingly as Anabaptists. They rejected infant baptism in favor of believers' baptism, state religion in favor of church-state separation, and the Old Testament in favor of the New Testament.

At the other end of the spectrum was the Church of England, the Anglicans, who appreciated royal privileges and retained numerous Roman formalities. The reformation of the Church of England came primarily through its archbishop of Canterbury, Thomas Cranmer, who compiled the *Book of Common Prayer* as the primary resource for church worship. Based squarely on the Bible, it reacquainted scores of believers with the Psalms, the Gospels, and Paul's letters—all in their own language.

If Roman Catholicism could not escape worship reform, neither could Anglicanism. Puritans sought to change the Church of England so they could remain members in good conscience, while Separatists became impatient and bolted from the flock to offer worship that was built more on Scripture than on tradition. One hundred years later, the brightest lights in the reform of Anglican worship were John and Charles Wesley. They organized spiritually hungry Englishmen into small groups of genuine biblical community where they studied the Scriptures, listened to lay preaching, sang joyfully, and served the poor. By the time the

Wesleys died at the end of the eighteenth century, worship in Europe was fragmented: one could find formal Romanists and Anglicans, semiformal Lutherans, less formal Calvinists and Puritans and Separatists, and informal Zwinglians, Anabaptists, and Wesleyans. Worship in America would show even more variety.

The earliest colonists in the New World brought their Anglican, Puritan, and Catholic faiths with them. Worship along the East Coast largely mirrored worship in Europe. But once the East Coast was settled, Americans moved west across the frontier. The religion that sprang up in this context was unexpectedly different; it became known as revivalism, named after its dominant emphasis on personal conversion via revival services. Frontier worship did away with formalities. Out went prayer books, educated ministers, and pipe organs. In came brush-arbor tents, song services, evangelistic sermons, and extended public invitations. In the process, the aim of worship changed dramatically. Worship was no longer for God. It was for the lost sinner who needed to be saved. The shadow of revivalism remains in much of our current worship practices.

While white Americans were worshiping out in the open as free men and women, black Americans were worshiping in private as slaves. If America's original sin was institutional slavery, then slavery's salvation was black worship. How slaves who were unjustly treated could accept the religion of their masters is beyond explanation. But the worship that was birthed in the midst of this evil and suffering has become a doxological treasure within American Christianity. Marked by dynamic and exciting preaching, lively audience participation, emotionally powerful music, heartfelt prayer, and otherworldly hope, these services called downtrodden slaves to patiently await the day when justice and goodness would prevail.

Pentecostal worship built on African-American worship, capturing its emotionality and adding an expectation of the Holy Spirit's immediate interruption into everyday life to bless, heal, and empower. Paying almost exclusive attention to the charismatic passages in Acts and 1 Corinthians, Pentecostals rejuvenated glossolalia (speaking in tongues), recovered body life in worship so that every member had a part to play, and reveled in prophecy, miracles, and singing in the Spirit.

SIX VIEWS OF WORSHIP

Theology, Bible, and history all unite in this witness: Worship has never been practiced in all places by all people in one way. God is too profound and people too diverse for that to happen. The question now becomes: Can we identify specific ways that people are worshiping today and explain why they are the most common approaches?

Some years ago I realized that the world of worship was changing rapidly and looked very different from what I knew growing up. That observation led me to visit numerous churches, participate in multiple worship services, and experience the richness of divergent liturgies and doxologies. At the same time, I began to read every book on worship that I could find. This time of hands-on exploration and academic research coincided with a request for me to teach a course on Christian worship at Beeson Divinity School, Samford University. Eventually I put my thoughts on paper. The result was *The Worship Maze: Finding a Style to Fit Your Church.*[9]

Soon after the book's publication, I realized that many people still failed to "get it." They were so busy defending their own approach to worship as "God's obvious preference" that they could never see the blind spots in their thinking. Then another idea occurred to me: Why not invite representatives from the most prominent schools of worship to present their views in a format where both strengths and weaknesses would be readily apparent? Why not provide a forum for interactive dialogue among scholars and practitioners who know their particular world of worship inside out? Thus was born the idea for *Exploring the Worship Spectrum: Six Views on the Church's Worship.*

Concluding that followers of Jesus Christ in North America are currently expressing their worship to God through six major approaches, I decided that my next task was to enlist capable writers who would clearly represent these views in an irenic spirit. God blessed the church in providing the authors who have contributed to this work. They are renowned for their leadership, writing, and speaking on worship. The contributors and their topics are the following:

Paul Zahl,   Formal-liturgical worship
Episcopal rector

Harold Best, retired music professor	Traditional hymn-based worship
Joe Horness, worship leader	Contemporary music-driven worship
Don Williams, Vineyard pastor	Charismatic worship
Robert Webber, theology professor	Blended worship
Sally Morgenthaler, consultant and speaker	Emerging worship

Each chapter summarizes a particular view of worship. The author explains the philosophy and practice inherent in this approach, examines its strengths and benefits, and acknowledges its limitations. Then each of the other five authors responds from his or her specific viewpoint by celebrating commonalities, suggesting inconsistencies, and highlighting blind spots. By the time you finish reading this book, you will understand the richness of worship as practiced in six major traditions as well as recognize clearly the strengths and weaknesses of the dominant approaches to worship in today's world.

It has ever been the case that worship is multiform, not uniform. God is not threatened by this reality—he ordained it; he expects it; he glories in it. As followers of him who said, "God is spirit, and his worshipers must worship in spirit and in truth" (John 4:24), we should celebrate every honest attempt to express love and devotion to God. Concurrently, our commitment to truth calls us to offer humble critique whenever we believe that a worship style has failed to provide a faithful expression of praise and sacrifice to God.

This book intends to be a forum where this kind of healthy dialogue can take place. May God use it to renew his people— the body of Christ—and make our worship more and more worthy of the One who deserves our all.

Introduction Notes

[1]Ralph P. Martin, *The Worship of God: Some Theological, Pastoral and Practical Reflections* (Grand Rapids: Eerdmans, 1982), 9.

[2]Horton Davies, *Christian Worship: Its History and Meaning* (Nashville: Abingdon, 1957), 105.

[3]Evelyn Underhill, *Worship* (New York: Harper, 1936), 3.

[4]James B. Torrance, *Worship, Community and the Triune God of Grace* (Downers Grove, IL: InterVarsity Press, 1996), 20, as quoted in D. A. Carson, ed., *Worship by the Book* (Grand Rapids: Zondervan, 2002), 42.

[5]William Temple, as quoted in Franklin M. Segler, *Christian Worship: Its Theology and Practice,* 1st ed. (Nashville: Broadman, 1967), 4.

[6]See Paul Basden, *The Worship Maze: Finding a Style to Fit Your Church* (Downers Grove, IL: InterVarsity Press, 1999), 19–25.

[7]Ibid., passim.

[8]Ibid., 44–45.

[9](Downers Grove, IL: InterVarsity Press, 1999).

Chapter One

FORMAL-LITURGICAL WORSHIP

FORMAL-LITURGICAL WORSHIP

Paul F. M. Zahl

It was during Dr. Bedell's ministry and well into the 1860s that the Church of the Ascension was called the "Low Church Cathedral," because, while its pulpit stood for a broad evangelical Christianity, it was marked by unusual fondness for good music and for a dignified service.

—James W. Kennedy, *The Unknown Worshipper*[1]

I believe in Bible-based verticality, which is another way of saying formal-liturgical worship. There is nothing like it for taking you outside your problems and also bringing you back to them a renewed person, better able to cope and to endure. Bible-based verticality is a glorious thing. This chapter seeks to offer its principles, its roots, and its virtues. It also seeks to parry some familiar objections to it.

Formal worship means dignified service that is not governed by the spontaneity of the moment or the spontaneity of the officiant. It means service in a form, within a mold. It is not off the cuff or as mood would govern. Rather, it accepts the constraint of a consistent and predictable pattern.

Liturgical worship means prescribed worship, service that is required for a given occasion. So if it is Sunday, you have a required act of worship for that day. If a baptism is to take place or the sacrament of Holy Communion is to be celebrated, you conduct the service according to a previously set format. You do not make it up as you go along.

Thus, for example, Episcopal ministers and most Lutheran pastors approach Sunday without giving particular thought to the shape of the service itself. It is formal (i.e., in the form given in a prayer book) and it is liturgical (i.e., set, depending on whether the service is to be one of the two sacraments or whether it is to be Morning Prayer, a service purely of the Word).[2] There is freedom in worship within a form, just as J. S. Bach worked within specific musical forms like the cantata and the Mass, just as Shakespeare worked within the sonnet and Giovanni Bellini within the *sacra conversazione* and the triptych. Form is able, somewhat counterintuitively, to stimulate fineness and quality, even innovation and renewal, in the context of traditional givens.

At the same time, formal-liturgical worship rules out the approach that makes it up as you go along. It is true to say that a high percentage of nonliturgical, nonformal churches ad-lib from Sunday to Sunday. You are not able to know from week to week whether it is going to be a mother-daughter service, a stewardship service, an evangelistic guest service, a youth Sunday, or a Scouting Sunday. F. Scott Fitzgerald was not the first American novelist to write about Americans reinventing themselves. But thousands of churches reinvent the service, or appear to, every Sunday. That, at least, is one burden this writer, as a minister of a liturgical denomination, does not carry.

We are concerned here with formal and liturgical worship. We are thereby also concerned with vertical worship. Vertical worship looks up first, before it looks out. It is transcendent before it is horizontal. It is faced north before it looks around. This means that it is not pastor- or preacher-centered. It is, or ought to be, Word-centered. It is not "man/woman"-centered, nor is it concerned, in the initial situation, with community. It does, almost always, engender family feeling. The worship of which I speak is, to use the expressive German, *senkrecht nach oben:* straight up and down, looking right up.

The first principles, then, of formal-liturgical worship are its setness, its givenness, and its direction. It is not informal, it is not nonliturgical, and it is not horizontal. Nor, however, is it cold. Nor is it confining. Nor is it excluding, or non-user-friendly. How can this be?

LEX CREDENDI LEX ORANDI

Formal-liturgical worship must be based on the truth if it is to endure. In fact, if it is not based on the truth, it will finally fall down in pieces on the ground. If vertical worship is not rooted and grounded in truth, specifically Bible truth, then it should not stand. It should "morph" into casual and horizontal worship. The reason why many evangelical and/or Protestant Christians have rejected liturgical worship over the centuries is that they have associated dignity and formality with unbiblical Roman Catholicism or Anglican Catholicism or just high churchianity that seemed to exist at the expense of Christianity.

The Latin phrase that covers the philosophy of worship I am presenting here is this: *lex credendi lex orandi*. That means: What we believe determines how we pray. Quite a few liturgical scholars and theologians today want to reverse the order and write: *lex orandi lex credendi*, or how we pray (i.e., worship) determines what we believe. There are even some writers who claim that our belief systems come after and follow from our language of praise, whatever that is. This is an entirely opportunistic view of worship, which subordinates truth to practice. *Lex orandi lex credendi* must be completely rejected.

For Anglicans—yet it is important for all Christians who value forms of worship—the *lex orandi lex credendi* falsehood goes back to a "power play" in the 1970s by which the Reformation anthropology and Reformation Christology of the old sixteenth-century Anglican prayer book were muted drastically in favor of a more contemporary picture of the Christian faith and the human condition. A new and very different prayer book was the result for American Episcopalians. As soon as this prayer book was passed by the Episcopal Church's General Convention (1979), everyone could announce with authority that the prayer book teaches thus and so. But which prayer book? By whose authority? The new one, just achieved? Or the old one, so convincingly and pastorally tested from the 1540s up until the 1970s? And yes, it has come true in experience that twenty-five years of praying the Christian faith in new words and new forms has created a very different church. Those liturgical politicians who piloted the fundamental changes in the 1970s could now observe by the 1990s, with some sad justice: *lex orandi lex credendi*. It was a self-fulfilling prophecy. Church people who now prayed Sunday after Sunday without the old confessions and penitential prayers became, well, a lot less penitential.

The fact is, theology has to precede the act of worship. You pray what you believe, not vice versa. It is an axiom here—it has to be an axiom in this consideration of formal-liturgical worship—that truth grounds prayer, not the other way around. Right thinking about God, Christ, and the condition of the human race is essential in forming and creating worship. "The hour is coming, and now is, when the true worshipers will worship the Father in spirit and truth, for such the Father seeks to worship him. God is spirit, and those who worship him must worship in spirit and truth" (John 4:23–24).

BIBLE VERTICALITY

What is right thinking about worship? For an evangelical Christian, there can be only one answer. It is Bible-truthful worship. *Sola scriptura* is the objective measuring stick for the propriety of all prayer, be it adoration, thanksgiving, confession, or repentance. If adjectives used to describe God are not in the Bible or they are inconsistent with Bible attitudes, then they are out. If Jesus Christ is described or portrayed as a woman—although he was tender and solicitous and generative of all good—then those terms are out. Services of blessing for same-sex unions are out. Blessings of the animals, which are still the rage in some mainline circles, are out unless they are shorn of ideas that put animal life on terms of equivalent status with human life.

Right (Bible) thoughts of God, right (Bible) thoughts of Christ, right (Bible) thoughts of the human being—these must confirm the value of all formal liturgy. Where liturgies cannot pass Bible scrutiny, they are worthless and worse than useless.

Here it could be objected that Bible truth is a Noah's Ark concept, which itself covers a multitude of potentially conflicting possibilities. How can one know what Bible truth is when there is evidently more than one "canon within the canon," when it is possible, for example, in the New Testament to find evidence of catholic ideas of ministry right next to charismatic views right next to paedobaptist views right next to free-church views and so forth?

Objectors who say this usually have their own agenda and are pumping for a special view that is found in one or two specific phrases or verses. We ought to subscribe to Luther's maxim on the understandability (what he called the "perspicuity") of the Bible: If you come upon a verse in Scripture that is inconsistent with others on the same subject, always interpret the exceptional verse in light of the more common ones. In other words, always interpret a hard verse in light of easier ones.

When you take Luther's commonsense rule of interpretation, you almost always find that the Bible as a whole is univocal on the big issues: God, Christ, and sin. God is unapproachable and perfect, Christ is his unique Word to us, and human nature is irreducibly flawed, double minded, and deceived about itself. On those three core truths hangs everything else. Thus formal-liturgical worship depends on its fidelity to the Bible understanding of God, Christ, and us. No evangelical Christian can be comfortable with set worship that exists in forms unless those forms are true in principle to the Book.

THE HOLY COMMUNION AS APPLE OF DISCORD

A further, very important element in the Bible-truth foundation for Christian worship concerns the Lord's Supper or Holy Communion, sometimes called the Eucharist. When a worshiping community holds unbiblical ideas of the Holy Communion, which is regarded by almost all Christian traditions as the most solemn act of worship, attempts to represent formal-liturgical worship lead to shipwreck.

To be specific, if the bread and wine of the Lord's Supper are considered to represent God's presence objectively, or tangibly and corporeally, then worship is due them. With that understanding, the ministers of the celebration are charged with a specialness over and above their status as Christian people, a specialness that they would otherwise share in principle with all whom they serve or with all who are present during their act of worship. The pendant to this high or catholic view of the Holy Communion is a high and catholic view of the priesthood.

Conversely, when the Sacrament is viewed as a sign or symbol of that which it represents, then the minister of the altar becomes a presiding elder or "president" (per Church of England parlance). The doctrine of the Body and Blood is the star, the ascent or descent of which determines the status of the ordained ministry. The higher the status of the elements, the higher the status of the clergy. Theater and theatricality follow. It is exactly such theater, or the presentation of surface for its own sake, that Bible worship shuns.

Is it possible in anything like a few sentences to settle the question of what constitutes the Bible truth of the Holy Communion? No. It was the apple of discord during the Protestant Reformation, and since then there has never been consensus among Christians concerning the theology of the Holy Communion.

What I believe we can say is this: Jesus instituted a commemorative meal, which was to become proclamatory in the now and not a dramatic reenactment of a past crisis. St. Paul affirmed that the enacted meal would always "proclaim the Lord's death until he comes" (1 Corinthians 11:26). At the same time, John 6 interprets the presence of Christ through the bread and wine in graphic and nonmetaphysical terms. Biblical realism requires that we take the Lord's words seriously: "This is my body"—both the verb and its present tense. And yet we are also warned stringently in Scripture against taking the symbol for what it represents (Acts 7:48) and thus laying hold of God and capturing him. God will not be had or held.

All this means that we steer, in matters of the Sacrament, between the Scylla of pure memorialism and the Charybdis of transubstantiation. All the Protestant churches of the Reformation retained formal-liturgical worship, officially at least, and all the Reformation churches without exception rejected transubstantiation.[3] What is required is unconditional reverence for that which the Supper represents and for that which it continues to proclaim. Yet the sign is not the thing signified. The thing signified is spiritual, invisible, and intangible, even elusive. It cannot be pinned down. If it is to be objectified in any form of any kind, it can be discovered in the preaching of the one thing, the re-creating forgiveness of sins through the God-man Christ Jesus. That Word gives life to the Sacrament. Without the Word of the Gospel, the Sacrament is sterile and entirely empty.

So Word creates sacrament, but not the opposite. And a Christian priest is a contradiction in terms, for there is only one priest (Hebrews 5:4; 7:3, 22–28). And a Christian minister is steward of the Word that makes all things new, including the believer who discerns the Word under the bread and wine in the evangelically grounded celebration of the Holy Communion.

Right views of the Holy Communion keep the community of faith from extremes or, better, from errors that have gross consequences for us. Right views of the Communion restrain the clergy and people from misplaced reverence. They keep the focus on the one creative entity of human transformation: the Word of God's grace.

MUSIC IN FORMAL-LITURGICAL WORSHIP

Music has almost always been an important component of formal-liturgical worship. Music is essential for two reasons. It is required, first, because it catalyzes emotion as nothing else. It is part of the "sighs too deep for words" (Romans 8:26), which the Holy Spirit breathes when rational words fail. The release of suppressed emotions is able to occur for many worshipers through the instrument of music, melody, and text. That is why people cry during hymns. Familiar hymns possess the quality of bringing emotion to the surface. Thus music is a sort of charismatic prophecy, in the sense of 1 Corinthians 14:24–25, by which the human being's true interests, intentions, and aspirations can come out. We need music in order to worship God, disclosing the archaeology of our temperament in nonverbal communication upward.

Second, we need music for the communication of teaching. Shaping texts (the expression of Word, hymns, and songs that convey Bible truth) form the people who sing them. Like the King James Bible and the old Anglican prayer book and *The Pilgrim's Progress,* the hymns of Isaac Watts and William Cowper, Frances Ridley Havergal and Edmund Hamilton Sears shape all who hear them and learn them. Solid texts deepen and sustain solid Christians. The combination of a singable melody with a Christ-exalting and sin-abasing poem is uniquely powerful.

Formal-liturgical worship will always, or almost always, require music of quality married to words of substance. The reason I prefer generally, but not exclusively, music from sources inherent in Western civilization is that European and English church music developed closely parallel to the Christian church for almost the entire period from Pentecost to now. The sources are so deep and rich, so developed and refined. For formal-liturgical worship, Western music will continue to be the principle source and feeding.

This does not mean fussiness or snobbishness or artificiality. The soundtrack of Piero Pasolini's 1966 film of *The Gospel According to St. Matthew* displayed radically and freshly the aptness of African liturgical music and Negro spirituals to portray the Redemption, the events of Christ's life. But those sources are simply outnumbered, in terms of variety and sheer quantity, by the liturgical products of the Western Christian canon. Moreover, much contemporary praise music is repetitive in melody and flaky in text. This is simply true, and I write as one who has conducted hundreds of contemporary services since the mid-1970s.

THREE OBJECTIONS

From the very beginnings of Christianity and in every period of revival or renewal in church life, at least three serious charges have been laid against formal-liturgical models of worship. They all boil down to one objection, but each reflects a different aspect or symptom of the one.

1. The first charge, the fundamental and central one, is that formal-liturgical worship quenches the Holy Spirit. That is to say, by addressing God in forms and by doing it the same way within an ever-repeating cycle of occasions—such as Sundays, baptisms, marriages, and funerals—the church is trying to tie God's hands. The church is conspiring to limit the way in which he speaks. Forms of any kind, setness to any degree, is a human attempt to tell God when to appear and how to appear.

The New flamed up like a rocket in the Corinthian congregation. It almost derailed the Wittenberg Reformation of Martin Luther. It created the Methodist Church. It has bequeathed a legacy of suspicion among Pentecostal Christians, not to mention most free-church sects, toward the old denominations. The accusation that we muzzle the Spirit of God, or try to, will probably never be laid to rest.

The best response to this charge is to admit its substance. Yes, formal-liturgical worship has suppressed and can weaken the receptivity of human beings to the spontaneous and hardly controllable eruptions of the Pentecost Spirit in the world. And yes, if our forms chain us to the appearance and not the reality of intercourse with God, then the forms must go! I believe a Bible Christian has to concede the potential and also the actual justice of this ancient tax on liturgical worship: Liturgy can represent the victory of form over substance. It has often worked that way.

On the other hand, human sin is able to create out of free worship some set and predictable forms of worship of a different kind. All you need to do is visit a classic Pentecostal Sunday-evening service, of any particular stripe or numerical size, and you will quickly observe that there is a pattern to it as well. The minister preaches and exhorts; the tongues, interpretations, and prophecies start to fly; they crescendo usually in a *choro continuo* of glossolalia; then the minister puts in a word or two; some more music follows; then the tongues, interpretations, and prophecies begin to fly again; they climax one last time in a *choro profundo* of "Yes, Jesus" and "Thank you, Jesus"; the pastor segues on; and on it goes.

I observed when visiting Bishop T. D. Jakes's preaching services at Potter's House in Dallas, in which the Bishop preaches with astonishing power, that an altar call followed every single one of his addresses. I saw that the same people went forward again and again—the usual suspects—and that his numberless anointings corresponded to people in my own parish going forward Sunday after Sunday to the Communion rail to receive the Sacrament.

What is truly free and what is truly formal? The Spirit can bless and attend both. The Spirit can absent himself from both. "Lord, take not thy Holy Spirit from us."

Another response to the ancient objection that forms constrain the Spirit is that forms can steward Bible truth such that in engagement with it, worshipers can connect with the very Spirit who attends his Word. Forms grounded in Galilean, Pauline, or Augustinian truth humble the sinner and exalt the Savior, as the English preacher Charles Simeon never tired of saying. With warmth, conviction, and prayerful expectation, a liturgical service can bear the Word, accompanied by the Spirit, straight to the heart. There is no decisive absence of the Spirit within the form if the form is presented in Pentecostal sincerity. I have seen sinners converted again and again within services that bear a set form.

2. The second enduring objection to formal-liturgical worship, which is really a subset of the first, is that it is, or usually is, cold and dead, with the quality of a performance. As with the first objection, we ought to admit the aptness of this second one. Liturgical worship can easily come across as chilly and alienating. It can become the coded signals of those alone who know and understand. We winced in the American Episcopal context when the Reverend Joel Pugh asked why it is that more Episcopalians know the reason why the color purple is proper for Lent than know the reason why Christ died upon the cross. Dean Pugh's words were an arrow straight into our hearts!

For liturgical worship not to be distancing and abstract, two things are required: sincere conviction on the part of the leader that the ideas behind the words are true, and unaffected personal warmth. It is possible to read a centuries-old service with passionate belief. It is also possible to give a personal touch, with the right smile and person-centeredness at the altar rail, with the right eye contact of recognition as you walk down the aisle. Moreover, a good sermon can cover a multitude of sins. A resonant word of grace is able to triumph over forty-five minutes of rote. Yet the experience of church history and actual parish life does warn that John Bunyan was correct in his salutary caricature of "Mr. Formalist" in *The Pilgrim's Progress*.

3. The third classic objection to the formal-liturgical model, especially on the part of evangelical Christians, is that it is not user-friendly. Specifically, it is bad for evangelism.

Again, I concede the substance of the charge. Hundreds of times during my ministry, I have watched as people from nonliturgical backgrounds have struggled with prayer books and hymnals, with getting up and sitting down, with versicles and responses. A liturgical service can make a person who is not used to it feel stupid and "out of it." And some formalist people seem almost to enjoy the discomfiture of nonliturgical visitors. "Those unlearned Baptists!" they seem to be thinking. The Episcopal service of Holy Communion can truly feel like the rite of a secret society.

As with the other two objections, there is a response to this third one. The minister in charge of a liturgical service needs to bend over backwards to make the nonliturgical visitor feel welcomed. The right sort of greeting, the right sort of (short) introduction to the hard parts of the service, warm but not patronizing instruction at junctures in the service—all these steps are required. They can make all the difference. With a little TLC and forethought, an atmosphere of inclusion can be engendered. Then maybe the uncomfortable visitor can receive the plus of the experience: transcendence, a little noble feeling, reverenced truth concerning God and man, and the right degree of emotional lead time or preparation in order for the sermon to connect.

All three objections we have lined out need to be heard. They are the proper correctives of legitimate criticism. But they lose their power when formal-liturgical worship is conducted within the context of prayer and faith in the present-speaking Spirit, within an atmosphere of warmth and sincerity on the part of the minister, with kind attention devoted to the newcomer or visitor. These criticisms, all of which are expressions of the one criticism—that formal worship quenches the Spirit—collapse, or at least diminish hugely, when liturgical worship is conducted properly. They collapse when the service is led in a spirit of conviction and love.

THE IDEAL

I wish to conclude by listing the specific qualities of liturgical worship that are able to make it ideal and optimal. We return to the short description at the beginning of this chapter. Those few phrases should be parsed, for they identify the characteristics of liturgical worship at its best:

> The Church of the Ascension was called the "Low Church Cathedral," because, while its pulpit stood for a broad evangelical Christianity, it was marked by unusual fondness for good music and for a dignified service.

The Church of the Ascension, on lower Fifth Avenue in New York City, was one of many Evangelical Episcopal parishes in the period before the American Civil War. The Evangelical or low-church tradition vanished after 1874 for reasons that have been discussed elsewhere.[4]

For it to be true to the Bible, formal-liturgical worship has to be grounded and rooted in broadly evangelical preaching. The preaching needs to be broadly evangelical, because the Christian religion is neither sectarian nor legalistic. The preaching needs to be evangelical, because the *Evangelium,* or Gospel, is the octane of the engine. Without public declaration of the salvation message of Christ and the Cross, there is no worship at all, or no worship I would wish to be part of. As I have said all along, Word must always precede, and also create, sacrament and praise, confession and blessing.

Anglican Evangelical worship was, and is in principle, marked also by an appreciation of good music. Music that is under-rehearsed, shoddily or self-indulgently presented, or superficial in text does not cohere with formal-liturgical worship. We cannot make peace with it. It is not a question of taste. It is a question of quality. We affirm the Western tradition of hymnody and liturgical music because it is time-tested and has been fed by many artists of genius. Non-Western music can add and enrich and also deepen. Contemporary Christian music can stir and also comfort. But good music in this particular context usually means the Western canon, and especially hymns, the texts of which have endured because they have addressed real people.

Anglican Evangelical worship has been, and is in principle, dignified. This is to say, ordered, objective; predictable, or better, consistent; and most important, vertical and transcendent. It is God-centered, not minister-centered. It is vertical rather than horizontal. It is not created from whim. It is not crafted by a committee, and certainly not weekly. Nor does it vary from Sunday to Sunday, except in alternating between Communion and Morning Prayer (i.e., the preaching service with hymns, prayers, and anthem). It operates within tested norms.

I wish to affirm that formal-liturgical worship relies on a broadly evangelical pulpit; a dignified service focused on the object of worship (i.e., God and Christ Jesus) rather than on the subject of worship (i.e., the pastor/minister); a warm and sincere interest in the lives and souls of the worshipers; and a conscientious simplicity that subordinates unfailingly the symbols of Christianity to the realities they symbolize.

As with the State of North Carolina, our motto as formal-liturgical Christians has to be, and remain, "To be rather than to seem."

A NOTE ON THE CANTERBURY TRAIL

A quite striking development in the United States in recent decades has been the migration of some high-profile, free-church evangelicals into formal-liturgical churches. Specifically, I am thinking of the phenomenon known as "the Canterbury Trail." This is a pilgrimage in church and worship that sometimes leads to the Episcopal Church.

What this entails is a discovery of the vertical factor in worship. Evangelicals who are on the Canterbury Trail report that they have been so burned out by pastor-centered, hymn-sandwich models of worship that when they strayed into formal-liturgical air space—i.e., when they wandered by happenstance into an Episcopal Eucharist—they were vividly impressed with its transcendence and God-centeredness. The Canterbury Trail is a quest for verticality among sincerely religious people who have soured on the cult-of-personality church that is centered on the preacher.

I am naturally sympathetic with pilgrims on the Canterbury Trail. But I am also skeptical. Protestant formal-liturgical models are sometimes just a way station for Canterbury pilgrims. In other words, if it is God-centered liturgy that is the point, then why not go all the way, to Rome or to the Orthodox? In fact, this is where most Canterbury "pilgrims" actually end up.

Protestant liturgical congregations still emphasize the sermon, even if they emphasize also the sacraments. The preaching ministry in Roman Catholic and Orthodox parishes is seldom the focus of worship. (Orthodox churches also have the barriers of ethnicity and sometimes even of language.) If you are in reaction to "free-church" evangelical worship, you may find yourself drawn to Rome (as in EWTN: Eternal Word Television Network) if you are really honest with yourself. This is in fact what has actually happened with many Canterbury pilgrims; they have sojourned in Canterbury on the way to something else. As an Episcopalian, I find it hard to think of my ambiguous denomination as a destination—that is, if denomination or ethos as such really matters to the seeker.

Furthermore, many Canterbury pilgrims have hit that road in search of consistent authority. If it is doctrinal or moral-theological *magisterium* that you want, not one of the Protestant formal-liturgical churches can give it to you. Look at the mainline Presbyterians, the mainline Lutherans, and the mainline Episcopalians. The Canterbury Trail is a wide thoroughfare. For better or for worse, the doctrinal parameters are broad.

My point is, Protestant Anglicanism, with its yoking of Sacrament and Word, with its priority of Word over Sacrament, will not satisfy your itch, if it is an end to pastor or sermon-centeredness you want. Better pass "Go" and sprint straight to Rome or, idiosyncratically, to Constantinople.

A TRADITIONAL WORSHIP RESPONSE

Harold Best

In this response I want to extract one item from Paul Zahl's chapter and treat it extensively. In the remainder I will only highlight other matters.

The one item has to do with the fixity-spontaneity dilemma and the somewhat superficial way Zahl treats it. I start with a question: Must liturgical worship be all that fixed, and is spontaneity the crass "make-it-up-as-you-go" caricature that Zahl so negatively says it is? In scanning the traditional prayer book,[5] I find this: ". . . the Minister, in his discretion, may use other devotions taken from this book or set forth by lawful authority within this Church, or from Holy Scripture; and *Provided further* [italics not mine], that, subject to the direction of the Ordinary [prelate or bishop], in Mission Churches or Chapels, and also when expressly authorized by the Ordinary, *in Cathedral or Parish Churches, or other places, such other devotions as aforesaid may be used, when the edification of the Congregation so requires, in place of the Order for Morning Prayer, or for the Order for Evening Prayer*" (italics mine).

The teasers are, of course, found in the words "devotion" and "lawful authority." From my uninformed side, I would assume "devotion" to include anything, whether by praying, reading, or reciting, that is found elsewhere in the prayer book. I assume that "lawful authority" has to do with some kind of approval from above. But since a great number of Episcopalians, including authorities from above, do not pay very close attention to several of the Thirty-nine Articles (the set historical/doctrinal core of Anglo-Episcopalian practice), it seems that a Bible-based freedom within the larger liturgical construct is warranted. I do not know how Zahl would respond to this because, in his presentation, there is an unresolved tension between what is Bible-based and what is liturgy-based.

I could wish that the standoff and mutual stick-tossing between so-called fixity and so-called spontaneity folks would be forgotten in favor of another model: composition and improvisation.[6] I know these words initially betray my musical training, but I want to take them out beyond the arts and apply them to the issue at hand. As much as I love and respect the time-tested dignity, truthfulness, and Word-smithed beauty of the liturgy, I could wish for similarly constructed variants, the responsibility for the creation of which would lie directly and fearingly in the hands of a Spirit-filled priesthood. (Zahl would rightly call this a ministerhood.) Let us call the established liturgy the master composition. Doing this allows us to acknowledge it as the first among all possible equals. But it also forces us to acknowledge that it did not appear liturgically *ex nihilo*. It was gradually realized over a certain expanse of time and through the creative input and interchange of many devoted ministers and practices, only to be set down after agreement (with no little amount of disagreement) had been reached. In other words, the final composition was realized improvisationally.

Composition is really improvisation slowed down and codified. Improvisation is composition sped up and on the spur of the moment, but impossible without countless painful and disciplined hours of practice and study that include both the gathering of information and the twin continuations of composing and improvising. One need only read up on expository preaching without notes—an actual book title[7]—to understand how improvisation and composition, fixity and instantaneity are bound together by continued study and practice. The kind of so-called spontaneity that Zahl criticizes is really a blurring of composition and improvisation, in that spontaneity is theoretically championed but not usually realized unless the patterns of so-called spontaneity are legitimately broken. Only the Holy Spirit, the Infinitely Trustworthy Improviser, is capable of this kind of breaking in, and all Christians, especially the charismatics, should understand that spontaneity of this kind can appear within fixity, so as either to confirm or disturb it, and spontaneity, so as to fix and control it. There is no such thing as *ex nihilo* spontaneity, even in the most Spirit-driven contexts, simply because the all-preceding fixity of Truth must be honored and adhered to.

Now back to the liturgy and my personal desire to see improvisation and composition in league with each other. What minister, having deeply studied the conciseness, elegance, and truthfulness of the collect prayer form, should not be allowed, even obligated, to improvise in this fashion? Let's go into deeper waters. Given the rich content of the *Sanctus* or the *Gloria* or the prayers at the altar in the Eucharist; given the enormous amount of study necessary to launch into the meanings behind the established words of these—why not have the minister create paraphrases that, in content and intent, walk alongside the originals? After all, all preachers, including the homily crafters in the liturgy, regularly put together their own versions of what the Word—the chief fixity—is saying. If this chief fixity that cannot be broken is regularly and legitimately turned over to homiletical composition and improvisation, why not the lesser fixities of the liturgy? It is in this sense that the form/freedom question could be innovatively and dynamically handled. Let me repeat: I love the liturgy, and I work hard in the exercise of my faith to be sure that each iteration is fresh to me, as if heard or read for the very first time. But I could wish that ministers would be forced to enter into it with the full content of their experience and training in Christ, taking responsibility for saying it with other words. This might take a reinvention of Lutheranism and Episcopalianism. So be it.

Please permit these few brief comments about the whole of Zahl's presentation.

- I cherish Zahl's placing the Word at the forefront. This is the real secret to the liturgy and the final judging point for all practices treated in this book.
- It is unfortunate that "making it up as you go" was used to describe certain kinds of worship. Almost nobody does this.
- The *lex credendi lex orandi* priority is spot-on and should be a firm reminder to all liturgy and worship crafters about what is causal and what is symptomatic.

- Article XXVIII of the Thirty-nine Articles should be read by every Christian. It compresses the facts and doctrine of the Lord's Table into a wonderfully biblical statement. It, as well as the words of delivery in the liturgy, comprehends everything from pure memorialism to the mysterious borders of body and blood. If it errs, it is in omitting any mention of hope, the eschatological side of memory. But almost all practices omit this.
- Zahl disappointingly cites a mere secondary reason for the use of music (its emotionally catalytic quality). The primary reason is that the church is commanded to sing (and play), purely and simply. The "too deep for words" idea carelessly subordinates the idea of the primacy of the Word.
- Overall, Zahl tends to be defensive instead of apologetic. There is no need to put a negative spin on what others do. This simply breeds comparativeness instead of exposition.
- As to the user-unfriendliness of liturgical worship, much of contemporary worship is not that user-friendly either. Unless you have memorized text and tune—that is, submitted to the habits of oral tradition tribalism—you will be lost in the flow. Furthermore, learning completely new tunes and texts, in the absence of printed music and given the soloistic/ornamentalistic origins of many tunes, makes for some fairly empty, sloppy, disengaged singing.
- As much as I resonate with Zahl's defense of good music, I find that he does not fully understand the diversity within the Western canon that he applauds, nor does he seem to make room for the need for new kinds of classical music. Does canon apply only to the past, or is there a twenty-first-century extension of it? Of course there is.
- Thank you, sir, for your critique of the liturgical nomads, the wanderers, and the ecclesiastical rolling stones. I fully agree that the Canterbury Trail syndrome needs the strong ecclesio-pharmaceuticals of stability and persistence.

A CONTEMPORARY WORSHIP RESPONSE

Joe Horness

At the heart of every great contemporary worship leader is a secret longing for elements of the liturgical. As contradictory as this seems, I think it is true, and I think this is why there is such an attraction to the liturgical among contemporary audiences these days. The orderliness and predictability of a liturgy frees us from the challenge of filling the empty page we face week after week. A depth of thought and theology challenges our minds and sometimes stands in stark contrast to the "all I need is you" themes of contemporary worship music. There is a time-tested truth and dignity to liturgy that sometimes seems more in keeping with the God we come to worship. Indeed, one middle-aged worship leader I know recently told me that, given the choice between purely liturgical and purely free worship, he would pick the liturgical because "at least somebody has thought it through."

Any great worship expression should help us really know God. In contemporary worship we sometimes get lost on the way to this goal. We can easily crank up three songs to fill the space before the message. We can repeat fairly meaningless phrases over and over as if they were some profound thought that needed real rumination in order to understand. We evaluate worship by how we felt or how the people emoted rather than by whether or not truth was spoken and God was lifted up. And in those moments we secretly sense that all is not well. We perceive what Paul Zahl is trying to say: that our worship needs to be rooted and grounded in the truth of God's Word, that our focus must be the Unknowable One, and that our hearts and minds desire something of greater substance than we are offering. We understand, at least on a heart level, that "right thoughts" of God, of Christ, of the human being "confirm the value" not just "of all formal liturgy" but of all worship. Liturgy provides expressions of truth that are sometimes fuzzy in contemporary worship. It provides stability and predictability that can sometimes feel lacking amidst all of our contemporary creativity. And at its best, it brings a reverence for God that the contemporary-worship set can often miss.

Yet, as contemporary worship leaders we understand that delivering great content about God is only half the battle. For the worshiper in the pew, worship cannot be just about receiving great truth or theology, however profound that truth is. Worship is about giving. Worship is the response we offer to what we have received. It is one thing to use a form to deliver the truth. It is another thing altogether to inspire a heartfelt expression of our response to that truth. It is one thing for my children to receive a gift at Christmas. It is quite another when they jump around and cheer and throw their arms around me with heartfelt thanks. That is the piece that a set liturgy can miss.

That is why, as contemporary worship leaders, we love the freshness that creativity brings and the authenticity that contemporary worship inspires. Those who opt for contemporary worship at its best are absolutely committed to offering heartfelt, fully engaged, jubilant expressions of love and thanks to the One who so wildly loves us. And unfortunately, we have experienced too many times how repetitive, predictable liturgy can fail to compel us to that place. To the contemporary worship leader, variety, for all of the challenges it brings week to week, brings life! Fresh approaches to worship lead to fresh experiences of God. Variety moves us off autopilot. One week we celebrate. Another week we may be led to be broken and repentant before him. But our experience of him, like our experience of any relationship, is ever-changing. And finding new ways to engage our hearts with him, to experience our relationship with him, and to help us respond week to week to what he is doing in lives is a labor of love. It is never a burden. The act of creating is itself an act of worship! The weekly exercise of that offering allows us to respond to events taking place in our lives and in our world.

We would rather remain in the mystery and unpredictability of relationship than to opt for the stability of set form, as comforting as that may be.

While I am on this subject, several authors in this volume have taken mild shots at what Zahl refers to as worship that is "created from whim" or "crafted by a committee." They phrase this in a way that seems to assume that we can all see how absurdly silly this is. But for those of us in a contemporary worship setting, or even an emerging worship setting, crafting the service week to week is not a negative. In fact, we might argue that a time of worship crafted by godly, surrendered, united, and creative people (who, under the direction of the Holy Spirit, are prayerfully and actively employing the gifts and talents that God has given them to design moments that have the potential to engage hearts and transform lives) may be an option that is at least equal to, if not better than, quoting by rote something that was crafted several centuries ago.

I say this with a smile, although there is a fair measure of truth to it. For the contemporary worship leader, imparting truth through worship is only half the battle. Leading people to a place of heartfelt response to the God we adore is the other.

The challenge for us as contemporary worship leaders is to remember that great worship must be built on great content, and liturgy certainly brings that to the table. The prayers and forms and creeds from liturgy that were crafted centuries ago have stood the test of time. They bring the Word to life for us in ways that many of us could never express. And in that sense, all of us worship leaders would be wise to study and learn from our liturgical brothers and sisters. For a contemporary worship form to flourish, or for it to even remain worshipful, it needs both the variety that our gifts can bring to it and the depth of thought and dignity that liturgy can bring. As Zahl states, great theology must always "precede the act of worship." Contemporaneity should never be an excuse for wrong thinking or irreverence. As contemporary worship leaders we must not simply be contemporary musicians. We must be contemporary pastors who are students of the Word, who learn from great liturgy and lead our congregations to great expressions of worship based on God's unchanging truth.

Any worship form is partially dependent on those who present it. None of us involved in the leading or direction of worship can afford to simply pick our style and rest in it. Rather than allowing the safety and familiarity of forms to permit our hearts to disengage, or allowing a hip beat or guitar rift to generate superficial emotion, it is imperative that our walk with God remain real, that our dialogue with his Spirit be moment to moment, that our communication of his truth be accurate, engaging, and authentic. When this fails, our method fails, be it liturgical, hymn driven, charismatic, contemporary, or other. For some reason still unknown to us, God still chooses to build his kingdom through surrendered, Spirit-filled people, not through the most time-tested forms or the most modern methodology. Forms and methods are the tools used by the people who are being used by God. The goal is to help people fully engage their hearts in offering authentic expressions of worship to God. Choose the tool that best helps your church do that. Learn and glean all that you can from the others. And walk with God in such a way that you can use them well.

A CHARISMATIC WORSHIP RESPONSE

Don Williams

Paul Zahl offers a reasoned, irenic, evangelical appeal for liturgical worship. First, he tells us what liturgical worship is. It is vertical, God-centered. It is Bible- or truth-based. It sees Scripture as univocal on the big issues: God, Christ, and sin. For liturgical worship, theology precedes worship. It is formal, predictable, structured, dignified, consistent, and simple. It looks up before it looks out. Its freedom is found within its form.

Second, Zahl tells us what liturgical worship is not. It is not human- or community-centered. It is not informal, horizontal, cold, or confining. It does not depend on the creativity of the moment or the whim or personality of the preacher. Neither is it based on a sacramental view of ordination, fostering clericalism.

Liturgical worship, in the evangelical tradition, holds to the Reformation cry *sola scriptura.* For Anglicans, the classical *Book of Common Prayer* establishes the principle that what we believe determines how we pray. If the Word creates worship, then the Word also creates the sacraments. The Lord's Supper is neither magical nor mystical; it is evangelical. It represents and proclaims the cross of the crucified Lord. But in contrast to Catholic theology, the signs are not the substance.

Music is essential for liturgical worship. It catalyzes emotion and aids our upward communication with God. Music also teaches. Solid texts make solid Christians. Zahl asserts that for formal-liturgical worship to work well, it needs Western music. With a strong Eurocentric bias he writes that good music usually means the Western canon (largely British?). Where does this leave the Third World, where Christianity is exploding? Where does this leave a whole generation in the West that no longer identifies with classical culture?

Zahl admits the basic objection to liturgical worship: It too often quenches the Holy Spirit. But for me, if liturgical worship is "vertical" and "God-centered," this must go both ways. As our worship ascends, where is the freedom for the Spirit to descend? If liturgical worship is Bible- or truth-based, what about the biblical, truthful spontaneous worship of the Corinthians that Paul both encourages and disciplines? When Zahl argues that even the freest Pentecostal church has its own liturgy, he begs the question. Is the Spirit free to move within whatever form we create? Zahl has already told us that liturgical worship is formal, predictable, structured, dignified, consistent, and simple. These words would never apply to the church at Pentecost or the Christians in Corinth. Zahl never faces this dislocation from primitive Christianity. Liturgical worship eliminates the free expression and sharing of the Spirit's gifts that are so much at the heart of the New Testament.

The second objection (following from the first) is that liturgical worship is a cold, dead performance. Again, Zahl admits the aptness of this criticism. His way out is for the leader to believe that "the ideas behind the words are true" and exhibit "sincere conviction" with "unaffected personal warmth." I find this shallow and burdensome. Is it the leader's responsibility to keep the church alive and have the personality type to do so? This puts us all squarely back under the law. The Rev. Mr. Warmth usurps the Spirit's presence and power.

The third objection (to me the hardest to overcome) is that liturgical worship is "not user-friendly"—i.e., it is bad for evangelism. Having thumbed through the prayer book or missal and having stood when I should have knelt, lagging behind in the rote response "Christ, have mercy upon us," I know the feeling of an outsider. Zahl must admit that liturgical worship is not "seeker sensitive." He should also notice that Protestant liturgical churches are aging and shrinking.

Zahl concludes that these objections lose their power "when formal-liturgical worship is conducted within the context of prayer and faith in the present-speaking Spirit." Has he opened the door to charismatic worship in a liturgical form, as, for example, practiced by charismatic Episcopalians? This is doubtful. The burden again lies on the minister's warmth and sincerity—offering kind attention to newcomers. There is more than a hint of clericalism here. "It's what's up front that counts."

Zahl's case is not convincing. Contemporary or charismatic worship can be as God-centered as liturgical worship, especially when it is focused on the presence of God, not just his manifest gifts. Christian worship in community will always function in the tension between freedom and order, the vertical and the horizontal. Paul addresses this in 1 Corinthians 14. But in liturgical worship, as defined by Zahl, order is overbearing, freedom vanishes, and little horizontal (community) is left. What does Zahl think of Paul's telling the Ephesians to address each other in Psalms and hymns and spiritual songs (Ephesians 5:19)?

To set Zahl's chapter beside Sally Morgenthaler's "Emerging Worship" is a shock to the system. We realize that we are operating in two different worlds, two different cultures, and almost two different worldviews. Zahl's ordered worship may connect to the modern world, but what of the postmodern? They may be similar in shared sacred space and symbols (candles, incense, and stained glass), but what goes on in that space seems light-years apart.

My conclusion is that many tribes make up the people of God. To be culturally current is to leave the liturgy and setting of Elizabethan England. To be culturally current is to welcome multiethnic and multicultural diversity. To be open to fresh moves of the Spirit and the full gifting and participation of the body of Christ is to leave pulpit-centered, altar-centered, controlled worship. Our unity is not our uniformity. Paul calls us not to create unity in the body by adopting one culture or approach to worship, but to maintain the unity of the Spirit already given (Ephesians 4:3). Where Jesus is confessed as Lord, the Spirit is at work (1 Corinthians 12:3). All things must be subject to the authority of God's Word and the life of the Spirit. For Protestants, the church is to be continually reformed and reforming.

Paul teaches that true worship is the marker of the Christian. Circumcision (external form) no longer counts. As he writes in Philippians 3:3 (NIV), "For it is we who are the [true] circumcision, we who worship by the Spirit of God, who glory in Christ Jesus, and who put no confidence in the flesh" (read: externals, human accomplishment, or achievement, even on Sundays at 11 AM).

A BLENDED WORSHIP RESPONSE

Robert Webber

It is extremely difficult for me to respond in any critical way to Paul Zahl. Having been fed on liturgical worship for three decades, I find myself saying "amen" to practically every point he has made. What I have particularly found to be true, he eloquently summarizes in simple pithy statements: "there is freedom in worship within a form"; "worship must be based on truth"; the sacrament must be steered between "memorialism" and "transubstantiation"; good music "catalyzes emotion." Furthermore, the fairness with which Zahl accepts the criticisms leveled against liturgical worship is impressive. His call for all liturgy to be done with "sincere conviction" and "unaffected personal warmth" as an antidote to these criticisms is on target. He simply is right. Where liturgy is being done as he expresses, people—especially the young—are flocking. They know that where they do engage in worship, they are fed and transformed. However, because there are so few liturgical churches that meet these standards, many young evangelical leaders are borrowing liturgical content for worship in the postmodern world.

Now on to one slight quibble. Zahl refers to the *lex credendi lex orandi* (what we believe determines how we pray) as the historic sequence between truth and practice, then states, "There are even some writers who claim that our belief systems come after and follow from our language of praise, whatever that is. This is an entirely opportunist view of worship, which subordinates truth to practice. *Lex orandi lex credendi* must be completely rejected." Permit me to respond with a yes and a no.

First, the no. The phrase *lex orandi lex credendi* (prayer shapes belief) emerged in the early church to explain the relationship between worship and truth. Historically, the origins of Christian truth found expression in the liturgy and then were formed into creedal statements. A case in point is the Trinity. The New Testament does not use the word "Trinity," but forms of worship expressed the Trinity before the doctrine was formalized in the Nicene Creed. In the New Testament, doxologies, benedictions, and baptismal formulae are triune. In the early church, the Apostles' Creed, the Eucharistic prayers, and forms of worship were triune long before Arius opposed the Trinitarian doctrine in the fourth century. Athanasius, the defender of the Trinitarian form within the liturgy, used the liturgy as an argument against the non-Trinitarian views of Arius. Why, he asked, is the liturgy triune or, to put it another way, how can you deny the Trinitarian nature of Christian worship from its very beginnings? My point is that in the development of Christian doctrine, the church was practicing Orthodoxy (right praise) before it developed more formed universal creeds of faith (Nicene Creed).[8]

But I know what Zahl is saying and agree with the spirit of what he says. Historically one could say that worship hands down truth, the early Christian community reflecting on its worship formalized this truth in creeds, and therefore these creeds and the truths they teach must shape our worship. Perhaps it could be put this way: *lex orandi lex credendi lex orandi*. Prayer shapes believing, believing shapes prayer.

I think Zahl wants contemporary worshipers to listen to this ancient wisdom. I feel confident that he would agree that current pop worship that is inattentive to truth will shape a worship that hands down a Christianity that may no longer be true. Pop worship creates pop faith that creates pop worship. And so the saga goes. Another way to say the same thing is, "Show me how you worship, and I'll tell you what you believe." There is much we can learn about both worship and truth from the historic liturgical tradition. Thanks, Paul, for reminding us.

AN EMERGING WORSHIP RESPONSE

Sally Morgenthaler

THE VERTICALITY OF WORSHIP

If Christian worship is about and toward God, it should be unabashedly vertical. Unfortunately, if there is a dimension of worship that evangelical American Christianity has sacrificed most in the past twenty-five years, it is precisely the vertical. Paul Zahl has zeroed in on one of contemporary evangelical worship's greatest weaknesses: its appalling lack of transcendence. In our zeal to relate to people's everyday worlds, our worship experiences have too often adopted the performance models of the 1980s and 1990s: emcee-driven and podium-centered. In our rush to dispense a religion that works, we have tokenized the Word, building services around life-management techniques and generic moral principles while inserting just enough Scripture verses to assure ourselves that we are indeed a church.

As much as we need to restore verticality to our contemporary worship experiences, we must remember that Christian worship is not one-dimensional. It involves at least three dimensions: height, depth, and breadth. That is, Christian worship is about God (height), but it is also about us in relationship to God (depth) and us in relationship to each other (breadth). We see this three-dimensional phenomenon in Acts 2:42–47: "They devoted themselves to the apostles' teaching" (height and depth), "and to the fellowship" (breadth), "to the breaking of bread" (all three dimensions), "and to prayer" (depending on the kind of prayer, possibly all three dimensions). To say "worship looks up first, before it looks out" is accurate. It matters supremely who it is we are worshiping. Thus Zahl's crucial and astute assertion: "theology has to precede the act of worship."

But we must be careful. To say "worship looks up first, before it looks out" is not to say, "Worship looks up first and never looks out." Zahl makes the statement, "Worship is transcendent before it is horizontal," then follows it with a phrase in the next paragraph that seems contradictory: "[formal-liturgical worship] is not horizontal." I will give him the benefit of the doubt here and assume that he is simply reiterating that worship is not, first and foremost, horizontal. On that point I would agree. The person and works of God should be worship's initial focus. Yet historic Christian theology celebrates the person of God as three persons—community exemplified. Faithful worship affirms who God the Creator, Redeemer, and Sanctifier is, what he has done, and what he is doing. In worship we experience restored communion with that three-in-one God, and restored communion with other human beings (that marvelous reciprocity expressed in the reference to "fellowship" in Acts 2:42). Certainly Zahl as an Anglican would agree: The celebration of the Eucharist is not simply a private participation in God's saving work through Jesus Christ; it is an intensely horizontal, bonding, communal rite.

WORSHIP THAT IS WORTHY IS
(MOSTLY) WESTERN AND CLASSICAL

Zahl unabashedly links formal-liturgical worship with Western, classical religious music—i.e., "music of quality married to words of substance." He acknowledges that there are other sources of music for religious use. But, he explains, "those sources are simply outnumbered, in terms of variety and sheer quantity, by the liturgical products of the Western Christian canon. Moreover, much contemporary praise music is repetitive in melody and flaky in text."

To limit God-encounters to Western, classical forms either because they are seemingly the most abundant sources or because they are considered more elevated for sacred use is exclusionary and inward—the opposite direction from the gospel. If other sources seem outnumbered, perhaps it is because a strong cultural bias prevents non-Western and generally non-classical sources from appearing on the formal-liturgical radar screen. And when other sources do surface—especially those of popular culture origin—it becomes easy to dismiss an entire body of material because some are inadequate, musically and/or theologically.

If our praise choruses are inadequate musically (which, let's admit, is often the case), we need to increase our skill level and get past the cheesy, 1980s compositional formulas. If our praise choruses are inadequate theologically (which many are), we have a responsibility to write better, deeper lyrics. The answer is not to stereotype popular music as unworthy for divine use. The answer is to get better and more faithful at using both popular and non-Western forms. We have had a five-hundred-year filter to cull out the bad—i.e., inadequate—hymns, and to be honest, we still have some less-than-model selections in the lexicon. Conversely, we have only had a scant thirty years to sort through thousands of newly composed hymns and praise choruses. Pastors and worship leaders, I invite you to become more intentional about choosing and writing contemporary music that has musical and theological excellence. And don't forget all the historical forms that are at your disposal: hymns, creeds, psalms, kyries, the Gloria Patri, Eucharistic prayers, Scripture readings, etc. These ancient conduits are awaiting rebirth in celtic, rhythm and blues, urban, alternative rock, and even ambient techno styles. But whatever we do, let us not default to one form of music as the apex of quality and religious acceptability. God is far too creative and God's world far too diverse to be limited to a single cultural expression.

SPONTANEITY AND PREDICTABILITY

Zahl asserts that one strength of formal-liturgical worship is that it is "not governed by the spontaneity of the moment or the spontaneity of the officiant." Spontaneity can definitely be abused. Stream-of-consciousness prayers can sacrifice direction and depth, while end-of-praise-chorus mantras can function as so much service filler rather than purposeful encounter. And true, the blank-slate, "whatever-we-feel-like-doing-this-week" approach to worship planning can fall short of worship substance.

That being said, the abuse of spontaneity does not mean we need to do away with spontaneity. Neither does the absence of spontaneity (defined by Zahl as worship that is more "dignified") ensure that a worship experience has been more sacred or somehow more acceptable to God. (One has only to read in 2 Samuel 6—the story of David's wife, Michal—to find out what God thinks of our notions of what is dignified in worship.)

The crux of the matter is this: Must we depend on four-hundred-year-old service formats—intact, without alteration—to ensure right worship? Or have we learned enough from these laudable models (i.e., have we done enough of our own theological and historical homework) that we are able to weave God's Grand Story into fresh, new forms—worship experiences that meet people where they are—and also give them the unchanging person and reconciling immediacy of God? Luther, Calvin, and other Reformers deconstructed the Mass and then reconstructed it for a new era of biblical understanding and a new culture. They were practiced in the art of incarnational ministry: God's divine pattern of meeting human beings at their specific point on the timeline, at their place on the globe, and in the languages and aesthetic expressions they speak. In hymns and Psalms set to popular folk tunes, theirs was the "mangerized" God—the servant deity who became sacrificially present to humanity in the mundane, immediate, and oh-so-particular circumstances of late Roman civilization.

Are we as preachers, worship leaders, and worship directors willing to be sacrificially and particularly present to our culture as God was and is through Jesus Christ? Are we, like the Reformers, willing to decipher the essence of faithful worship and recast it in the languages that people speak and understand today? It is extremely disconcerting to read Zahl's solution to the weekly task of worship crafting: essentially, open the book to the prescribed service for that Sunday and follow along. Worship that, in Zahl's words, "accepts the constraint of a consistent and predictable pattern" may be well meaning. It may default to several-hundred-year-old forms in order to ensure that the person and works of God remain the staple of worship (a commendable goal).

But if "the way we've always done it"—regardless of what tradition we favor—is the only means to attain worship faithfulness that we have to offer, we need to ask ourselves, "Are we punting? Are we simply taking the easy way out?" Leaders who, as Zahl describes, "approach Sunday without having to give particular thought to the shape of the service itself" are not functioning as true leaders. Rather, they are operating as curators, preserving a worthy but increasingly wooden past.

Zahl cites one of the chief benefits of formal-liturgical worship as eliminating any room for ad-libbing (the tendency to make things up as you go along). He extends this view to the concept of worship planning, claiming that contemporary services attempt to reinvent worship each week and, in doing so, fail. Again, this hard-line support of prescribed service formats may be sincere and well meaning. But it may also indicate both a lack of faith and no small degree of laziness. Let's face it: It takes courage to hold form and function, style and substance in tension; to take the old and put it in new wineskins. Quite honestly, it also takes persistent, weekly sweat. To wrestle with the issue of Christ and culture is one of the most challenging tasks we are given as ministry leaders. Zahl seems uninterested in taking up this challenge, unwilling to put out the effort it takes to balance roots and relevance. Referring to the weekly recrafting of faithful worship, Zahl concludes, "That, at least, is one burden this writer, as a minister of a liturgical denomination, does not carry." We have a choice. We can view worship crafting as a burden, or we can see it as an opportunity to reimagine faithful, living God-encounters for a new world.

Chapter 1: Formal Liturgical Worship Notes

Proposal: Paul Zahl

[1]James W. Kennedy, *The Unknown Worshipper* (Harrisburg, PA: Morehouse, 1964).

[2]The Roman Catholic Church as well as some schools of thought within the liturgical Protestant churches number seven sacraments. In addition to the Reformation's two Gospel or Christ-mandated sacraments, baptism and the Lord's Supper, such groups would number confirmation, penance or confession, marriage, ordination, and extreme unction as sacraments of the church. In their founding or confessional documents, however, all Protestant churches recognize only baptism and the Holy Communion as commands given by Jesus.

[3]Thus the Church of England's Article of Religion XXVIII (1563): "Transubstantiation (or the change of the substance of Bread and Wine) in the Supper of the Lord, cannot be proved by Holy Writ; but is repugnant to the plain words of Scripture, overthroweth the nature of a Sacrament, and hath given occasion to many superstitions."

[4]See Diana Hochstedt Butler, *Standing against the Whirlwind: Evangelical Episcopalians in Nineteenth-Century America* (New York: Oxford University Press, 1995); E. Clowes Chorley, *Men and Movements in the American Episcopal Church* (New York: Scribner, 1948); and Allen C. Guelzo, *For the Union of Evangelical Christendom: The Irony of the Reformed Episcopalians* (University Park: Pennsylvania State University Press, 1994).

Response: Harold Best

[5]"Concerning the Service of the Church," *The Book of Common Prayer* (New York: The Church Pension Fund, 1945), vii.

[6]Composition and improvisation are, in fact, applicable to a whole range of human action and in my estimation comprise a ready model for the ways in which God himself acts, for he is the ultimate composer and, within the fixity of many of his composed things, is the quintessentially ingenious improviser.

[7]Charles W. Koller, *Expository Preaching without Notes* (Grand Rapids: Baker, 1969).

Response: Robert Webber

[8]See also Prosper of Aquitaine (c. 390–463), *legem credendi lex statuat supplicandi* (the rule for interceding should establish the rule for believing),in Jacques-Paul Migne, *Patrologia Latina* 51:209.

Chapter Two

TRADITIONAL HYMN-BASED WORSHIP

TRADITIONAL HYMN-BASED WORSHIP

Harold M. Best

What is the rhyme and reason behind hymn-based or traditional worship and what might this practice look like to those who prefer it? Let me begin with this question from a perspective that takes in anybody's worship preferences. I believe they are generated in one of two ways.

First, individuals live long enough within an ecclesiastical tradition to become one with its particular dialects and to hear and respond easily within its constraints. They feel no urgent desire for radical change even though, in the cultural whole of their living, they may enjoy styles and dialects that are quite different from the one(s) with which they choose to worship. To this extent, one might say that traditionalism is a function both of time and association. The longer people enjoy a tradition, especially if they have grown up within it, the more reluctant they are to see it change. The more the tradition appears to be unique to the context in which it is practiced, the more it becomes one with the context. We might call this combination of time and association "traditionalism from the inside."

Second, others choose a worship style that most comports with an already established perceptual need to which they have culturally (instead of ecclesiastically) become accustomed. They then import this into the worship context. In reality, this is another kind of traditionalism. The difference between it and the first kind is that this tradition seems newer and closer at hand, having already been chosen and enjoyed outside of the ecclesiastical context. But it cannot be chosen and enjoyed without the passage of time and without a certain amount of accommodation. The passage of time turns it into a tradition, however new or "contemporary" it might seem to be. We can call this second type "outside" or "imported" traditionalism.

Ultimately this means that any tradition, including the so-called contemporary worship tradition, is obligated to join with the same question that the church has faced for centuries: What do we do next, and with what degree of resistance will nextness be met? In fact, there is already ample evidence to suggest that "contemporary worship" has settled into recognizable predictability after only twenty or thirty years of existence on the North American scene. In recent years we have also seen stirrings within some churches to form yet other worship styles, for example, for emerging millennials and/or postmodernists. Even as the possibility of further stylistic fragmentation presents itself, the tradition question will inevitably come back to address every fragment. This creates a further question, this one growing directly out of our immediate culture: Will worship styling continue to go along with a political, consumerist, and age-divided culture by continuing to answer to increasingly subdivided interest groups, or does it strive to create a dynamically relevant indigenous culture to which all interest groups must eventually say yes or no?

Please remember that in stating things in this way, I am not attempting to sneak up on any contemporary practice in the name of hymn-based worship. I fully believe that when the Spirit of God introduces his reforming power to the body of Christ, all practices are up for grabs.

We are not in a worship war. Well, yes we are, but not the one some commentators like to refer to. There is only one worship war, and it is between God and Satan, each the supreme object of someone's worship, either redeemed or lost. We are self-absorbed when we use the "war" word as a working term for the petty and overly self-indulgent skirmishes that we enter, almost always over transient, not eternal, things. The other contributors to this volume are people of peace, gentility, and unity. The object of a book like this, then, should be to show options within wholeness; better yet, to create wholeness out of options; even better than that, to long for a new synthesis of the things that are separated and to pray for a cadre of artistic and ecclesiastical leaders who will bring us into startlingly brilliant territory: hitherto unseen, uncrafted, and unified around the person of the Savior. Some might argue that this is too much to ask of artists and leaders, but it is certainly not too much to ask of the Lord of Pentecost. It is in this light and in this spirit that these few thoughts about hymn-based worship are offered.

HYMN-BASED WORSHIP AND AUTHENTIC WORSHIP

The subject of hymn-based worship has little meaning without a theological understanding of worship itself. It makes little sense to me to speak of hymn-based worship (or contemporary worship or blended or liturgical worship, for that matter) as if these either generate or are based on separate notions of what worship is, or as if worship were limited to the ways these notions were worked through within the time-style space-span allotted to them. I would much rather speak of worship-based hymnic practices or worship-based liturgical practices than the reverse.

Here is why.[1] We were not created to worship—this suggests that God is a being who needs that kind of attention. Rather, we were created worshiping—already at worship, already outpouring to the eternally continuous Outpourer, God himself, who, even before he breathed his image into our dust, was eternally pouring himself out to his triune self: Father to Son to Spirit, in unending bliss and love-riddled conversation;

who pours himself out in the endless wealth of his creatorhood;

who poured himself out in creating a race *imago Dei;*

who pours himself out in self-revelation;

who poured himself out in the atoning and reconciling work of his Son; and

who continues to pour himself out through the work of the Spirit and the Son in bringing the church closer to the stature and fullness of the Christ.

We fell. But this did not stop our worship and our outpouring. Rather, we exchanged gods and continued our worship. This is the only way we can explain the plethora of religions, religious systems, and gods, along with our continual and continuously varied efforts to reach, serve, and placate them, always and everywhere. True worship—that is, godly and Christ-centered worship—is the redemption and washing clean of this continuum. It comes into being, not out of nothing, not out of the blue, but out of a divine work in a lost and fallen heart. It comes only when we, as continuous but inauthentic worshipers, give ourselves to Christ, who alone can take our falsified condition, turn it right side up, wash it in his blood, and direct it to his glory throughout the remainder of time and into the infinite arrivings of the eternities to come. Unceasing worship—continuous outpouring—marks the way of the entire world. God through Christ takes this infected glory and restores it. Thanks be to God.

Hence the conviction that all of our redeemed living is unceasing worship, continuous outpouring. Hence the assurance and the challenge that we do not as much go to church to worship as journey there to continue our worship in company with brothers and sisters as a local manifestation of the gathered body of Christ himself—his bride, washed and newly virgin, for the marriage supper of which he is the one and only Holy Groom.

As I proceed, I want to avoid definitional quandaries concerning what a hymn is, compared to, say, a gospel song, or a spiritual or a chant or a chorus. This would take too much time and offer very little to the core of the issue. Therefore I shall extend the idea of hymn-based worship to everything contained in hymnbooks, for it is the book part that interests me far more than typological definitions of "hymn." I realize that hymnbooks vary in content, scholarly accuracy, and artistic quality. I further realize that there is a fine line between certain kinds of hymn-based worship and formal-liturgical worship in that both practices make good use of hymns and each makes use of a liturgy of one sort or another, given the root meaning of liturgy as a service or work performed in light of a task at hand. If I happen to venture into formal-liturgical territory, it is because of the near-seamlessness of worship forms that employ hymns and also because many hymn-based practices have their historical roots in the classic liturgies. I would urge all readers to see these connections in a positive light and, for that matter, to forge connections on their own among all of the practices mentioned throughout this book.

Allow, then, this brief definition of hymn-based worship. In its usual structure, it is directed toward a seamless linkage, in no particular order, of:

- Sung text (congregational, choral, and solo) and instrumented music
- Instructional and responsorial sentences, said or sung
- Selected Scripture(s)
- Prayers of three general kinds:
  —Brief invocations/petitions/benedictions
  —Congregational prayers of confession, praise, and intercession
  —Pastoral prayers, offered on behalf of the congregation
- A sermon or brief, interconnected homilies
- Offerings of temporal goods in a spiritual manner
- Periodic (usually monthly) celebrations of the Lord's Supper, with its own self-contained musical, textual, instructional, and devotional actions

In some congregations a set order is established with little or no variation from week to week, while in others, variation, resequencing, and even wholesale borrowings from classical liturgies are common.

Given these actions, what is it that makes hymn-based worship a vital and persistently dynamic part of the total worship of the body of Christ? All along, I want to think about what should be vital about it and not what might happen to be the case in this or that hymn-based assembly. I put it this way because spiritual vigor and structural imagination are not always evident. This is not the fault of the practice but of the practitioners. You also must know that I am not personally pushing hymn-based worship over other kinds, given my long-standing love of liturgical worship coupled with a fervent desire for synthesis, wide-ranging creativity, and reform within all aspects of the church's worship life. In fact, if I were to have been given the assignment of critiquing the current worship scene, I would have, among other things, taken hymn-based worship to task for its failure to understand that the best traditions are dynamic, culturally alert, and ever-changing. Finally, it might be useful for you to know that over the span of nearly a half century I have worked as an organist, pianist, choir director, or organist-director in the following contexts: Episcopalian, American Baptist, Conservative Baptist, Presbyterian, Mennonite, Christian and Missionary Alliance, Reformed, Evangelical Covenant, interdenominational Bible, and military chapels.

TEXTED SONG IRRESPECTIVE OF STYLE

Please permit a few words about texted song of all kinds and in all styles, for that is what all church music is fundamentally about. In texted song we have a marvelous example of the union of truth and artifact. Call this union by any one of several names: chant, hymn, gospel song, psalmody, praise chorus, anthem, solo, oratorio, cantata, or response. Call it old or new, useful or useless, traditional, contemporary, popular, classical, relevant or irrelevant. But whatever you call it, you are talking about one thing: texted song. The puzzling thing about all this song is that most of the debate about it, both now and in times past, is not about the absolute side of it—truth—but the artifactual and relativistic side of it—music. Let me put this negatively: That which should unite our practices—namely, truth—takes second place to what so often divides us—namely, music. There may be opinions and debates about how truth is to be expressed in a text, or what truth might be chosen for expression—whether through the strict iteration of the Psalms or through metrical versions of them or through Christocentric paraphrases of them or through freely composed texts that range over the entire counsel of God; and whether to emphasize a particular doctrine or counteract a certain heresy. But these are all about the permanent stuff of truth and not about the transient stuff of music. Nonetheless, music often turns out to be the line in the sand, as it certainly is at this time.

If there is a difference between the current scene and historically earlier ones about musical style, it now rests in the antipathies of classical and popular (read traditional and contemporary) rather than sacred and secular (read churchly and worldly). For a number of reasons—some good, others questionable—the majority church no longer seems troubled over the sources from which its musical styles are drawn.[2] This has come to mean that imitating secular creativity is not as problematic as imitating traditional. This new distinction makes matters more difficult for church leadership because tradition itself—the traditions handed down, the succession of traditions, the heritage of many centuries, the very stuff that leads on to further change—is questioned.

THE HYMNBOOK ITSELF

Above all, one cannot talk about the value of hymns in worship without first of all acknowledging the unique value of the hymnbook. There is no time here to go into the history of its evolution, from simple collections of tunes and texts to complex and multi-useful documents. Suffice it to say, the best hymnbooks are treasure troves of theology, prayer, Scripture, song, hymnic information, stylistic variety, and liturgical opportunity. Wisely and creatively used, they form the backbone and primary sourcebook of church music, the center around which all remaining song and instrumental practices are to be gathered.

The hymnbook is one of three texted sources without which authentic hymn-based worship is impossible. The other two are the Word of God and optional prayer books and liturgies. In any case, the Word of God is the primary and indispensable dayspring for the remainder. I shall not deal with prayer books here except to say that their validity depends solely on their faithfulness to the Word, and prayer books and liturgical documents should comprise a significant part of the working library of all church leaders, whether or not their use is actually required.

What about this time-tested book of hymns? What is it capable of doing? Here are a few responses to these questions.

The hymnbook is a temporal and artifactual servant of the Word of God. Let us take this sentence in reverse. It is a servant of the Word of God in that it has regularly proven itself in the task of putting to words (most often rhymed and metered) the entirety of the character of the triune God, his works, his plans, and his accomplishments. It likewise scans the condition of humankind in its worth, its plight, its needs, its varying circumstances, its responsibilities, and its ultimacies. In this sense, the hymnbook is, in its own way, a comprehensive exegetic work; it is metrical theology. Over centuries of thought and practice, hymn writers have virtually left no topical or theological stone unturned.

Hence, we can safely say that a properly compiled hymnbook is a primary and indispensable source for thinking and singing biblically.

The hymnbook is artifactual in that, despite its truth moorings and except for its Scripture readings and lectionaries, it is a human construct. It is temporal in that it is impermanent, noncanonic, evolving, and on occasion, unbiblical or theologically careless. Despite limitations and lapses, the hymnbook has historically been true to scriptural truth in examining the whole of its disclosure to us. In fact, hymns have been not only theologically proactive but counteractive as well, in that more than once they have been specifically composed to counteract heresy and infidelity.

The hymnbook is a remarkably diverse stylistic archive. The worshiper is not only exposed to, but comes to be conversant in, a plurality of literary and poetic styles, from the earliest free-form chant texts to a variety of rhymed and metered shapes. While no one should base the validity of the hymnbook on aesthetics alone, no one should deny that it contains countless examples of poetic expression that as literature rank extremely high. In this sense alone, the hymnbook continues to serve the body of Christ as one of its primers in poetic excellence. It has shown the Christian how theological eloquence and clarity can be pared down to a simple couplet, yet expanded into more extensive forms that are both architecturally sound and eminently singable. The church cannot afford to turn her back on this rich storehouse. Except for the current group of excelling hymn writers—of whom mention will be made subsequently—the church has no current alternative.

But beyond mere poetic quality, the same is true of the content. The Lord, working through his company of poets, has seen to the composition of texts that cover every quarter of the human condition and every aspect of the counsel of God. In that the literature of the contemporary/praise and worship practices has so far done little to cover the full scope of God's workings, the human condition, and its responses, it behooves every leader to find a way to fill this vacuum. For this reason alone, the hymnbook should remain at least one of the working parts of all worshiping bodies and worship styles. True, there are many hymns that are out-of-date and many that are qualitatively insecure, but excellence, irrespective of style, is timeless, therefore contemporary.

Just as the textual content of a good hymnbook is stylistically diverse and poetically excellent, so is its musical content. Once again, the worshiper has the opportunity to take to heart, mind, and ear an amazing variety of musical styles. What other cultural source—sacred or secular—offers so many functional musical options in so little space? Two thousand years of musical evolution are offered: chant, psalmody, carols, folk tunes, ethnic tunes, curving Welsh ballads and hearty English melodies, Germanic stoutness, French clarity, early American forthrightness, gospel tunes (both black and white), nineteenth-century sweetness, twentieth- and twenty-first-century freshenings and asymmetries.

Some of the greatest examples of simple tune writing come to us in the hymnbook. I have a doctorate in composition and for years taught composition at the undergraduate level. I can tell you that one of the most difficult things for any composer is to imagine and craft a good, simple, and singable tune. Yet, in the hymnbook we have scores and scores of them, some good, others great. Out of the twelve pitches that we Westerners have at our disposal, some of these tunes have sprung to life using only four. Hundreds of them use just five pitches, and the overriding remainder of them confine themselves to seven or eight. Beyond the use of this limited pitch inventory, hymn tunes must also humbly serve the text and comport to its curvature, various meters, and size. In Johannine terms, the music must decrease so that the text can increase. On top of it all, these tunes are meant to be mastered by the laity, not the trained professional. While they must welcome and gratify the untrained ear, they must not confound its limitations. Hence, just as hymn texts are miniature theological, poetic, and aesthetic primers, the tunes are miniature musical primers. The legacy and literacy of tunefulness among the laity is a remarkable value, and in this way hymnody has served both general and ecclesiastical culture admirably.

The hymnbook and hymn-based worship thrive on hands-on printed material. A hymnbook is a portable, readable, concrete body of work. The words are there, easily at hand and available even when the projection screen is turned off. The music is printed. It can be read and learned by being seen. It is in its own way an excellent primer for sight singing. Even those who cannot read music in the academic sense of the word learn to see and follow pitch curves, rhythms, and harmonic textures simply by watching them move around on the page. And often this approximate reading leads to precise reading. When printed music is used with children and children's choirs, they pick up indelibly on a kind of musical literacy that will remain with them for the rest of their lives. In fact, public school music education at its best still looks back to, and honors, the New England Singing School tradition founded by none other than the hymn writer Lowell Mason. To the extent that many contemporary practices have overlooked the value of visual musical literacy and carry-around texts, and in a literal sense have reverted to preliterate oral tradition, they are failing—not just the church, but culture. The hymnbook easily corrects this lapse. We must remember that a musically educated singing church—congregation, choir, and above all, carefully trained children—not only comprises a fitting worshiping community, but enriches a musically wayward culture itself.

The history of choral music, especially in the Protestant church, is tightly interwoven with the hymnbook. As was said early on, the hymnbook is the backbone of all church music. This is true not only because congregational song is the heart and soul of all church music, but also because all other church music must answer to the centrality of congregational song. Many choral works—long and short, new and old—are nothing other than hymn arrangements, in that hymn texts and/or tunes are the source of the larger work. The songs of the congregation fuel instrumental pieces, often called chorale preludes, chorale fantasies, partitas, or just plain arrangements. ("Chorale" is another word for congregational song.) The tune becomes the *cantus firmus,* the fixed song of a particular arrangement. Thus, what is sung by the congregation, what is performed by choral ensembles or soloist(s), and what is played on instruments are kin to each other, discrete members of a large family, each of whom graces and welcomes the other.

Therefore, with the Word as the center of all church song, the hymnbook as its singable exegetic companion, and a significant body of hymn-related church music, we have a living organism that is virtually without parallel in the life of the church.

Because of this organic union, it becomes quite easy and often desirable to construct the entire musical part of a complex liturgy around hymns and hymn tunes. This is a tremendous binding mechanism, an aesthetically pleasing and theologically informative structural device. It is something that thinking leaders and responsible laypersons come both to treasure in its use and lament in its absence. This aspect of traditional worship has very little to do with "We've always done it this way, so why change?" and everything to do with "Here is an incomparable repertoire in which truth, art, and liturgy cohere. Join with us in its surprises and rewards." If there is anything that the traditional hymn-based worshipers need to do in this respect, it is to become newly awake to this rich potential, to make varied use of it with a hearty faith and lively imagination.

The hymnbook is a working history of the creative struggle to go beyond the singing of pure Scripture. Do not misread this. I am not by any means speaking against the intonation or melodizing of pure Scripture. I could wish that this practice were a regular part of the song of all worshiping bodies. But hymnody is a testament to something else, something of supreme importance: Thinking biblically allows ordinary people to think alongside the Scriptures, in direct faithfulness to them, while setting its truths to their own poetic frames of reference. In this sense, all hymn writers participate in the Word first of all, only then joining their creative skills to its truths. Thus, singing the Scriptures and scripturally surrendered hymns turns out to be a wonderful and massive metaphor for the union of divine revelation and human response. The very existence of hymnody is tantamount to God saying, "Now that I have said all that I need to, let me hear you talk and sing back to me on my terms using your own creative devices." Or, put it this way: As the Word of God is read in a worship service, the hymns in that same service talk back to the Word and onward to God in faithful concord. In this sense, congregational song joins prayer and homily in prophesying: It speaks up, speaks out, and speaks truth.

The hymnbook is a magnificent instrument for private devotion. I speak first of all as a musician. I have real trouble singing text in corporate worship because my mind is fixed on the musical side of the equation: Is it good music? What makes it good? How would I play it or direct it were I up front? What changes and variations would make it even more dynamic? And so on. But I also speak as one who finds it difficult to repeat something without thinking slowly and deeply about what I have just repeated. When I sing hymns in corporate worship (or for that matter, repeat prayers), they go by too fast, so I stop singing and begin to think about what I have just sung. I fall behind.

But let me have a hymnbook in the spiritual time warp and quiet of my home. Give me time to read and reread, to ponder, to paraphrase, to conjoin my reading with Scripture and private prayer. Let me sink my spiritual teeth into the meat of a great Watts or Wesley or Dudley-Smith text. Let these texts metamorphose into personal prayers and longings. Let these and more come together as the Spirit wills. Let them spring toward the Scriptures that have inspired them and then back to the hymn text. Let the Bread of the one furnish the crumbs of the other with heavenly nourishment. Let even one line of a hymn walk around in my heart and mind for a day or so. In all of these activities and more, I find in the hymnbook a companion—a lifelong companion; I find a devotional instrument of extraordinary strength and wisdom.

If the hymnbook suffers neglect in our times, it is not so much because shortsighted and thoughtless pastors and worship leaders have discarded it, but because it is sequestered away in sanctuaries and used only on Sundays. Over the course of a singing year, maybe twenty or thirty percent of its contents, give or take, will have been used. But give every parishioner a copy of a great hymnal and challenge each one to absorb and integrate its contents fully into an eager and farseeing devotional regimen, and you will have a revival of interest, not just in hymn singing, but in the Lord himself. No concept of hymn-based worship is complete without vigorous attention to the hymnbook as a permanent part of everyman's devotional apparatus.

The hymnbook is both a scholarly undertaking and a cleverly flexible musical resource. Hymnology is a respected professional discipline. Its leading scholars have not only furnished human culture with conceptual, historical, bibliographic, narrative, and theologically centered thought, but have set the example for hymnbook compilers and editors to proceed carefully and accurately. An examination of hymnbooks such as *The Worshiping Church* (Hope), *Worship II* (GIA), and *The Covenant Hymnal* (Covenant) will demonstrate the extent to which editors, compilers, committees, and task forces have labored to produce collections that contain a wealth of carefully researched information.

One of the joys of going through a good hymnbook is to peruse its Scripture readings and lectionaries, stories, prefaces, indices, creedal statements, devotional commentaries, suggested orders of worship, and prayers. The subtitle of *The Covenant Hymnal* is "A Worship Book." The case for a good hymnal could not be better stated.

A good hymnbook is also clever—or maybe I should say a good hymnbook in the hands of a clever worship leader is a remarkably flexible tool. Through the use of metrical and tune indices, new matchings of tunes and texts can be found that allow for variety and freshness. For instance, in a church with a limited music budget, a modest but eager choir, and minimum arranging skills on the part of the leader, new combinations of tune and text can be turned into fresh, singable, and accessible anthems, and not a penny has been spent on music.

THE HYMN AND THE LITURGY

The foregoing has already included much information that bears on hymn and liturgy. But a few more matters can be added that are directly associated with the orderly flow of corporate worship. All along I am using the word "liturgy" the way others might use the word "service." As already suggested, a hymn-based worship service is a liturgy of one kind or another. I prefer "liturgy" over "service" because of its linkages to the whole round of public and private action, each a liturgy to the Lord, each a composite of bowing down and serving.[3] Furthermore, I can use the word "service" to refer more aptly to a quite common practice in hymn-based contexts, the traditional song service.

There is an interesting and easily ignored relationship between those song services and current praise and worship practices. In each case the song part is a distinct and separated module placed at the beginning of the entire service. It can be of any length, it can include spontaneous choices, the leaders and accompanists usually are more prominent, there is a marked degree of informality throughout, it is seldom knit to what follows, and its overall ethos is one of personal and subjective piety. The old line service (a free combination of hymns, gospel songs, and choruses) is more correctly called a service—a liturgy—whereas the terms "praise" and "worship" imply that these describe but one part of the corporate gathering. This is in contrast to the biblical directives that praise and worship should not only take in a single action but also comprise a continuous way of living.

However, as valuable and spiritually uplifting as the traditional song service is, it does not completely fit the classical idea of hymn-based worship. In the latter, hymn singing is a continuous part of the overall tapestry, an intrinsic part of the flow of the liturgy. As already suggested, it links with other musical and textual actions throughout the liturgy: choral music, instrumental preludes, interludes, offertories, postludes, and the like. This linkage is sometimes direct in that hymn texts and tunes comprise the thematic content of the whole. At other times it is corollary when texts and music are not hymn-related. Even so, hymn singing is not a module but an organic part of the whole. In that the design of the hymnbook is meant to cover the church year for formal-liturgical worship and to cover topically the entire work of God, discerning hymn choice invariably folds into the flow of the service. In this sense the congregation understands its ministerial, even priestly, importance as well as its participation throughout the liturgy, making hymnic comment on sermon, prayer, sacrament, invitation, entering, and leaving.

This unity further suggests that leading worship in a hymn-based context is an ongoing task instead of an upfront responsibility for just one segment. In many churches, in fact, more than one person may be designated as assisting (rather than leading) in worship, undertaking different actions at different times. The sharing of leadership carries with it the assumption that no one individual really leads worship, as if this were biblically possible in the first place.

I want to refer back to an earlier mention of a cadre of imaginative, fresh, and theologically alert hymn writers. These come quickly to mind: Bishop Timothy Dudley-Smith, Fred Kaan, Fred Pratt Green, Margaret Clarkson, Brian Jeffrey Leach, and Carl P. Daw Jr. Hope Publishing Company (Carol Stream, IL) has done a noble job not only in publishing the hymnal *The Worshiping Church,* but in producing, quietly and at no small cost, readily available collections of hymns by a majority of these writers. No leader should ignore them, and no stylistic practice should exclude them, for they are with the times, well written, often pithy, and always singable.

OF ORGANS AND PRAISE BANDS

This is as good a place as any to bring up the subject of keyboard instruments, especially organs. I would contend that organ playing is indispensable to hearty congregational song, despite the thoughtlessness with which the validity of this instrument is questioned as part of outmoded traditions and listening habits. Before going further, I want to be the first to acknowledge that the organ has been misused by being overused by zealous, solo-minded performers. I would also acknowledge that the organ world has often sired a kind of snobbery that has impeded the concept of church music as humble service. Finally, I acknowledge that for many, the organ has turned out to be a mystically overpowering idol. More than the legendary king of instruments, it has often been seen as the king of kings, with many organists choosing their church jobs on the basis of the quality of the organ rather than on the call of God to quiet, meek service.

Even so, the baby should not be thrown out with the bathwater. Let me say why. The very basis of the design of even the most modest organs flows directly out of natural, God-given laws found in the overtone series. I want to avoid the massive technicalities of physics and acoustics, so let me say it this way: Without any doubt, the organ is the most naturally supportive instrument for singing that Western culture knows of. Its very design and its intelligent use in hymn singing are meant to accomplish one purpose: to support singing by the intelligent use of registers chosen to fill in the cracks—to provide both an underpinning and a blossom to the work of the congregational voices. The result is a synergy: the whole greater than the sum of the parts. People are moved to heartier song without being overpowered or displaced, and their natural untrained voices are significantly validated and enhanced. True, there are those times when the organ soars above and beyond its normal collaborative task in the provision of free accompaniments and occasional iterations of brilliance and dash. But in the hands of a good organist, these should be reserved for those momentary or seasonal and festive times when clear hymnic water is turned into the polyphonies of rich wine. An organ does not have to be gargantuan to accomplish these tasks—not when it is well designed and properly played.

I want to be respectful and thoughtful in these next words, and I realize that I might be wandering into the territories and preferences of other contributors to this book. But as valuable as the instruments and sounds of the typical praise band might be, they often do little to bolster and enhance congregational song in the pure sense of physics and acoustics. They can easily overwhelm to the point where congregations no longer hear themselves sing and end up accompanying the worship band, when the reverse should be true. This does not mean praying for good riddance. That would be evil. Rather, it means that musicians who truly understand the laws of sound, the acoustical congregational voice, and the rigors of instrumental collaboration must make use of their instruments in radically different ways. I attend a church in which the worship band—especially the drummer—understands how delicate and understated their work can be. As a result, there is better singing and less watching than I have observed in so many other churches and colleges around the country. By the same token, organists must be more insightfully trained as to how the instrument is to be played beyond the often boringly slow and tedious sound masses that are enough to put a thunderstorm to sleep.

I long for the time when all instruments together comprise a worship band, where insightful musicians will come to understand the orchestrational aspect of instrumental music. I mean this: A skillful orchestrater understands that all the instruments at his or her disposal do not play all the time—no, not even the drum set. Rather, through sensitivity to the rich variety of musical contexts and, in our case, to the wide-ranging contexts of congregational song, instruments and instrumental combinations are chosen that remain in perpetual ebb and flow, showing sensitive shifts of color and texture based both on the art of musical action and the nuances of text and context. This is not impossible; it is simply difficult. But what isn't when it comes to doing things well?

A PRAYER FOR THE CHURCH

I conclude with the quotation of two stanzas of a hymn by Carl P. Daw Jr., with the prayer that the body of Christ will stay awake and alert to the fullness that continues to come in tune and text.

Sing to the Lord no threadbare song, no timeworn
    toothless hymn,
No sentimental platitude, no empty pious whim;
But raise a song just off the loom, fresh woven, strong
    and dense,
As new as God's eternal now transcending time and
    sense.

Let earth's diverse, melodic tongues declare in telling
    phrase
The glory of the only God who merits thanks and
    praise.
All other hopes will disappoint, their brittle luster fade,
But sure and strong remains the Lord by whom all
    things were made.[4]

A LITURGICAL WORSHIP RESPONSE

Paul Zahl

Harold Best's treatment of "Hymn-Based Worship" approaches being a masterpiece. This is because it distills a lifetime of leadership within traditional churches. It covers the big issues, such as the continuing relevance of hymnals; the volume and core significance of the organ (as well as its potential idolatry); the whole long repertoire of Western hymnody; and the relation of hymns to liturgical worship on the one hand and to "contemporary" worship on the other. The author also writes in an endearing style.

What I take Best to be presenting is very much what Episcopal worship, speaking from my own tradition, was all about until 1979, when the prayer book was changed. What Best calls a "brief definition of hymn-based worship" is the order and presentation exactly of traditional Anglican Morning Prayer. I find this model to be crisp; Word-centered but not waterlogged by texts; dynamic, even fluid; and eclectic in appeal, assuming sympathetic and faithful leadership on the part of the minister.

Sadly, Episcopalians, together with most Lutherans, have thrown out this familiar model. What Harold Best is talking about here is *dead* within the mainline Protestant churches. Dead and extinct. Gone with the coelacanth.

Now this picture of hymn-based worship as liturgy is in fact not antediluvian! It is radical. Dr. Best's chapter is radical.

The essay is radical, first, because it puts the church in continuity with classic Protestant hymn writing, which is interconnected to the theology of grace enunciated vividly and enduringly by William Cowper and Isaac Watts, Charles Wesley and A. M. Toplady. Seventeenth- and eighteenth-century Protestant hymnody is much less legal than it is graceful. When we chuck the old hymnals, we open a massive stone door for the Orcs of legalism. Life is better when John Newton rules!

Best's essay is radical, second, because it sees through the false allure of overemphasizing the Eucharist, a mischief characteristic of late-twentieth-century liturgical churches. The Eucharist is not a converting ordinance. It is a sustaining one. The Eucharist every Sunday bespeaks a chaplaincy model of the local church—"I'm in with the 'in' crowd."[5] In contrast, hymn-based worship, as Harold Best enfleshes it, is much more evangelistic in intention.

The essay is radical, third, because it is emotional in the hidden recesses. Here I am picking up on Best's idea of "traditionalism from the inside." It is not true that the average American does not know—subliminally at least—a whole drawer full of old hymns and hymn tunes. The old standbys are deeply anchored in our individual and cultural unconscious. When apparently secular people wander into traditional churches out of personal need and hear old hymn-tunes and texts, they weep. We do not live in the U.K.—not yet. People here still have this material in their bones.

I remember listening to Philip Kaufmann, director of the 1984 version of *Invasion of the Body Snatchers*, explaining why he used the tune "Amazing Grace" at the climax of that haunting science-fiction movie. He said the tune evokes hope to almost everyone—even in Hollywood. You don't have to be a practicing Christian to have heard and ingested "Rock of Ages."

When the church uses these old tunes and texts, we are making a radical emotional catharsis available to returning POWs from the secular world's aggressive superficiality. Our traditional hymns are cathartic. When we forget this, we enter the moist zone of the insipid.

Fourth and finally, Best's ideas about the organ are radical. This is because the organ is the instrument given us by God to allow the human voices to sing over it. It does not drown out the congregation. (Of course it can, but only in the bondage of a prima donna.) Unlike many amplified praise bands—and we honestly have a fine one, a discreet one, at my parish in Birmingham—the organ is able to support the singers, not render them uncommitted. The organ is able to nurture emotionally faithful participants.

All this means that I give Harold Best's argument an "A." I wish, in fact, that he were still looking for a job. Has he been able to reproduce himself? I feel certain that in relation to his concept, time is on his side.

A CONTEMPORARY WORSHIP RESPONSE

Joe Horness

Because I grew up in a traditional church environment, hymns were almost a part of my DNA. My mom, a world-class organist, could play any hymn from any hymnal, by memory, in whatever key you started singing in. I grew up hearing those songs before I even entered this world! As I grew older, my dad often led the singing on Sunday morning (and again on Sunday night), and my three sisters and I, left unattended in the second row, would do our best to cover all four vocal parts with great gusto. Reading Harold Best's chapter on hymn-based worship brought back many rich memories.

Best's chapter also stirred in me a renewed appreciation for all that I received, often unknowingly, from those years of "hymnal-based" training. It seems as if I have always known that my God is "a mighty fortress," a "bulwark" (although it took me some years to figure out what that was!) that would never fail. I have always known that he is holy, have been amazed at his matchless grace, and have found myself humming "Great Is Thy Faithfulness" at times when life seemed most unsure. Best reminded me again that the hymnal has indeed been a treasure trove of theology, prayer, Scripture, and song that has played a very central role in much of my understanding about God. As I read his chapter, I looked at the hymnal on my bookshelf with a renewed sense of wonder; it is an amazing book that has largely been taken for granted in my life. It has taught me great truths around which, as Best states, our hearts should be united. I couldn't agree with him more.

For these reasons and a myriad of others, I love the old hymns. So, given the rich resource that Best has described, and even my own rich heritage with hymns, why would I challenge us to integrate what is best about hymn-based worship with the ongoing expression of what God is doing in worship today? Why not just shout a hearty "amen" and let's get on with life as we've known it for the past hundred years?

Three primary reasons come to mind. The first is that hymn-based worship, as we know it today, too often leads to complacency and causes us to miss the explosion of God's creativity and the movement of his Spirit that is ongoing in the world. The second is that it tends to negate those who are writing modern-day hymns, those who are continuing the tradition of giving testimony to what God is doing in their generation. The final reason is that hymn-based worship is often clung to by churches that would rather look inward to the likes and dislikes of the already convinced than to look outward to a world in need. Churches filled with people who are passionately praying that friends they love will come to know the saving grace of Jesus usually find that they can be more effective in helping them do that when they put the great theology of the hymns and the Word into a language those friends can understand.

The hymnal, as Best describes it, is indeed a diverse, flexible, and theologically rich tool. But the truth is that no matter how wonderful the tool, its effectiveness is still determined by those who use it. When we worship, God has called us to engage not only in learning comprehensive theology but also in authentically communicating our love and adoration to him. It is one thing for theologians and writers to claim that when we sing a hymn "the congregation understands its ministerial, even priestly, importance," but it is another thing entirely to sit in the back row of a typical church and sing a few. Not many church members, if any, are considering how the hymns are part of the overall tapestry of history and liturgy, covering the entire work of God in partnership with the living Word. The reality is that all too often the members of the congregation are disengaged and disinterested, lulled by familiarity and repetition into going through the motions while our churches foster and maintain a culture that keeps us distant from a dying world. Just as contemporary worship races onto shaky ground when we mindlessly clap and settle for trivial lyrics propped up by rhythmic guitars, so hymn-based worship is stripped of its power when the very book in our hands gives us an excuse to simply flip pages, forgo creativity, and passively mouth words that flow from minds set on autopilot because we've been here too many times before.

My struggle is not with the tool, nor with those who wrestle to use hymns in a way that truly causes people to engage their hearts and minds in expressing their worship before our worthy God. On the contrary, my desire is to renew and reclaim the best of what is found in hymn-based worship for the contemporary church. The problem arises when the church refuses to grow and learn, when we cling to the historical at the expense of the spiritual, and when the subtle goal of using hymns is to maintain tradition, not to deepen worship. The difficulty continues when the priority becomes preserving our indigenous church culture at the expense of remaining inaccessible to the culture outside our church walls.

Our job as worship leaders is to help move people's hearts, both the churched and the unchurched, toward the truth of God, toward the wonder of his grace in all his holiness and mystery, and to help us respond to the truth of who we are in his presence. Hymns creatively chosen, thoughtfully expressed, and musically prepared in a relevant way can be a part of helping us do so. And to that end, by all means they should be used. But sometimes, when used almost in defiance of new styles and expressions of worship being written today, they become the tradition that binds us to the overly familiar, and that quietly suffocates what is genuine and real in our praise. More often they remain one more hurdle that those outside the faith must clear simply to enter God's fellowship with us. That which once made him more accessible to people often obscures him now.

Jesus has called the church to be a light to a lost world. Especially in today's culture, the music we use to communicate our message plays an enormous part in that effort. If we believe that the church was created by God to be the messenger of his love to the lost; if we believe that the church is not simply for the edification of believers but is the hope of the world; if we believe that the arts can communicate the love of Christ effectively and powerfully to those who desperately need to know him; then we have a choice to make. We can communicate the love of God through music and worship in a style and language that our unchurched friends can relate to and understand, or we can ask them first to enter into, then to understand, and finally to accept a churched culture (including the organ) that has become woefully out of touch with them before we even begin to tell them of Christ.

In essence we tell the newcomers, "Learn my language and then I'll describe God to you." This is simply unthinkable to me, and I believe that it breaks the heart of God! Jesus himself worked hard to enter into the world of those he came to heal and to save. When he taught, he communicated in stories and idioms that his culture would relate to. In centuries past, the church music some of us love so much today was written in an effort to do the same. The old hymns were written, just like many of the contemporary hymns being written today, as powerful, educational, and culturally relevant expressions of what God was doing in the lives of the people of that generation.

The practice of giving voice to what God is doing in the current generation simply continues today. Old songs give birth to new songs in a never-ending testimonial of the activity of God. The styles have changed, but the intent is the same. The truth is the same. In our efforts to applaud the rich heritage of the past, we must not negate the efforts of those who are giving expression to who God is through music today.

Fanny Crosby wrote five thousand hymns. About ten of those made it into the hymnbook. Similarly, there are hundreds of songs being written and recorded today that will never be counted as classics. But there are many amazingly gifted contemporary "hymn writers" today who continue to put God's activity into song. Writers like Tommy Walker, Darlene Zschech, Chris Tomlin, and Brian Doerksen are writing songs that also flow right from Scripture.

Many of those songs paint us theologically rich pictures of God and truthful pictures of our human condition, just as the hymns do. And yet these songs call us to respond to those truths in ways that this culture knows and understands. The church is to be a city on a hill, a light in the darkness (Matthew 5:14). The experience of God we offer to those who enter our walls should be one that glorifies him in all of who he is, but does it in a way that invites the uninitiated to participate in that with us.

I love the hymns. As Best so beautifully states, there is no worship war! I am moved by the wonderful reminder he has painted me of the heritage, the theology, and the rich culture my worship experience has afforded me. As a worship leader I will continue to write hymn arrangements that can bring some of the richness of that past into the church of today. But I also want to continue that heritage by writing and leading songs that give fresh expressions of who God is. Even the Psalmist implores us to "sing to the LORD a new song" (Psalm 149:1)! I want to be a part of that movement as well. He is not just the God of yesterday. He is still God today. And because of that, my priority will always be to find the most effective and relevant ways to engage the hearts of the church in authentic expressions of love to him and to make his amazing grace as accessible as I possibly can to all who would seek him.

A CHARISMATIC WORSHIP RESPONSE

Don Williams

Harold Best begins his chapter with the sociological observation that the longer you live within a tradition the more comfortable you become with it. When the tradition appears unique to its context, it becomes one with it. So we have sacred spaces where we do sacred, religious things little connected to the outside world. No wonder the mainline denominations are graying and shrinking. They have lost most of the next generation, starting in the radical 1960s, unable to respond to the massive cultural shifts that came with the times.

The comfort of tradition explains why older congregations fight innovation, but of course this applies or will apply to contemporary worship as well. The radical and new becomes standard within a generation. As Luther said, what is gospel today becomes law tomorrow. There was a time when hymns reflected the outside culture rather than an ecclesiastical world all their own. But now they have become more and more remote. As the church walks through its traditional liturgies, it seems distant, archaic, dated, and unappealing to the contemporary, secular world. It has little connection with outsiders seeking to become insiders. It also reinforces the generation gap, blind to the whole postmodern culture that the church must reach or die. Best himself, if invited, would critique hymn-based worship for its failure to understand that traditions must be "dynamic, culturally alert, and ever-changing." And, I would add, responsive to the presence and power of the Holy Spirit, as evidenced in 1 Corinthians 14.

No doubt hymns have much good and even some great theology, possess rich musical styles, maintain continuity with past generations, honor and enhance organs, fold easily into liturgies, may (and I stress "may") enhance congregational singing, and, in hymnbooks, are portable, contributing to private devotions. Although Best hardly acknowledges it, no doubt hymns can also be used in contemporary, blended, and charismatic worship.

We must remember that contemporary and charismatic music came to the church from the "outside" during the Jesus Movement and the worship revolution that it sparked. Indeed, masses of new converts tried to carry their culture into the traditional church and even embrace its hymn-based culture as their own. But most mainline churches rejected them. ("Too experiential, too weird looking, too apocalyptic, and they even played guitars!") For this new generation to sustain and grow its own life, it had to find its way with little or no help from established denominations.

Best's hope that the church will someday find a "dynamically relevant indigenous culture to which all interest groups must eventually say yes or no" is a dream. The church never has found one—from Episcopal liturgy to revival services to Black Gospel. In a postmodern world with massive pluralism, it may even be a bad dream. We have never risen above H. Richard Niebuhr's social sources of denominationalism,[6] and today's pluralism makes this even more improbable. In fact, such pluralism (a market-driven, disestablished church in the U.S. with all its denominational diversity) is good for church growth and keeps many groups in a state of revival.[7] As mainline decline continues, hymn-based traditional worship will weaken as the mature (pre-World War II) generation passes.

When Best writes, "I fully believe that when the Spirit of God introduces his reforming power to the body of Christ, all practices are up for grabs," those who delight in charismatic worship couldn't agree more. This worship continues to develop. It seeks the freedom and leadership of the Spirit in every service. It welcomes pluralism in musical expression, including time-honored hymns as they are woven into a new worship tapestry.

Best attends a church that has a worship band. He himself, apparently, has moved beyond simply hymn-based worship. I would love to hear how hymns fit into this setting. To rewrite Jesus' saying, "Therefore every worship leader who has been instructed about the kingdom of heaven is like the owner of a house who brings out of his storeroom new treasures as well as old" (see Matthew 13:52). The same Spirit who inspires the best of charismatic worship hasn't missed the last 1,900 years of church history. To hear from him is to hear all that he has done in every generation, including our moment, and receive it with gratitude.

A BLENDED WORSHIP RESPONSE

Robert Webber

I find it very difficult to respond to Harold Best's contribution on "traditional hymn-based worship" for several reasons. First, Harold and I are friends and colleagues, having taught together for more than two decades at Wheaton College (in different departments). Second, my expertise is in theology, not music or hymns, so when I am put into music discussions I am a neophyte. And third, I regard Harold as the premier thinker in the area of music in worship and prefer, if anything, to sit at his feet.

This chapter is full of profound insights set forth in eloquent poetic language. Harold's mastery of worship—its theology, history, interface with culture, and bearing on spirituality—is evident on every page. I have no contention with anything stated in his chapter. So what I am going to do is to interact with the profound statements made on the theology of worship.

Harold rightly speaks of the triune God who "pours himself out" in Creation, in revelation, in Jesus Christ, and in the Holy Spirit, "bringing the church closer to the stature and fullness of the Christ." True response to God's "outpouring" is found in Christ alone, who takes the "infected glory" of God's creation and restores it. Thus, our worship is an "unceasing worship, continuous outpouring" of our life journey in the "manifestation of the gathered body of Christ himself." This is an abbreviated look at his fuller definition. Now to my comments.

First, this understanding of worship rightly begins with God, not the self. And it points to a balanced triune nature of worship as opposed to a worship that is Father-driven or Son-driven or Spirit-driven. Worship is the work of the triune God, and the worship (service) that is most pleasing to God the Father is the work of the Son—his incarnation, death, resurrection, eternal intercession at the right hand of the Father, and return to vanquish all the powers of evil and rule as Lord over all creation. The war is between God and the powers of evil. Who will win this war? Who will rule over God's entire creation? God in Jesus Christ through the power of the Spirit has won back creation and creatures to his glory. "Every creature in heaven and on earth and under the earth and on the sea, and all that is in them" are singing: "To him who sits on the throne and to the lamb be praise and honor and glory and power, for ever and ever" (Revelation 5:13).

Second, once it is in place that worship is all about God and the *missio Dei*, then we can begin to understand what it is that we do in our public gatherings of worship and in our lifestyle of worship. We tell and enact God's story in our gatherings. In this we proclaim the meaning of human existence from beginning to ending. And as we rehearse this story through music, the arts, preaching, and the Eucharist, we are formed and shaped by this story so that our lives—personal, family, work, recreation, social communion—express a continual and unceasing praise, as Harold has so well stated.

I hope every reader will listen to what Harold has said. This biblical understanding of worship will turn us away from the narcissistic preoccupation with worship as self-gratification and restore worship as God's work of renewing the face of the earth. This worship will stimulate our gratitude, spoken and acted out in the assembly and lived in all of life to the glory of the One who creates and redeems to recreate.

Thanks, Harold. I hope my theological musing has done your thinking right.

AN EMERGING WORSHIP RESPONSE

Sally Morgenthaler

I grew up in a hymn-infused world, plunking out my first hymn melodies at age two. By age five I was playing hymns such as "Onward Christian Soldiers" and "The Old Rugged Cross" two-handed, by ear. Throughout elementary and junior high school I accompanied the school Christmas programs (improvising my versions of Christmas carols) and accompanied hymn-sings at nursing homes, Sertoma meetings, and church potlucks. Around age ten I was working daily through the big blue book of Bach chorales, an assignment given me by my very astute piano teacher. By age twelve I was transposing those chorales into several keys. By college I was singing all manner of marvelous hymn arrangements as a member of the St. Olaf Choir. Great hymns have nurtured both my faith and my musical progress. Consequently, Harold Best's chapter resonated with me in a personal way. I freely admit a resultant lack of objectivity on the subject (I'm partial to hymns!). Best's chapter only helps to increase my admiration for this marvelous song form and the services built around it.

First, I greatly appreciate Best's distinction between a service that merely inserts hymns and a service that uses hymns texturally and theologically or, as he puts it, liturgically. If one wants to know what is beyond praise and worship, it is that mostly uncharted frontier beyond the familiar twenty-minute song set (handed down, as Best points out, from hymn-sing practices). In the new worship frontier, artfully tapestried, eclectic new liturgies are being created, including hymns both new and old, readings, poetry, newly composed litanies, biblical narrative, dance, meditations, and prayers. This new frontier of emerging, cross-centered churches is a present-tense reality that, for whatever reason, Best could only assign to the future. His lofty vision—"a new synthesis of the things that are separated ... a cadre of artistic and ecclesiastical leaders who will bring us into startlingly brilliant territory: hitherto unseen, uncrafted, and unified around the person of the Savior"—is, as I write, already being realized. Yet it is taking shape largely outside the high-culture circles that for decades have dominated discussions surrounding faithful liturgical practice.

Best makes the rhetorical statement that such a synthesis may be "too much to ask of artists and leaders." He then follows this statement by the conviction, ". . . but it is certainly not too much to ask of the Lord of Pentecost." Perhaps we need to ask the Lord of Pentecost to free us from the constrictions of the "higher/lower" culture debate and let the Spirit create rich and faithful liturgies out of all the languages of the people: digital art, photography, and video; neotribal, techno, and popular music; indigenous, community-derived prayers (in all the various historical forms); street-level, theologically rich readings accompanied by multimedia; the Lord's Supper as multisensory celebration; Scripture as told narrative versus life manual; and of course, new songs that capture the sweep of the Grand Story of God rather than simply the immediate current of personal emotion.

Best's self-proclaimed passion, a "long-standing love of liturgical worship coupled with a fervent desire for synthesis, wide-ranging creativity," just so happens to be the newfound passion of many twenty- and thirty-somethings as well as increasing numbers of those in their forties-through-seventies who are disenchanted with the limitations of the traditional/contemporary split. Best asks, "Will worship styling continue to go along with a political, consumerist, and age-divided culture by continuing to answer to increasingly subdivided interest groups, or does it strive to create a dynamically relevant indigenous culture to which all interest groups must eventually say yes or no?" Again, Best may not be familiar with what has been emerging in nascent worship cultures over the past decade. Increasingly, the age and ethnicity scope is enlarging, producing exactly the "dynamically relevant indigenous culture" attractive to a wide variety of interest groups.

Although an awareness of specific emerging worship patterns seems to be lacking in his essay, Best's evaluation of hymnology as treasure troves of theology and anthropology could not be more on target and is, in my estimation, one of his pivotal paragraphs. Hymnology, he says, "has regularly proven itself in the task of putting to words (most often rhymed and metered) the entirety of the character of the triune God, his works, his plans, and his accomplishments. It likewise scans the condition of humankind. . . . We can safely say that a properly compiled hymnbook is a primary and indispensable source for thinking and singing biblically."

Having made a case for the educative role of hymns, Best then makes this claim: ". . . the literature of the contemporary/ praise and worship practices has so far done little to cover the full scope of God's workings, the human condition, and its responses." I would have agreed with his statement until about six years ago. Since that time, there has been a flood of new hymns coming initially out of the United Kingdom and then inspiring a fresh depth in North American hymn writing. These fresh compositions do not come from the fine, albeit more traditional sources Best mentions—*The Worshiping Church* (Hope), *Worship II* (GIA), and *The Covenant Hymnal* (Covenant)—but out of a younger version of the praise and worship movement. Here are but a few examples of fresh, popularly derived lyrics, which, I daresay, accomplish theologically and anthropologically what Best seems willing to attribute only to classically styled hymnology.

Breathe

> Silence fills a formless void
> Darkness spills over the deep
> The spirit of the Lord hovering
> Then you breathe
> You spoke the word
> And life begins
> You spoke the Word
> And life begins
> Deep calls to deep wondering

Then you breathe
And everything begins here
But you saw more
Everything begins here
You must have known
You'd shed your blood for me
Dust to flesh
You formed a man who
Falls from grace and knows his sin
But love chose redemption
Love chose redemption and you
Breathe.[8]

Beautiful, Scandalous Night

Go on up to the mountain of mercy
    To the crimson perpetual tide
Kneel down on the shore
Be thirsty no more
    Go under and be purified
Follow Christ to the holy mountain
    Sinner sorry and wrecked by the fall
Cleanse your heart and your soul
    In the fountain that flows
    For you and for me and for all
At the wonderful tragic mysterious tree
    On that beautiful scandalous night you and me
Were atoned by His blood
    And forever washed white
    On that beautiful scandalous night
On the hillside you will be delivered
    At the foot of the cross justified
And your spirit restored
    By the river that pours
    From our blessed Savior's side
At the wonderful tragic mysterious tree
    On that beautiful scandalous night you and me
Were atoned by His blood
And forever washed white
    On that beautiful scandalous night.[9]

Best seems deeply concerned with preserving the specific literacy (print) that hymn-based worship has traditionally required. He states,

> To the extent that many contemporary practices have overlooked the value of visual musical literacy and carry-around texts, and in a literal sense have reverted to pre-literate oral tradition, they are failing—not just the church, but culture. The hymnbook easily corrects this lapse. We must remember that a musically educated singing church—congregation, choir, and above all, carefully trained children—not only comprises a fitting worshiping community, but enriches a musically wayward culture itself.

To dub North American culture as "musically wayward" is a serious claim, one that reveals a deeply held bias—one that also happens to be deeply flawed. Musical intelligence can certainly be enhanced by an ability to read musical notation. But as a musician myself, I fully understand that the ability to read notes comes nowhere near to encompassing musical intelligence. If that were true, many of our most gifted gospel, jazz, and pop musicians would be rendered musical idiots.

But there are even more foundational issues here. In light of Howard Gardner's pioneering work on multiple intelligences,[10] Best's fixation on print is, at the very least, anachronistic. Yet, when one considers that North America moved into a print-plus-image-and-sound world in the latter part of the twentieth century and is fast moving to an image-plus-sound-and-print world, confining literacy to ink on a page smacks of cultural arrogance. In theological terms, such a view is the antithesis of incarnational, for God came and continues to come to us in the languages we speak and in the very cultures we inhabit (Philippians 2:5–11). It just so happens that most North Americans no longer inhabit the world of print.

In Best's own words, "That which should unite our practices—namely truth—takes second place to what so often divides us—namely music. . . . [We should be most concerned about] the permanent stuff of truth and not about the transient stuff of music." One could very well add, ". . . the transient stuff of books and screens." Either we believe truth is no respecter of form, language, or intelligences, or we do not.

There are enduring reasons why both hymns and hymn-based worship structures should be a part of every worship leader's palette. I appreciate the incisive work Best has done in this chapter identifying the prodigious doctrinal and musical gifts resident in both hymns as compositional form and the services hymns co-create. My hope is that his lyrical and musical benchmarks for excellent hymnology will inspire—in profusion—a new wave of Christocentric, passionate songs, and worship services in the church, regardless of style.

Chapter 2: Traditional Hymn-Based Worship Notes

Proposal: Harold Best

[1]I refer the reader to my book *Unceasing Worship: Biblical Perspectives on Worship and the Arts* (Downers Grove, IL: InterVarsity Press, 2003) for an extensive treatment of worship as a lifelong continuum of which corporate worship is but one aspect.

[2]In a chapter this short, it is impossible to develop the good and bad reasons. However, a few of them may be listed here for further thought. The good reasons consist of at least the following:

- A theologically sound questioning of artificial boundaries between the sacred and the secular
- Fruitful efforts among Christian thinkers regarding the absoluteness in Truth and the relativity in artifacts
- Theologically positioned thought about the dignity and worth of the artifactual side of all cultures
- Efforts of missiologists, ethnotheologians, ethnomusicologists, sociologists, and anthropologists in the area of contextualization

Questionable reasons might include the following:
- Among some leaders, a naïve equation of relevance and immediacy
- Careless or unconscious flirtation with postmodernist relativism and political multiculturalism, each one spiritualized and methodologized
- With some leaders, the creation of a new practitional dualism through the wholesale separation and/or rejection of traditionalism and the adoption of the "contemporary"
- Related to this, a failure to understand that cultural diversity is the theologically proper basis for unity

[3]See David Peterson, *Engaging with God* (Downers Grove, IL: InterVarsity Press, 1992), 55–70, for a useful discussion of the distinction and relation of bowing down and serving.

[4]"Sing to the Lord No Threadbare Song" by Carl P. Daw Jr. © Copyright 1995 Hope Publishing Co., Carol Stream, IL 60188. All rights reserved. Used by permission.

Response: Paul Zahl

[5]From the song "The 'In' Crowd," by Billy Page, recorded by Dobie Gray (Charger Records, 1965).

Response: Don Williams

[6]H. Richard Niebuhr, *The Social Sources of Denominationalism* (New York: Meridian, 1957).

[7]See Roger Finke and Rodney Stark, *The Churching of America 1776–1990: Winners and Losers in Our Religious Economy* (New Brunswick, NJ: Rutgers University Press, 1992).

Response: Sally Morgenthaler

[8]Matt Brouwer and Jill Paquette. "Breathe," on *Imagerical* (Reunion Records, 2001). Brentwood/Benson Music Publishing Company, 741 Cool Springs Blvd., Franklin, TN. Used by permission.

[9]Bob Bennett, Derald Daugherty, and Julie Miller, *At the Foot of the Cross* (Imaginary Music, vol. 1, 1997). Brentwood/Benson Music Publishing Company, 741 Cool Springs Blvd., Franklin, TN. Used by permission.

[10]Howard Gardner, *Frames of Mind: The Theory of Multiple Intelligence* (New York: Basic Books, 1983).

Chapter Three

CONTEMPORARY MUSIC-DRIVEN WORSHIP

CONTEMPORARY MUSIC-DRIVEN WORSHIP

Joe Horness

THE HEART OF THE MATTER

While reading through the Old Testament recently, I was caught by surprise. I expected to get a renewed picture of the holiness of God, and I did. I knew that I would once again stand in awe of his power, and I did. The verses that commanded me to fear him and obey him jumped out at me and convicted me, just as I thought they would.

But the more I read, the more I was moved by something else. Above all, our God—the God of the Universe, the God who is above all gods, the God who is holy and powerful and wants our obedience—longs for relationship with us. Can you imagine? God longs for something! The One who is above all and who created all still desires something. And that is to be our God. To be *my* God. To be in relationship with all of us. I was surprised to find that in the Old Testament. Somehow I expected it to be a New Testament theme, found primarily in the story of Jesus and the early church. But here it was, written across page after page of the Old Testament in the story of God's covenant with Israel and the world.

Listen to God's heart as he expresses it here to Moses, just after leading the Israelites out of Egypt:

> I will consecrate the tent of meeting and the altar; I will also consecrate Aaron and his sons to minister as priests to Me. I will dwell among the sons of Israel and will be

their God. They shall know that I am the LORD their God who brought them out of the land of Egypt, *that I might dwell among them*; I am the LORD their God" (Exodus 29:44–46, italics mine).

Time and again this longing springs from the heart of the God of the Old Testament. He yearns for his people to be obedient not just because he is holy, but because it is an indication of their relationship to him. He longs to be honored and loved for who he is and for what he has done among them.

You can feel the divine pathos as God implores, "How long will this people spurn Me? And how long will they not believe in Me, despite all the signs which I have performed in their midst?" (Numbers 14:11). He desires their worship, not to somehow meet the needs of his heavenly ego, but because it is an indication of the relationship he shares with the people he loves.

This is the pattern of God's faithfulness and his people's unfaithfulness. God draws the people to himself, longing to be honored as their God. The people rebel and serve other gods. God brings judgment upon them. They cry out, not so much in real repentance as in a desire to be freed from the pain. God hears their cry and is faithful to his promises in spite of them. Slow to anger and abounding in loving-kindness, pursuing relationship once again, he brings them to a place of healing and blessing. The people get comfortable and rebel. And on it goes.

In the book of Isaiah we find God preparing to judge the people of Israel once again. He gives them fair warning. He is very clear about the rewards of repentance and obedience and about the consequences of their disobedience. He proclaims his desire simply to be their God. Above all, we glimpse the longing of his heart as he informs the people why this judgment is about to take place: "This people draw near with their words and honor me with their lip service, but they remove their hearts far from me, and their reverence for me consists of tradition learned by rote" (Isaiah 29:13).

God is not condemning huge sins or child sacrifices or debauchery. Something else is breaking the heart of God: dutiful worship, expressions of love that are not really expressions of love at all, tradition that becomes rote, going through the motions, lip service.

Impossible as it seems, the people's hearts simply are not moved in any real way by the continued love and mercy and faithfulness of their God. And in essence, God replies, "I hate dutiful worship. If your heart is not moved by who I am, then better that you not go through the motions at all."

Jesus echoes this theme in the New Testament. Confronted by the Pharisees, Jesus quotes this same passage from Isaiah and follows it with the powerful statement, "in vain do they worship me" (Matthew 15:8–9). Jesus makes the point very clear. If our worship is just about singing songs, getting people in the door before the announcements, or killing twenty minutes before the message, then do not bother. If we are reciting creeds simply because that is our tradition, knock it off. If we seek supernatural miracles simply for our benefit and for what we will receive, we have missed the point. If our hearts are not engaged in authentic expressions of love for him, if this is not about a relationship with our Creator and Redeemer, then God is not honored.

John Piper expresses it this way:

> If God's reality is displayed to us in His Word or His world, and we do not then feel in our heart any grief or longing or hope or fear or awe or joy or confidence, then we may dutifully sing and pray and recite and gesture as much as we like, but it will not be real worship. We cannot honor God if our hearts are far from Him. The engagement of the heart in worship is the coming alive of the feelings and emotions and affections of the heart. Where feelings for God are dead, worship is dead.[1]

A few years ago I was asked to participate in a debate at a Christian college and seminary. The discussion was to revolve around what the professor called "the dumbing down of worship." Predictably, the conversation revolved around the rich theology of hymns versus what people perceived to be the emotional shallowness of contemporary choruses. Eventually the discussion included topics like the majesty of the organ versus the earthiness of drums. I did my very best to listen, which was not easy for me, and to respectfully consider what each group was offering. Finally, I had listened for as long as I was able.

"Do you mind if I share something here?"

"Oh, Willow Creek! Yes, please, go right ahead."

I had a sneaking suspicion that since I came from a very contemporary church, they did not expect my opinion to be on the majority side.

"I think you've raised some great points about the depth of hymn lyrics and about the rich history of music in the church," I said. "But if I'm really honest, I do not think that God is overly concerned about whether we are singing a chorus or a hymn. And I do not think he really cares whether you are playing the organ or the drums. What I think he cares about is this:

"'A mighty fortress is our God a bulwark never failing . . .'"

I sang it as listlessly and unenthusiastically as I could.

"Or similarly," I added, "'Jesus draw me close, closer Lord to you . . .'"

I sang it the same way: one hymn, one contemporary chorus, total boredom.

"What I think God cares about is the disengaged heart. I do not think that he is particularly interested in our theories or techniques of worship except as they are effective in genuinely drawing hearts to him. Worship that is not heartfelt and authentic simply does not interest him."

This passion to see hearts fully engaged, to radically eliminate dutiful, going-through-the-motions song times, and to bring people into a powerful time of relationship with our living God is what is at the heart of contemporary worship renewal. At its best, contemporary worship was born not simply out of a desire to swap the organ for a guitar, but out of an intense longing to somehow move from the casual, disinterested reciting of creeds and singing of hymns into an authentic time of loving and grateful interaction with the One who shed his blood for us.

UNDERSTANDING CONTEMPORARY WORSHIP

Contemporary worship endeavors to use modern instrumentation (e.g., guitars, drums, synthesizers, percussion, horns), contemporary musical styles (e.g., rock, jazz, hip hop, rap, gospel), and freshly written or arranged songs (both new choruses and fresh treatments of traditional hymns), in the language of this generation to lead people into authentic expressions of worship and a genuine experience of the presence of God. In addition, contemporary worship often combines these musical forms with other creative elements, such as Scripture, prayer, liturgical elements, and visual images, in an effort to help people fully engage their hearts in worshiping the Lord.

Unfortunately, the move toward contemporary worship is often seen as a jettisoning of old values rather than as a move toward engaging hearts more fully and using a language that the next generation can relate to and understand. Without a clear vision of the goal, the organist and the choir director simply feel rejected. Those of us who grew up on the old hymns miss the familiar songs and decry the seemingly trivial and emotional lyrics of many of the new choruses being written today. What once at least had a sense of reverence and holiness to it, even if hearts were not particularly engaged, often has been lost in the latest vocal fills and guitar rifts of the new worship leader. Unfamiliar with and unclear about where this new genre is supposed to be taking us, churches fight over the obvious changes and hunger to retreat to what once was familiar ground. Plug in the organ. Bring back the Easter cantata. Lose the microphones. But contemporary worship, when properly employed, has the opportunity to be so much more than what we see at first glance.

The move that many churches have made from traditional to contemporary worship involves very visible changes that often obscure the underlying values that should be driving the change. Most of us would recognize traditional worship as worship that includes the hymnal, organ, choir, and a song leader. We would probably associate liturgical worship with robes, responsive readings, and the reciting of various prayers and creeds. Similarly, when I ask people to define contemporary worship, they immediately list things like drums, guitars, choruses projected on slides, a worship team on microphones, and a worship leader. And on the surface, they are pretty close.

But just as traditional worship is more than a hymnbook and liturgy far more than the reciting of the Apostles' Creed, the first step to understanding contemporary worship is to understand the goal of the changes that are being made. Most of the struggles and boardroom discussions taking place in churches seem to revolve primarily around issues of instrumentation, volume, traditional versus contemporary song selection, and how our constituency will react. On the negative side, decisions are made to "keep worship the way it is" simply so that no one will be offended. Conversely, changes are often made not because of the joy it would bring our Savior but because someone thinks it would increase attendance. "How quickly we forget what it's all about," says Tommy Walker, a good friend of mine and a well-known contemporary worship leader. "We can get so strategic that we worship so our church will grow, not because He is worthy. But we're doing all this because God is worthy and we want to worship Him."[2]

If you were to take away only one insight into contemporary worship from this chapter, let it be this: People of this generation are longing to experience the genuine presence of God. And God is longing to move in and among the hearts of his people. If we will learn to worship from hearts that are fully engaged, God will be glorified and set free to move in us and among us.

The twenty-five years I spent in my traditional church, with Mom at the organ and Dad leading the singing, awakened a deep longing in me, as it has in the people of this generation. The great hymns of the faith taught me wonderful things about God, enriched my theology and my understanding of who God is, and in many ways painted a picture of God that laid the foundation for what was to follow. But I began to realize that singing about God was somehow not enough. I wanted to know him. I wanted to interact with him. I wanted to experience the things I was singing about and find them to be true. I began to understand that worship, as it is described so vividly in Scripture, was meant to be a dialogue, flowing from the outpouring of a relationship with God.

Sally Morgenthaler describes the problem well: "We are not producing worshipers in this country," she writes. "Rather, we are producing a generation of spectators, religious onlookers lacking, in many cases, any memory of a true encounter with God, deprived of both the tangible sense of God's presence and the supernatural relationship their inmost spirits crave."[3]

William Hendricks has documented that the question the occasional church attendee of this generation most asks is "Where is God?" This question, writes Hendricks, "lies at the heart of why people come to church. They expect to find God there. And why not? If you can't find Jesus in a church, then where can you find Him?"[4]

For some, the goal of traditional worship may be to impart great theology through the hymns of John Wesley and others. Other traditionalists have expressed to me the desire to "preserve the classic music of our faith." For some of my charismatic friends (some, not all), the goal of worship seems to be to experience the miraculous—to see healings, to receive words of knowledge, and to feel the Spirit of God move in tangible ways. But for the contemporary worshiper, the main goal is relationship. We are beginning to understand that worship is more than one-way communication from us to God. It is a two-way communication between God and his people. We exalt God. He reveals his presence and changes our hearts. We pour out our hearts and remember his greatness. Refusing to be outdone, he meets our needs for intimacy and grace.

"Essentially, Christian worship is the spirit and truth interaction between God and God's people," writes Sally Morgenthaler. "It is an exchange."[5]

To assist this generation with such an exchange, the contemporary worship movement has indeed made adjustments in how people approach God. For much of post-Christian America in the 1970s, church music had become a stumbling block rather than an avenue for connecting with God. Organ music and choir pieces, while having rich significance to the elderly in my church, no longer bore any resemblance to the music that so deeply stirred the hearts of my generation. Hymn lyrics, while full of rich poetry and deep theology, focused wonderfully on who God is but often failed to give worshipers an opportunity to express to God how they felt about those things. And for a growing number of us who watched with alarm as the church became less and less able to communicate in a relevant way with our unchurched friends, there was an increasing awareness that the church would somehow have to learn to speak a language our friends would understand. For us and for our friends, to draw near to God in an authentic and heartfelt way was going to require a new way of communicating with him.

Out of these longings and concerns contemporary church music began to emerge. Groups like LoveSong and singers like Larry Norman began to play and sing songs that communicated to this new generation. Though not widely accepted at first, the thought that guitars could be used by God and that new, contemporary lyrics could be penned by those who love him was out of the box—and once out, there was no turning back.

SEEKER SERVICES VERSUS WORSHIP SERVICES

Willow Creek Community Church was on the front edge of this change (at least among noncharismatic churches) when it began in the mid-1970s. Most of us from those early years had grown up in very traditional churches and certainly appreciated the education and heritage they had given us. But we had also seen firsthand how poorly the traditional church communicated to our unchurched friends. Bringing a nonchurched friend to church was like bringing them to Mars. The music was different and unfamiliar. The quality was often poor. Even the language we used often made it difficult for them to understand the life-giving message we were trying to communicate. The whole experience was designed for the already convinced. Church was certainly not a place we wanted to bring our friends and almost mercifully was not a place they wanted to come. But it was unthinkable to us that our unchurched friends, and thousands like them who lived all around us, would simply be left to drift away from God into a Christless eternity. So we continued to ask ourselves the questions "Why do our unchurched friends not attend church? If we designed something with them in mind, what would that look like?" And we began to craft services designed to bring the gospel to our friends in a way they could relate to and understand.

From early on we believed that the arts, including contemporary music and drama, could be used to draw people's hearts to God. We decided from the very beginning to devote our weekend services to evangelism and outreach, reasoning that if our unchurched friends were going to attend church, they would most likely come on Sunday. So we wrote dramas, created multi-image slide shows, and gathered in the wee hours of the morning each Sunday to set up some basic sound and lighting equipment in the local movie theater. The modern seeker service was born.

Even then, people reacted. "Willow Freak" was a term I often heard tossed around. Somehow this idea that we could use contemporary forms of art to reach people with the love of Christ was just too much of a leap for folks back then. People who had never been to Willow Creek accused us of "watering down" the gospel. But that never happened. The idea was not to build a big church. The idea was to see our friends follow Jesus. Therefore we were committed to God and to each other to preach the whole gospel, in all of its truth, without apology. And we did. We simply decided to try to teach God's truth in a way that our unchurched friends would be able to understand and apply to their lives.

Some people lamented the lack of God-referenced worship in deference to evangelistic services on Sunday mornings. But frankly, back then, if we found our worship experience to be meaningless, we were pretty sure that it would not be any different for our unchurched friends! And our weekend service, after all, was not designed for us. It was designed for our friends who still did not know Christ. So we usually sang one or two new worship songs in a weekend service, then leaned more heavily on special music, drama, and video to communicate the ideas we were trying to convey. We had a lot to learn. But we persisted, and God was faithful.

While our church has learned over the years to covet and cherish our times of worship together, and while the look and feel of our seeker services has continued to evolve and change as our culture shifts and changes, we still commit every weekend to providing a place where our unchurched friends can understand the amazing grace of Jesus.

If weekends were for outreach, however, then we quickly realized that we would need an additional time designed to grow and deepen our believers' relationship with God. With that in mind, the core of our young church would gather each Wednesday night for a time of singing and teaching. This service was completely different from our weekend service in that it was completely designed to minister to the hearts of believers. Somehow we knew that an essential part of developing fully devoted followers of Christ would have to involve worshiping God in spirit and truth, but none of us had any idea of what that might really look like. So we did our best. There were not many contemporary worship songs written back then, but we began with the few songs we could find, wrote a few others, and tried to write arrangements of hymns that the band could play.

Then in 1982 our senior pastor, Bill Hybels, attended a charismatic church while on his summer break. For the first time in his life, Bill experienced the kind of worship that we had been dreaming about—worship that was rich and heartfelt, where the presence of God was deep and real, and where hearts were changed as a result of being there. Upon returning from his break, Bill emphatically announced to our staff that somehow, some way, we were going to learn to worship.

For the next three months Bill taught our church about worship. He taught us about the character and power of God, knowing that our worship of God could only grow in proportion to the picture of him that we carried in our hearts. He taught us about what worship is and gave us a vision for what it means to come to worship expecting to meet with God. And he taught us that it was our responsibility to bring something to worship. We were not there to be wowed by the worship team. We came to bring God an offering of love and thanksgiving. The job of the worship team was to give us the best possible opportunity to bring that offering. We determined as a church that we would never again settle for going through the motions of worship. When we came to worship, we came to meet God. We came to fully engage our hearts and our minds in expressing our love to him. Weekends were designed to help our friends learn about God, but midweek worship was our time to celebrate, to be broken, to be in his presence, to celebrate Communion, and to open his Word.

We made a million mistakes. The learning curve was slow, both up front and in the congregation. We were learning new songs, trying to teach a whole band to play in a worshipful way, and trying to learn what it meant to model this kind of worship from the stage. We had to learn what it meant to be worshipers in our private lives so that what we did on stage came from authentic hearts. And we had to learn how to lead worship times that would help people fully engage in meeting and participating with God.

It was a whole new deal to teach our people to emote and express their love for God freely as well. Most of us had spent a lifetime singing songs without engaging our hearts and our souls in what we were doing. None of us had ever raised our heads, our hands, or our hearts. I do not think that any of us had ever really experienced what it meant to meet with God in worship in a genuine way. In twenty years of traditional worship I could remember having a lot of fun swapping vocal parts with my dad and my sisters as my mom cranked it up on the organ, but I could not ever remember being changed or deeply moved. But we hungered for that, and we knew that we wanted to learn. And we knew that God longed to meet with us as well. So we pressed on.

Gradually we began to recognize that God's deepest desire is that we would bring him our whole hearts in worship and that he would be free to move in us. It was never just about instruments or hymns. It was always about using those tools to create a time and place for God and his children to meet together.

KEEPING OUR EYES ON THE GOAL

With that in mind, let me reiterate: If we reduce the contemporary worship movement to a definition of worship that uses guitars and drums, or if we define it to the exclusion of liturgy or hymns or charismatic movements of the Spirit, we miss the point. At the heart of the contemporary worship movement is this longing to connect with God. To that end we use the music that best helps us speak our language, which for us means guitars and drums and music with a modern beat. But for most of us who lead in this manner, on the day when those instruments no longer serve us best, we'll lose them. If the congregation we are leading best connects with God through liturgy, then that is the tool we will use. When there is a traditional hymn that expresses the character of God or our love for him better than anything else, then we rearrange it a little and keep it in play. The instruments, and even the worship style, are only tools. They are not ends in themselves. And there is no competition with other worship styles. Ours is no better than theirs. We simply use what will serve our people best and help them encounter God most readily. The end is to meet with Jesus, to know his presence, to fully engage our hearts in authentic expressions of love to him.

This is what cutting-edge churches are learning. This is what real worshipers are beginning to understand. Musical styles play an important part in helping each generation communicate with God in a way that is familiar and that frees their hearts to meet with him. But the goal is not style. The goal is to produce authentic worshipers of Jesus Christ:

- People who are more and more attentive to his voice, are yielded to his Spirit, and are falling more and more in love with him
- People who are obedient to his call and committed to his service
- People whose hearts are deeper and quieter
- People who are dedicated to prayer
- People who are sold out to sharing the saving love of Christ with lost people who are desperately in need of him
- People committed to unity and community
- People who not only sing songs but live lives that are expressions of worship to him

Our worship should lead people into fuller devotion to Christ. As Bill Hybels likes to say, "Ninety-five percent devotion to Christ is not enough." I want to lead worship that calls our church into one hundred percent devotion to him.

THE HEART OF GOD

One of the common (and often valid) criticisms of the contemporary worship movement is that it seems very consumer oriented. People might read what I've written here and judge that it sounds like a bunch of selfish children who want what they want when they want it. "I want to experience God, so meet my needs. If drums and guitars help me do that, then unplug the organ. I am hungry for a supernatural experience, so provide one or I'll find a church that can."

If this movement were based solely on people's needs and wants, I would agree that we have a problem. But the outpouring of God's Spirit these days in many contemporary services is not occurring because churches are suddenly giving people what they want. The worship revolution we are experiencing begins in the heart of God. Worship was his idea. Our longing to be in his presence is always initiated by him.

Jack Hayford writes,

Worship is God's gift to man. [Read that again! Can you believe it?!] Worship has never been intended by God to be an occasion for proving one's expertise in religion, but for satisfying one's hunger and thirst for God. A Bible-centered approach to worship reveals that worship is not a God-built device to somehow get man to stoke a heavenly ego. Scripture consistently shows God calling his creatures to worship in his presence that he might release, redeem, renew and restore them.[6]

God desires that we worship in his presence so that he can move in our lives! God desires our worship—not just because he is worthy, but also because he knows that when we fully engage in worshiping him, it puts our hearts in a place where he can move and stir in us as at no other time.

Over and over again the Scriptures call us to worship the Lord. The Psalms exhort us: "Come, let us sing praises. . . . Sing to the LORD a new song. . . . Praise God in his sanctuary. . . . Let everything that has breath praise the LORD." Even the sun, the moon, the stars, and the heavens are implored to worship the Lord. Worship is clearly one of the most important things God's people can do. It is their first and ultimate calling.

Peter reminds us,

> You also, as living stones, are being built up as a spiritual house for a holy priesthood, to offer up spiritual sacrifices acceptable to God through Jesus Christ. . . . You are a chosen race, a royal priesthood, a holy nation, a people for God's own possession, that you may proclaim the excellencies of him who has called you out of darkness into his marvelous light" (1 Peter 2:5–10).

When we do that, God will be there. Psalm 145:18 says that God will draw near to those who call upon him. In John's gospel, Jesus tells the woman at the well that an hour is coming when "true worshipers will worship the Father in spirit and truth." Then he adds, "For such people the Father seeks to be His worshipers" (4:23).

Just a quick reading of the Psalms can give you a powerful vision of what God will do in the hearts of his people when they authentically engage in worshiping him. I encourage you to read through the Psalms again. Every time the writer refers to worship, see what the result is in his life. After compiling my own list through this exercise, I found that David and his fellow writers tell us that when we worship, we will develop nothing less than a yearning for God, joy, a passion for God's presence, an increased faith, a love for God's Word, comfort, an increased love for God, adoration, exaltation, celebration, thanksgiving, praise, unity, and repentance.

Are there any of us who are not longing to see these kinds of things occur in the lives of the people who attend our church each week? We work so hard to see life-change happen in people. We build beautiful churches. We prepare great messages. We run small groups and countless ministry programs in the hopes that real life-change will take place. But Scripture is clear that much of God's work will happen in our hearts only as we truly learn to worship him from the heart.

A. W. Tozer reminds us:

> Until the hearers find God in personal experience they are not the better for having heard the truth. The Bible is not an end in itself, but a means to bring men and women to an intimate and satisfying knowledge of God, that they may enter into him, that they may delight in his presence, may taste and know the inner sweetness of the very God himself in the core and center of their hearts.[7]

The hunger we feel to be in God's presence is not just the yearning of young, disgruntled churchgoers. It is a hunger placed in our hearts by our maker, and one he longs to meet. The transformation taking place in our churches, when effectively led, is one that God himself has initiated and has longed for. When we come to him seeking his presence, he is eager to respond.

THE ROLE OF THE CONTEMPORARY WORSHIP LEADER

As a contemporary worship leader, I come to the table with these understandings firmly in mind. I understand that the modern church faces many difficult changes and that the changes in worship are some of the most difficult many people will face. But I know that God has awakened in this generation a deep hunger not just to know about him, but to experience his presence in all of his power and grace. And God has awakened that longing precisely because it is his deepest desire to meet with and move in us. My calling is to lead our church into times of worship where God and his people can come together, where he is exalted, where we express our love for him, where he is free to move in us, and where our hearts are changed.

At its worst, contemporary worship is none of this. Without a stranglehold on what it is we are really trying to do, contemporary worship degenerates quickly into a poor man's version of what it was we were trying to emerge from. We can quickly trade songs of great depth and theological truth for choruses of sappy sentimentality. We can quickly shift away from focusing our minds on Christ to focusing our minds on how I feel. The Apostles' Creed was written by early godly believers in order to clarify exactly what we believe. How many young people today know it? Handel's *Messiah* can evoke in us a sense of awe at the holiness of God that no contemporary chorus can capture. I often sit in contemporary worship services and discover that we have simply traded three hymns for three choruses and have fired the organist in order to purchase drums, alienating our older Christ-followers in the process.

Contemporary worship can also become a performance. Praise team members sing their hearts out on the stage while the congregation is often left behind. We choose songs people do not know, in keys they cannot sing, to beats they cannot follow, and then wonder why they are not engaged. We forget that worship rises or falls on our concept of God. We forget that one of our primary challenges is to paint for people a great picture of God to which their hearts can respond. We forget the power of Scripture. We forget the power of prayer. We can easily gear our worship times around what we think is hip or cool and forget that our primary calling is to serve our congregation and help them meet with God. I often cringe to watch young worship leaders perform worship music, apparently more concerned about the sound of their guitar or the solo line they will sing than whether or not the congregation is deeply engaged in worship. Our first priority is not to perform. Our primary purpose is to lead God's people to meet God. If the congregation is disengaged, we are simply back to where we started with a different cast of characters.

OUR RESPONSIBILITY

At its best, however, contemporary worship is an amazing thing. Guitars and drums, when played by gifted and humble musicians, can proclaim the majesty of God as well as almost any organ offertory that Mom used to play, while in a style that my friends and my children enjoy and understand. A gifted worship leader will work not just to fill twenty minutes with unrelated songs, but to craft a time of worship that allows people to truly meet with God. A worship team, rightly coached and led, can model fully engaged, heartfelt worship to the congregation, causing the people to engage more fully as a result of their example. And congregations, over time, begin to come to worship with a sense of expectation that God will be there. They begin to come with hearts that are ready to meet God and with spirits that are longing to proclaim their love to God. They learn to come prepared, not just to receive, but to bring an offering of worship to the Lord. And they come expecting God to move, to speak, to convict, and to encourage. They come knowing that having been a part of this time will change them.

In the last book of the Old Testament, God returns one more time to this theme of relationship. Throughout all of the pages of history, God has never given anything less than his best to his children—Creation, the Exodus, the Promised Land, the temple, the Prophets. Over and over again God has poured out his best for those he loved. But the people have figured out once again how to bring their worst. The prophet Malachi writes that they have figured out that it costs a lot less to put a lame lamb on the altar than to offer the best of the flock. They know that offering the sick lamb that will die anyway makes more economic sense. But they have missed the heart of God that simply longs to be honored as their God.

> "If I am a father, where is My honor? And if I am a master, where is My respect?" . . .
>
> "You bring what was taken by robbery and what is lame or sick; so you bring the offering! Should I receive that from your hand?" says the LORD. . . .
>
> "But when you present the blind for sacrifice, is it not evil? And when you present the lame and the sick, is it not evil? Why not offer it to your governor?" . . . says the LORD (Malachi 1:6, 13, 8).

After all that God has done, is this the best that the people could muster to bring in return? A lamb that costs them nothing?

An offering that is convenient? A dutiful, going-through-the-motions expression of thanks? Tradition? Lip service?

Listen to the heart of God breaking as he proclaims,

> "Oh that there were one among you who would shut the gates, that you might not uselessly kindle fire on My altar! I am not pleased with you," says the LORD (v. 10).

As congregations who practice contemporary worship, we must know that the offering that we bring to God each week is of utmost importance. It is not enough to preserve the classic hymns. It is not enough to utter ancient phrases. It is not enough to play the latest praise songs with a really hot band. It is not even enough to speak in tongues. It must be our passion, and our calling, to lay upon the altar the very best offering that we can bring to God each week.

Bringing God our best does not come without effort and sacrifice. It requires prayer and careful planning. It requires prayerfully listening to God about where and how he would like us to meet with him. It requires carefully crafting worship orders that will paint people a great picture of God, and then designing and redesigning services that will give the people uninterrupted time to be with him. (Hint: Save the announcements until after the worship time! We work hard to get people's hearts engaged. Once they are there, do not interrupt it.) It requires artists, musicians, and technical people who are genuinely gifted by God to do what they do. It requires showing up for rehearsals. Lack of excellence ruins worship moments and causes people's hearts to disengage. It demands servanthood. This is not about our performance. It is about serving the people in our congregations as they come to worship the Lord. It requires authentic, godly worshipers who will model to our churches what it means to love Jesus and to love being in his presence. And for our congregations it will involve their hearts, their minds, their souls, and their wills. Fully engaged. Emotional. Surrendered. Heartfelt. Pouring out authentic expressions of love to the one who gave his life for us. The band, the choruses, and the worship leader are all secondary. They are the tools we use to help engage the hearts of our congregation in meeting with God.

A final thought. Following the book of Malachi, God is silent for hundreds of years. No more prophets. No more visible activity. The people had brought the cheapest lambs they could find. Now they wondered, how would God respond? Would he respond? They waited.

The very next thing they heard from God was this:

> In the same region there were some shepherds staying out in the fields and keeping watch over their flock by night. And an angel of the Lord suddenly stood before them, and the glory of the Lord shone around them; and they were terribly frightened. But the angel said to them, "Do not be afraid; for behold, I bring you good news of great joy which shall be for all the people; for today in the city of David there has been born for you a Savior, who is Christ the Lord"(Luke 2:8–10).

God brought his best Lamb. Let us do the same. Give him praise!

A LITURGICAL WORSHIP RESPONSE

Paul Zahl

Joe Horness's plea for contemporary worship in our churches is unapologetic. It seeks to persuade. I, for one, am skeptical; but there are important strengths here.

The heartbeat of the essay is the author's desire and hunger for all Christians—for all people—to experience the presence of God. In the face of traditional worship's coolness and detachment, the call here is to connect with God. Here is the crux of it, in Horness's words:

> Contemporary worship endeavors to use modern instrumentation (e.g., guitars, drums, synthesizers, percussion, horns), contemporary musical styles (e.g., rock, jazz, hip hop, rap, gospel), and freshly written or arranged songs (both new choruses and fresh treatments of traditional hymns) in the language of this generation to lead people into authentic expressions of worship and a genuine experience of the presence of God.

Contemporary worship will build the relationship with God and also issue in personal holiness.

The author's style is different from that of the other authors in this collection. It is hortatory, pleading, and apologetic in the good sense and also carries a forceful surprise ending. There is not much theory here, but there is a lot of Scripture and a ton of good will.

My criticism, however, is of the idea as it works out in practice, not with the idea of contemporary worship itself. Contemporary worship is almost always held hostage to its musicians, who happen to love the sound of their own performance. (Who does not?) This is the reality. It is what happens. Only when the worship leader or pastor is extremely strong do the services escape the captivity of the musicians. The music team cannot help themselves. I have witnessed this again and again and again, in the United Kingdom, in New York, in San Francisco, and, well, everywhere. Only at Holy Trinity, Brompton (most of the time), and at Redeemer Presbyterian in New York City have I seen the right humility and controls braking the music for the good of the whole.

I fear, too, that the urge to connect emotionally with God will cross the thin line between out-reaching praise and libidinal interference—i.e., the unconscious projection of issues relating to sex onto the act of praise and connection. It is notorious that people get confused in this area, often without knowing it. For example, is that a Stevie Wonder song about the "Sunshine of my life" or the "Son-shine" of your divine heart, or . . . what? To whom am I singing those passionate words? I worry actively about the phenomenon John Steinbeck observed in *The Grapes of Wrath*, where the evangelical preacher lost his ministry because he could not distinguish the differing feelings engendered by free and spontaneous services of praise.

So I am skeptical, based on experience, while I am also open to the experience of praise. This is because I hunger to know God. That hunger I share with Joe Horness.

A TRADITIONAL WORSHIP RESPONSE

Harold Best

It does not take long in this culture of ours for something to become antique. Just go to a flea market, a swap meet, or even an antique shop and you will find things for sale labeled as collectible, desirable, or even nostalgic that, yes, have issued from as nearby a time as the seventies or eighties. The nineties are surely next, and given the speed with which the techno-commercial side of culture assures quick obsolescence, oldies may not have to become gold to be sold.

Contemporary worship is certainly here to stay and has fast become one of the forms of traditional worship and, in the sense just cited, an oldie. This certainly does not make it wrong or out of style, especially when we understand how the church has historically chosen to be out of style, both in the theological sense of scandal and foolishness and in the sense of stylistic slowdown and even stasis. In one sense, therefore, the question to the prospective churchgoer is "What brand of out-of-styleness do you prefer?" In another, it is "To what extent are you willing to change when leadership thinks it's time to change?" It appears to me that Joe Horness understands the possible discomfort and reality behind this last question for, in more than one place in the chapter, he comes across as one to want change when change is deemed to be necessary. The one remaining question then would be "Who decides on change, the leadership or the followership?"

I truly love ever so many kinds of popular music. They comprise a good half, if not more, of my listening, composing, and

119

improvising habits. Furthermore, I have truly come to admire the deep spiritual fervor that drives much of the contemporary worship movement. I have come to love and be anointed by so much more than classical church music. There is a vividness and excitement to a truly humbled, musically sensitive, and dynamic worship band that is not duplicable anywhere else. And given the wild shifts in American popular music—too many for any of us to keep up with—and given the wonderful returns in classical music and art to tonality, accessibility, neo-representation, and temporal compactness, who knows how soon the contemporary movement will be forced to reclassicize, and who knows whether the next generation of contemporary worshipers will turn out to be the unbudging traditionalists that are now so openly criticized?

So, in the midst of my appreciation and respect for the several musical dialects in the most forward-looking contemporary worship contexts that can be used "to lead people into authentic expressions of worship *and a genuine experience of the presence of God*," I have two questions. First, why do we need to assume that it takes contemporary worship "to see hearts fully engaged, to radically eliminate dutiful, going-through-the-motions song times, and to bring people into *a powerful time of relationship with our living God*" (italics mine in both cases)? I thought that this was the purpose of all worship, irrespective of style. I will put it another way: I have been to many contemporary worship services where the very dutifulness, etc., that contemporary worship is supposed to remedy turns out to be as problematic as in so-called traditional forms; and I've been in traditional and liturgically based settings in which the power of the Lord has anointed the singing for young and old alike that makes the words "traditional" and "contemporary" curiously irrelevant.

I thank Horness for his detailed fairness in criticizing poorly done contemporary worship, but this might only mean that style per se may not solve the problems that only the Holy Spirit can. I keep going back to this old saw: What is there intrinsically and inherently about God, Jesus, the Holy Spirit, our redemption, the Word, and the communion of the saints that we can either fully appropriate or ignore before we consider the fact and stylistic content of corporate worship, and only then choose a worship style within which we can fully engage our faith-, love-, and hope-driven responses and actions?

The second question issues out of the words I have italicized above and is asked more than once throughout my responses to the various models presented in this book. What drives what, faith-driven worship or works-driven worship? Does style, in Horness's thinking, lead people into a genuine experience of the presence of God, or does a faith-, hope-, and love-driven experience of God actually empower the styles that we choose to employ instead of the reverse? Unfortunately, I infer the former instead of the latter from what I read, especially in the first part of the chapter. Are the various kinds of music and art tools for worship (as Horness implies), or are they acts of worship? Just as a hammer, as a tool, cannot be the house that it builds, neither can music, as a tool, be a part of the worship house that it builds, yet we regularly want to include music as an intrinsic part of our worship instead of an outside tool that effects it. I think it impossible to have it both ways. I tried to make this distinction clear in the introductory comments in my chapter on hymn-based worship when I said that worship-based hymn usage is far more the issue than basing worship on hymn usage. It seems that the problem with most contemporary thinking about worship, whatever the style, is that Sunday morning starts it up, but only on the basis of having chosen the right style.

Nonetheless, elsewhere in the chapter, in speaking of Bill Hybels's teaching on worship, he writes clearly and eloquently about worship almost as if it were an all-preceding action—a way of life, really—that should inform and shape the corporate gathering instead of the reverse. He speaks of our bringing offerings in our worship, a much more biblical idea than using things as tools for what may not yet be at hand until the tools effect it. His comments about the differences between seeker-sensitive gatherings and worship times are wonderfully clear and nicely reasoned and a clear reminder to those who forget that true seeker sensitivity is based on the continued sensitive seeking to which all believers are continually obligated.

Let me say again: There is nothing wrong with choosing the right style, in that contextual appropriateness and subcultural awareness have always been the hallmark of a wisely directed program. But what if we took music (and by implication, the other art forms) away, as was done for quite a long time in Matt Redman's church in England? There the discovery was made that the gathered assembly had created a golden calf out of music and turned reformingly vital when it was taken away. Only then was music welcomed back, but now as a mere evidence of something far more grand, and no longer the central attractor.

And there is the issue of disconnection between the contemporary and the old, which to me, as an older person who has spent his life around young people, seems to be only fractionally addressed. Through quotes from Webber, Morgenthaler, Walker, and Hendricks about the overall worship problem, and then circling around through the perceived failures of traditional worship, Horness comes back to the idea that organ music and choir pieces have significance only "for the elderly."

My goodness, is it that bad? Are there no younger people who love the classics? Are there no classics that dovetail ever so neatly with the contemporary? Of course there are—otherwise, why, for instance, do "Jesu, Joy of Man's Desiring" or the film score for *The Fellowship of the Ring* grab young minds and ears so magnetically? In my travels around the country, I have met many such young folks. And the beauty of it is that they also love popular stuff. They are often more eclectic than the churches—contemporary or traditional—that they attend and could wish for some real mind-boggling and heartwarming variety. Furthermore, are there not ardent Christ-loving classicists who have fewer church homes than before because the contemporary church turns out to be the church of the majority? Should not the harvest-minded and experience-oriented church understand that the Great Commission also reaches out to underrepresented people—not just the elderly, but an entire class of Americans and Europeans for whom middle-road contemporaneity is entirely too conservative? All told, I would much rather hear Horness simply say that contemporary worship is one of several valid choices that people can pragmatically exercise in conversing with God and with each other. To defend a particular style as being the answer to dead worship or the open door to live worship can all too easily make way for the belief that authentic worship is style-based before it is Spirit-driven.

I too am heartily dissatisfied with much of what goes on in the traditional church, but my dissatisfaction is with its quality and its confusion of traditionalism and retrospection. And yes, I agree that classically driven church musicians have done way too much to obscure the true nature of church music as, above all else, the people's song. Far too many have made aesthetics and difficult accessibility their golden calves. I was trained this way by classically trained evangelical reactionaries and have spent a greater part of my later years repenting of this sin and attempting to forge a musically integrative path that is dissatisfied with limiting the speech of the church to only one or two opposing dialects. But doing that does not necessarily mean that I need forsake the musical and artistic ideals, now that they are no longer idols but offerings.

If there is anything singularly wrong with the contemporary, it is that it has developed no literature or repertoire that goes into the artistic depth of things. All people were created to go deep; otherwise the doctrine of *imago Dei* is little more than a commercial jingle. There is no deep and probing equivalent in the contemporary, say, to the Brahms *Requiem* or Handel's *Messiah*. There is only the popular, and as those of us who love the popular know, it must be legitimately shallow to be popular. So just as my prayer is for more Joe Hornesses, Fernando Ortegas, and The Newsboys, it is also for more Timothy Dudley-Smiths, William Mathiases, and Arvo Pärts, let alone the growing number of Christian jazzers who seemingly have little or no place in the so-called contemporary, charismatic, or traditional forms. Just as the usual contemporary approach to worship in many churches may be due for an unsettling reformation, so is the traditional and hymn-based. And all of us have to remember that the financial and demographic riches of a Willow Creek are certainly sufficient to take it further than small contemporary-based churches, and even further than where it now is, granting the passion of Horness's repeated concern for the next generation.

In the sections "Keeping Our Eyes on the Goal," "The Heart of God," "The Role of the Contemporary Worship Leader," and "Our Responsibility," Joe is really cooking. He hits the nail on the head over and over. I love to read this kind of passionate writing, and I am sure that the writing is a mere shadow of the even greater intensity of Joe's own heart. I would love to sit down over many coffees with him, to celebrate with him, to talk music and art with him, to learn from him, and to intercede for lost souls with him. I could hope that all worship leaders would articulate themselves this way—irrespective of the style(s) they espouse. And that, of course, is why so many of these words of Joe are so strong. They simply have nothing to do with style.

Finally, I join Joe in the fervor of this statement: "If you were to take away only one insight into contemporary worship from this chapter, let it be this: People of this generation are longing to experience the genuine presence of God. And God is longing to move in and among the hearts of his people." I would simply add that if we changed the word "contemporary" to "all," we would have a strong beginning for any chapter in this book.

A CHARISMATIC WORSHIP RESPONSE

Don Williams

Joe Horness takes us from his childhood worship in a traditional church to the intentional and radical departure known as Willow Creek. Under the leadership of Bill Hybels, innovative approaches to ministry moved in two directions. Weekends were famous "seeker-sensitive" services. All communication, including music, targeted the outsider. Midweek services welcomed the church core. Here true worship was pursued and developed. The strengths of Horness's chapter are his theological and biblical foundations and the integrity of his own insider journey as a worship leader. He takes us behind the forms to the content and function of the changes he experienced and led. Like Willow Creek, his story is a work in progress. This is both his strength and his weakness, as we shall see.

Horness's values are clear. First, God is the author of our worship. He longs for relationship with us. This theme courses throughout the Bible. When we are simply going through the motions, we are not worshiping at all. Second, God wants our hearts. Horness paraphrases the prophets, "If your heart is not moved by who I am, then better that you not go through the motions at all." Worship engages our whole selves. It expresses our love. Citing John Piper (who has Jonathan Edwards lurking behind him), Horness believes that God wants the affections of our heart. "Where feelings for God are dead, worship is dead." This means that the form (chorus or hymn) of worship is not the point. Theories and techniques only count as they draw our hearts Godward.

Horness defines contemporary worship as the passion to see hearts fully engaged, bringing people into a relationship with the living God. He shifts from Webber's stress on experience (in chapter 5) as the marker of contemporary worship to the affection of the heart in "loving and grateful interaction with the One who shed his blood for us."

But what form does this take in contemporary worship? It uses current language and instrumentation. The heart is engaged in the context of the present culture. What this does not mean is musical performance for effect. Underlying values drive what we do. Horness warns against changing format to increase attendance. Contemporary worship communicates because it uses the music that speaks our language. The question is not organ or guitar; the question is to serve this generation in its encounter with God, meeting Jesus and engaging in authentic expressions of love to him.

Horness asks that we understand that this generation longs to experience God's presence. Likewise, God longs to encounter us. With our hearts fully engaged, God is glorified and free to move in our midst. Rather than singing *about* God, we are to sing *to* him, to interact with him. Worship is not a spectator sport. It is a dialogue for participants with the living God. Its main goal is relationship.

Contemporary worship also responds to the massive cultural changes that began in the 1960s. Willow Creek Community Church was birthed in this response. Horness summarizes its history and goes on to say that the seeker-sensitive services left a need for a midweek gathering for believers that was "completely different." In 1982, as a result of Bill Hybels's attending a charismatic church, everything dramatically changed. Here was the worship he had been dreaming about: rich, heartfelt, with the life-changing presence of God. Worship grew as Willow Creek's picture of God grew. The midweek meeting celebrated God's presence among his broken people. Painfully at times, and slowly, this church learned to worship—with whole hearts and new freedom.

Horness answers common objections to contemporary worship. The focus is not on consumer Christianity or my needs and experiences. It is not on performance up in front. The focus is on the heart of God. He initiates our longing to be in his presence.

He knows that worship puts us in the right place for him to move upon us. It is our ultimate calling.

Sound advice is also offered for worship leaders. They must keep their purpose in worship clearly in mind; otherwise, disintegration will quickly set in. Their primary calling is not to be hip or cool, but to serve the congregation and help it meet with God. At the same time, they must practice and prepare. Excellence must be combined with servanthood. They come to bring an offering of worship. They come, expecting God to move.

Horness grounds contemporary worship in a strong biblical theology of grace. This is good. But based on this, is it really the case that where feelings are dead, worship is dead? Feelings change. Affections are not constant. Many psalms reflect this. Thus the need for revival. We do not worship because we feel like it. We worship because God alone is worthy. It is primarily about him, not us. Often this is also for our good, because as we worship, our affections are stirred once again.

The strength of Horness's autobiographical journey at Willow Creek is also his weakness. How can we generalize from one person's and one church's experience? What is the broader arena of contemporary worship? How can we appropriate it apart from traveling to Willow Creek for Wednesday night? These questions remain.

Horness speaks of traditional worship as potentially deadly, form without an engaged heart. He then traces his own journey. Clearly he has embraced what I would call the heart of charismatic worship: the whole self enflamed, engaged, and abandoned in the presence of God.

There is a larger picture that Horness suggests but misses. Contemporary worship, as he defines it, is merging with charismatic worship. My clear bias is that contemporary worship is a way station on the road to experiencing the fullness of the Spirit and the release of his gifts for the whole congregation. The forms that this is taking are many, but the substance is being poured out upon the church today. This means that all worshipers come with gifts to be given, not just the up-front leadership. This means that prophetic words may be released in the corporate setting. This means that healings may be experienced as people pray for each other. This means that anyone may lead out in open prayer. This means that the priesthood of all believers is being functionally restored to the church. Worship is personal but not individualistic. We are the body of Christ and individually members of one another (Romans 12:5).

My first contact with charismatic worship came in 1983 when I attended the Anaheim Vineyard, where John Wimber was the pastor. As the congregation sang through a set of songs led by their worship band, I was touched by the simple lyrics and moved by the sense of God's presence. But as a Presbyterian pastor, I was totally unprepared for scores of worshipers around me weeping: pain and joy in the presence of Jesus. Horness has captured this affection, and now the lines between "contemporary worship" and "charismatic worship" seem to disappear. Is this kind of worship the real secret to the healing of the church?

A BLENDED WORSHIP RESPONSE

Robert Webber

Joe Horness may not know this, but I have been at Willow Creek many times when he has led worship. Joe has a heart and passion for God that are always evident in his worship leading. He is the real thing.

His chapter speaks the same throughout. He makes it clear on the first page that "God ... longs for relationship with us." God is not honored, he writes, "if our hearts are not engaged in authentic expressions of love for him." He even defines contemporary worship as "a move toward engaging hearts more fully." And when we learn to worship from hearts that are fully engaged, God is both glorified and set free "to move in us and among us." According to Joe, when Bill Hybels taught the Willow Creek congregation how to worship, "we began to recognize that God's deepest desire is that we would bring him our whole hearts in worship." Therefore the end of worship is "to meet with Jesus, to know his presence, to fully engage our hearts in authentic expressions of love to him." Consequently, "when we worship, we will develop nothing less than a yearning for God, joy, a passion for God's presence, an increased faith, a love for God's Word, comfort, an increased love for God, adoration, exaltation, celebration, thanksgiving, praise, unity, and repentance."

I cannot help but think that Joe is sincere. I sense that his personal goal in worship is summarized in the emphasis he places on the heart. I know he strives to be and do what he considers to stand at the heart of worship.

But it is a tall order!

Who can do it?
Who can love God with all his heart, mind, and soul?
Who can achieve perfect union with God?
Who can worship God with a pure and unstained heart?
Not me!
Not Joe Horness, either.
Not you. Not Billy Graham. Not Bill Hybels. Not Matt Redman.
Not anybody I know or you know.
Only Jesus can. And he does for me and for you what neither of us can do for ourselves.

This is the message that is missing in the literature of contemporary worship. It is too much about what I ought to do and too little about what God has done for me. God has done for me what I cannot do for myself. He did it in Jesus Christ. Therefore my worship is offered in a broken vessel that is in the process of being healed, but is not yet capable of fullness of joy, endless intense passion, absolute exaltation, and celebration. But Jesus, who shares in my humanity yet without sin, is not only my Savior—he is also my complete and eternal worship, doing for me, in my place, what I cannot do.

It is true, as Joe points out, that we are created for relationship with God. But because we participate in Adam, who broke a relationship with God not only for himself but for all human creatures, we are incapable of establishing perfect union with God. But God, in the Incarnation, became one with us through the Second Adam, who in union with God paid on the cross the penalty for our sin. He won a victory over the powers of evil, and he dwells in eternal union with the very divine essence of God, where he is eternally interceding to the Father on our behalf. This is the good news of the gospel. And for this reason, our worship is always in and through Christ.

I am quite sure that Joe and other contemporary worshipers will read what I have written above and offer their "amen" to it. But why contemporary worship leaders never tell us this good news baffles me. It leaves me with the sense that I am asked to do the impossible. And when leaders lead us to believe they accomplish this kind of love, passion, and praise, then the rest of us either have to fake it or worry that maybe we are not spiritual enough.

Thanks for Jesus Christ, who is my worship. We are free! And in gratitude, we offer our stumbling worship in the name of Jesus with thanksgiving.

AN EMERGING WORSHIP RESPONSE

Sally Morgenthaler

A CONTEMPORARY WORSHIP PRIMER

Joe Horness has given the worshiping, culturally transitioning church a tremendous gift with this chapter. Here is a worship primer that transcends all styles; a short but powerful course on the essence of what it means to truly engage with God. Beyond what many of us tend to emphasize in the contemporary setting—the bells and whistles, the styles, the performance—Horness's emphasis is on gatherings that reflect an authentic, passionate relationship with God through Jesus Christ:

> If our hearts are not engaged in authentic expressions of love for him, if this is not about a relationship with our Creator and Redeemer, then God is not honored.... What I think God cares about is the disengaged heart. I do not think that he is particularly interested in our theories or techniques of worship except as they are effective in genuinely drawing hearts to him. Worship that is not heartfelt and authentic simply does not interest him.

Whatever worship model we use, Horness has helped us to see that this heartfelt, created-to-Creator exchange is at the core of what we do. Imagine distributing this primer among your staff and your congregations. Imagine using it for a month of study, prayer, and reflection around the ministry and calling of worship. If and when your congregation decides to transition its worship style, it will be firmly grounded in what pleases the heart of God and will most likely avoid the familiar worship-change landmines associated with a fixation on style.

REAL REASONS: TRANSITIONING LEADERS IN HONESTY MODE

I consult with many transitioning churches each year. When I ask their leadership, "What is motivating you to shift your worship style?" I get many answers. From boredom to satisfying a particular constituency, boosting a sagging church attendance, meeting budget needs, and keeping up with the big churches next door, I've heard it all.

Ideally, the reason to update a worship style would be, as Horness summarizes, "to use the language of this generation to lead people into authentic expressions of worship and a genuine experience of the presence of God." I have worked with a few transitioning churches that from worshiper to worship leader and pastor are motivated by this godly goal. However, I work with more congregations whose motivations are not nearly as deep or scripturally rooted. And herein lies the problem, as Horness acknowledges: "The move that many churches have made from traditional to contemporary worship involves very visible changes that often obscure the underlying values that should be driving the change."

The operative word in Horness's sentence is "should." The values that Horness delineates so carefully and so well in his chapter are, for whatever reason, missing in many of our transitioning churches, and primarily among their leadership. It is all too easy for those of us who minister in small congregations to look at large, contemporary churches and be overcome with church envy. Certainly, the desire for ministry effectiveness is positive. But let us be brutally honest. As pastors and worship leaders we sometimes desire to go beyond effectiveness (bringing more people into an intimate, worship relationship with God) to what will stroke our shrinking egos and seemingly provide us with a better standard of living. Those of us who have spent our ministry years in small churches may indeed long for the high of preaching and leading worship to a packed house. Year after year we see our numbers dwindle and the average age ascend. We may have experienced a golden period in the 1970s and early 1980s. People just came to church, and we did not have to hang from the chandelier and spit watermelon seeds to get them there. Now we are lucky if we can pay the light bill. What is more, we're living on salaries commensurate with our minuscule church size.

How easy is it to get pulled into worship change for personal reasons? Very! Growth (when defined as making more and better worshipers) is actually one of the best reasons for worship change. One of the most crucial principles that churches like Willow Creek have taught us is this: There really is a world out there and we are called to reach it with the love of God in Christ. However, when our motivation for worship change comes primarily from the personal perks derived from growth (status, fame, identity, money), it is then that we as leaders have gone off track. And I have seen literally hundreds of transitioning congregations pulled helplessly into the undertow of fixation on personal career agendas.

Transition that is motivated by leaders' career agendas is almost always headed for trouble. There is a leadership desperation that sets in early. Change tends to be driven from the top down and is marked by a lack of listening and pacing, a disdain for heritage, and an inability to compromise. The list goes on. Leaders desperate for worship change at any cost are leaders in identity crisis. We are all too familiar with the narratives of worship wars in our churches. Usually we hear the stories of members who dig in their heels and say, in effect, "Not in my neighborhood." One wonders how much of their hostility might be due to desperate, career-driven leadership that has sacrificed the whos and whys of worship in deference to the how. Then, as Horness portrays, the scenario becomes predictable:

> Without a stranglehold on what it is we are really trying to do, contemporary worship degenerates quickly into a poor man's version of what it was we were trying to emerge from. We can quickly trade songs of great depth and theological truth for choruses of sappy sentimentality. We can quickly shift away from focusing our minds on Christ to focusing our minds on how I feel.... [We] often ... discover that we have simply traded three hymns for three choruses and have fired the organist in order to purchase drums, alienating our older Christ-followers in the process.... We can easily gear our worship times around what we think is hip or cool and forget that our primary calling is to serve our congregation and help them meet with God.

WE HAVE A CHOICE: THE FUTURE OF CONTEMPORARY WORSHIP

Horness's definition of contemporary worship bears repeating: Contemporary worship uses "the language of this generation to lead people into . . . a genuine experience of the presence of God." Up until now, the generation that has been associated with the adjective "contemporary" has been almost exclusively the baby-boomer generation—roughly, those of us born between 1945 and 1963.

But if we take a look at the dictionary definition of "contemporary," it means, literally, "of the now." Two subsequent generations have emerged since the boomers: those born from 1964 to 1979 (now mid-twenty-something to about forty) and those born since 1980. When I hear many of these young people talk about the contemporary worship they grew up with in church (make note: they use that word not with its dictionary meaning, but quite accurately as a descriptor of the praise-and-worship styles of the past two decades), it is clear that the worship of their baby-boomer parents is as irrelevant to many of them as classical, European worship was to the baby boomers themselves.

Those of us who occupy the baby-boomer bulge in North American demography are used to having the world focus on us. For several decades now, we have occupied the attention of corporate America, the media, Wall Street, Congress, and since 1992, the presidency. But in the past five years that has been changing. Our children, nieces, nephews, and—for the oldest of us boomers—our grandchildren are becoming young adults. Their world—technology, family situations, lifestyles, learning styles, and aesthetic languages—is vastly different from the world of our youth. And if we are really honest, our world has shifted drastically along with theirs.

It remains to be seen whether we as baby boomers will be able to release our contemporary worship services from the compartments we created in the 1980s. It remains to be seen whether we can, for those who follow us, do what Horness describes: ". . . use the language of this generation to lead people into . . . a genuine experience of the presence of God." It is all too easy to keep "contemporary" in the box of worship tastes long since stale and increasingly irrelevant to our own generation. And if the rising worship wars of many churches founded in the 1980s and early 1990s are any indication, it is all too common to hear our own parents' words coming out of our boomer mouths: "What is good enough for us is good enough for you."

Joe Horness has accomplished in this chapter the very thing he calls worship leaders and pastors to do. He has painted "a great picture of God to which [our] hearts can respond." Contemporary worship paints a picture of God that new generations can understand, an image of God they can grasp—one that inspires them to give back to God all that they are.

It is my contention that we as baby-boomer leaders have no idea how ready most baby-boomer attendees are to move past the worship styles and formulas of the 1980s into a fresh, truly contemporary engagement with God. Our forty-to-late-fifty-year-olds have been morphing right along with their children and grandchildren and at the turn of the millennium are desperate to integrate the world they live in every day with the world inside the worship center. They do not want to reject the wisdom and lessons of the past, but they are hungering to worship God in the now of their existence.

It is a new day. Let us as the leaders of God's people rise up and meet it, as Joe implores, "fully engaged"—one hundred percent present to God and present in the time and space to which God has called us. That, and only that, is contemporary ministry.

Chapter 3: Contemporary Music-Driven Worship Notes

Proposal: Joe Horness

[1]John Piper, *Desiring God* (Sisters, OR: Multnomah Press, 1986), 83.

[2]Tommy Walker, worship director at Christian Assembly Foursquare Church, Los Angeles, CA; quoted in Sally Morgenthaler, *Worship Evangelism* (Grand Rapids: Zondervan, 1999), 35.

[3]Morgenthaler, *Worship Evangelism*, 17.

[4]William Hendricks, *Exit Interviews: Revealing Stories of Why People Are Leaving the Church* (Chicago: Moody Press, 1993), 265–66.

[5]Morgenthaler, *Worship Evangelism*, 47.

[6]Jack Hayford, *Worship His Majesty* (Waco, TX: Word Books, 1987), 48.

[7]A. W. Tozer, *The Pursuit of God* (Camp Hill, PA: Christian Publications, 1982), 10.

Chapter Four

CHARISMATIC WORSHIP

CHARISMATIC WORSHIP

Don Williams

In 1968 I made my first visit to Calvary Chapel, built on the edge of a bean field in Costa Mesa, California. The small church building was bursting at the seams with a new generation— "Jesus Freaks" the media would later dub them. As Lonnie Frisbee, a young, long-haired evangelist led in worship, the crowd opened their Bibles to the book of Psalms and sang through several passages, accompanied by the rock band LoveSong. As a traditional Presbyterian minister, I was jolted. Something new was up and, in retrospect, much of the worship in the Western world would never be the same. New charismatic worship was being born out of a political and cultural crisis.

Charismatic worship may be defined theologically as worship where the leadership and gifts of the Spirit *(charismata)* are evidenced or welcomed in personal and corporate praise, responding to a mighty act of God.[1] Rooted in Pentecostalism, it developed out of the mainline charismatic movement, flowed into streams of the Jesus Movement of the late 1960s and early 1970s, and continues in the "Third Wave" renewal to the present. In this chapter we will trace its history, reflect on its theology, and propose its future.

THE CHARISMATIC RENEWAL

American Pentecostalism finds its origins in the Azusa Street Revival of 1906.[2] Its specialty was the repetition of Pentecost (Acts 2) with the "baptism of the Spirit" signified by the gift of glossolalia—unknown tongues, unintelligible language, ecstatic speech. It has emphasized an experience of the Spirit after conversion, with tongues as the entryway into other spiritual gifts such as healing, prophecy, miracles, and deliverance from demons. This stream flowed to the nations, forming new denominations in the Wesleyan or Holiness tradition. Starting out as working-class and multiracial, it later spawned denominational structures and gained middle-class respectability. It was evangelical in its theology and revivalist in its worship.

Pentecostal experience was infused into mainline denominations in 1960 when Father Dennis Bennett, an Episcopalian rector in Van Nuys, California, experienced the baptism of the Holy Spirit with the gift of tongues.[3] For Bennett, this resulted in a disruption of his pastorate and subsequent reassignment. For the church at large it resulted in the spread of the power of the Spirit in mainline Protestant churches, modifying traditional forms of worship.

In 1967 a similar experience of the Spirit by Dominican Father Francis MacNutt and other priests and nuns led to the charismatic renewal in the Roman Catholic Church. MacNutt united the baptism of the Spirit with healing and took the charismatic renewal into the worldwide Catholic communion, with special attention to houses of prayer, clergy retreats, and healing services.[4]

How did this impact worship? As the charismatic renewal surged, singing in tongues became its marker. Free-flowing harmonies joined with verbalized glossolalia were mixed with some English repetition of spontaneous ejaculatory prayers like "Jesus, Jesus, Jesus," or "I love you, Lord." A variety of postures such as hands raised toward heaven, standing, or kneeling accompanied sung prayers. Shorter worship choruses, often repeated, developed along with them. Here is an example:

> I love You, Lord,
> And I lift my voice
> To worship You.
> O my soul, rejoice.
>
> Take joy, my King,
> In what You hear.
> May it be a sweet, sweet sound
> In Your ear.[5]

Other practices, along with evangelical calls for salvation, included praying for the baptism of the Spirit and ministering to the sick with the laying on of hands. In the Roman Catholic tradition this appeared in healing Masses. These new forms of ministry were incorporated into traditional liturgies. By the mid-1960s, however, as a result of the cultural dislocation of the civil rights movement and Vietnam protests, folk music appeared in the church, resulting in more sustained periods of free worship. These innovations blended with standard hymns and traditional liturgical forms to create a hybrid worship culture.

In all of this there was a conscious attempt to recover aspects of charismatic worship modeled in 1 Corinthians 12–14. This included time for spontaneous prophetic words, "words of knowledge" giving direction for specific prayers for the sick, and opportunities for more congregational participation: ". . . everyone has a hymn, or a word of instruction, a revelation, a tongue or an interpretation" (1 Corinthians 14:26 NIV).

While the charismatic renewal had a huge impact on mainline churches, bringing many nominal Christians to a vibrant faith, it tended, especially in its Protestant forms, not to impact evangelism, issues of social justice, or world missions.

THE JESUS MOVEMENT

The counterculture that surfaced in the 1960s brought massive changes. With linkage between the generations broken, institutions were suspect, including the traditional church. New music forms defined this period with a decidedly antiestablishment thrust. Through folk, folk rock, and soft and hard rock, youth editorialized to youth. Musicians wrote their own lyrics, and formal worship, using hymns from the eighteenth and nineteenth centuries, seemed as dated as the institutions that sustained them.

It was almost inevitable that the streams of charismatic renewal and the Jesus Movement, which was the countercultural revival in the late 1960s, would meet and often merge. Coffeehouses such as the Salt Company in Hollywood opened and nurtured new forms of musical expression. Professional musicians like Larry Norman, Randy Stonehill, and others wrote protest music in a Christian context.

As new churches sprang up or were transformed, it was predictable that many would leave the old hymns and liturgical forms behind and embrace "Jesus Music."[6] These congregations genuinely expressed their new faith in a countercultural context. Some within the mainline denominations tried to become current without the charismatic component. "Contemporary worship services" were born, replete with folk groups, clapping to up-tempo rhythms, balloons, and dressed-down leaders.

Much like rock concerts and "love-ins," worship in the Jesus Movement usually consisted of only the new music, leaving traditional hymns behind. Worshipers engaged in free forms of physical expression, singing for sustained periods of time with bands arranging worship sets of songs.

Wherever the Jesus Movement merged with the charismatic renewal, time was devoted to the expression of spiritual gifts— singing in tongues, speaking in tongues with interpretation, prophetic words, and spontaneous prayers—in an attempt to recover parts of Corinthian worship as directed and corrected by Paul. All of this was accompanied by a strong apocalyptic sense that Jesus was returning soon (often absent in the older charismatic renewal), hard-driving evangelism, and the simple biblical faith of a pre-critical era. Songs still did not often beckon congregations into intimate worship. They offered message music for evangelism, instruction, and exhortation. One of the best of the new genre came from the Calvary Costa Mesa group called LoveSong. A line went "With one [hand] reach out to Jesus and with the other, bring a friend." This was the spirit of the Jesus Movement.

THE THIRD WAVE

C. Peter Wagner of Fuller Theological Seminary defined the "Third Wave" as the next move of God after Pentecostalism and the charismatic renewal.[7] It no longer demanded speaking in tongues as the sign of the Spirit's baptism. This separated the Third Wave from earlier waves. In the early 1980s a new group of Vineyard churches, branching off of the Calvary Chapels of the Jesus Movement, formed under the leadership of former jazz musician John Wimber. Abandoning the use of contemporary music for evangelism and "warming up the crowd," Wimber saw worship as an end in itself. For him, it included both high praise and songs of intimacy, now mostly directed to God himself rather than merely sung about him.[8] It is estimated that today eighty percent of all white Protestant churches in the United States include Vineyard songs in their public worship.[9]

Wedding contemporary worship with his "kingdom theology," Wimber held that worship draws the heart of God to his people. As worship ascends, God comes down. He becomes experienced as immanent. In the midst of this worship, people are often convicted, converted, healed, and even delivered from evil spirits. The power of God is often manifest in this worship.

As with the charismatic renewal and its counterpart in the Jesus Movement, Wimber expected God to release prophetic words and visions during worship. Time was made to "wait on the Lord" and to "hear from God." Evangelism and healing through prayer teams were also incorporated into a "ministry time" at the end of a service. This is Wimber's formula for church services: worship (singing), the Word (preaching), and then the works of Jesus through prayer and the laying on of hands (ministry time).

Incorporating themes from the charismatic renewal, Wimber fostered worship music that is God-centered as well as culturally current as in the older Jesus Movement, but with a deeper sense of spirituality. Wimber taught that the whole congregation is the choir, singing to God and before God, who himself is the "Audience of One." Wanting to be "naturally supernatural," Wimber tended to downplay the culture of Pentecostal worship and practices and some of the overt-power manifestations of the healing evangelists.

Wimber developed a five-phase model for worship with the goal of intimacy with God.[10]

- Stage 1: "A Call to Worship," a time of invitation.
- Stage 2: "Engagement," which in Wimber's words is "the electrifying dynamic connection to God and to each other."
- Stage 3: "Exaltation." Wimber comments, "If you draw near to God, you're just going to want to praise him!"
- Stage 4: "Adoration." This is the time of "tenderness, bringing love songs before the throne of God's love."
- Stage 5: "Intimacy." Wimber explains, "We need a visitation of God. We need his presence and his work among us. We don't worship for that, though—but it is a by-product."

In the 1980s Wimber exported his message and ministry of charismatic renewal around the world, eventually impacting major denominations. In England, for example, he fed into the older charismatic renewal and the New Churches of the 1970s and 1980s (such as Frontiers and Pioneer). Today the press calls a portion of the Anglican Church's charismatic wing "Wimberites." Over seven hundred churches in the New Wine Network, including a majority from the Church of England, have adopted much of his theology and practices.[11]

Drawing on the charismatic renewal and the Jesus Movement, Wimber changed worship forms to a contemporary style, replaced organs and choirs with worship bands or worship teams, released younger musicians to write their own music, and opened services to charismatic gifts, leading to ministry teams and ministry times.

Wimber not only taught and led worship, but wrote some of the best 1980s Jesus songs, moving from high praise and witness to intimacy. For example:

Spirit Song

O let the Son of God enfold you with his Spirit and
    his love,
Let him fill your heart and satisfy your soul.
Give him all the things that hold you and his Spirit like
    a dove
Will descend upon your life and make you whole.

Jesus, O Jesus, come and fill your lambs,
Jesus, O Jesus, come and fill your lambs.

And:

Praise Song

Son of God, this is our love song.
Jesus, my Lord, I sing to you.
Come now, Spirit of God,
Breathe life into these words of love,
Angels join from above,
As we sing our love song.[12]

THEOLOGY

Charismatic worship, like all historic Christian worship, is Trinitarian: worship directed to the Father, through the Son, in the Spirit.[13] Perhaps its distinctive is the desire for worshipers to experience some measure of the full life of the triune God, including the Holy Spirit. A. W. Tozer writes,

> A doctrine has practical value only as far as it is *prominent in our thoughts and makes a difference in our lives.* By this test the doctrine of the Holy Spirit as held by evangelical Christians today has almost no practical value at all. In most Christian churches the Spirit is quite entirely overlooked. Whether he is present or absent makes no real difference to anyone.... So completely do we ignore Him that it is only by courtesy that we can be called Trinitarian. The Christian doctrine of the Trinity boldly declares the equality of the Three Persons and the right of the Holy Spirit to be worshipped and glorified. Anything less than this is something less than Trinitarian.[14]

The gift of "charismatic worship" to the church has been functionally to restore the Holy Spirit to our services. Charismatic worship, then, finds its source in the Father, is mediated through the Son, and is empowered and led by the Spirit. It makes Paul's dictum real: "For we are the true circumcision, who worship God in spirit ['by the Spirit of God,' NIV], and glory in Christ Jesus" (Philippians 3:3 RSV). True charismatic worship is not human-centered or emotion-centered. The Spirit comes to bear witness to Christ (John 15:26) and empowers and directs the church to that end. Honoring the Son honors the Father and keeps charismatic worship from becoming Unitarian or Binitarian by neglecting one member of the Trinity for another.

At the same time, the Spirit sensitizes worship with both freedom and order. Leaders of charismatic worship plan in advance. They also respond to the leading of the Spirit in the moment. At its best, this keeps worship fresh and relevant to each situation and congregation.

The Spirit comes not only to glorify Jesus but also to edify the church through the written Word of God. This deposit of Spirit-given revelation receives, in the moment, his illumination so that it can be understood, and his empowering so that it can be obeyed. Since the gifts of the Spirit are biblically grounded, charismatic worship welcomes their manifestation or release. When they are exercised in an orderly way, the whole church is built up. Confirmation by the written Word of God and edification of the Body are the tests of any given manifestation of the Spirit. The active exercise of spiritual gifts means that the whole congregation may be engaged in charismatic worship. Rather than passive observers, worshipers become active participants. In Wimber's phrase, "Everybody gets to play."

The personal effects of this worship are transformative. The Spirit indwells believers to change them to become more like Christ. The Spirit searches the hearts of God's people, exposing sin and pain, bringing forgiveness and healing. Paul expects worship to renew our minds (Romans 12:2). As New Testament theologian Tom Wright teaches, we become like what we worship.[15] If we worship the idols of our age, we become like them. If we worship the triune God, we become like him—incorporated into his community of eternal, holy love.

Increasing Christlikeness breeds increasing intimacy with God. We are broken before him in our sin and raised up to be like him in his grace. As we are with him, we become more and more like him, going from "glory to glory" (2 Corinthians 3:18 NKJV). Now we know his voice; then we will see his face.

We grow up in Christ in order to go out to this world. Worship leads to witness. The Spirit empowers us for mission: the evangelization of the world. Charismatic worship often effects just that. For example, Tim Hughes, worship pastor at Soul Survivor in England, writes,

> [There] was a group of young people who . . . would just hang around . . . rather than go to any of the meetings. As the days went by the group started attending. . . . One night some of the group gave their lives to Christ. When asked what it was that provoked them they responded that it was the worship. "We never thought Christians could worship like that." As they joined with others in worship they were moved, but more importantly the eyes of their hearts were opened to see Jesus as their Savior.[16]

FUTURE DIRECTION

Charismatic worship is dynamic, growing, and changing. One of the best clues as to its future is Matt Redman, thirty-year-old English worship leader and songwriter. In his music Redman reveals God-centered worship with spiritual depth, poetic power, and contemporary relevance. His songs are scriptural, revealing the tensions of the biblical revelation of God—transcendent and immanent, holy and loving, inviting us into the paradox of friendship and fear.

Worship is centered not on our needs but on God himself. Redman writes, "From a heart so amazed by God and His wonders, burns a love that will not be extinguished. . . . It will not allow itself to be quenched, for that would heap insult on the love it lives in response to."[17]

While public worship must be ordered and organized, it must also be free, surprising, "Spirit led." An unquenchable burning worshiper needs to be full of the Holy Spirit. "We talk a lot about 'Spirit-led worship,' but if we truly want to be led by the Holy Spirit, we need to make sure we're keeping in step with Him in our everyday lives."[18] This will lead to aspects of worship that are fresh and surprising—a sign of life. Redman proclaims, "Worship is meant to be an encounter, an exciting meeting place where love is given and received in an unscripted manner." Structure must not strangle life,[19] and God often calls worship leaders to do the unexpected. "If we do what the Father is doing, when He's doing it, God will break into our services in powerful and surprising ways."[20] Spirit-led worship can at times become "holy mayhem, burning through our pride."[21]

Redman warns that we cannot make worship happen. "No amount of striving or hyping can communicate real worship."[22] No amount of good musicianship or skillful arrangements will compensate for God withholding his presence. "Worship is a spiritual event long before it is ever a musical event."[23] As a spiritual event, it comes from meeting God in the "secret place." When worshipers "go public," they must check their hearts ruthlessly.[24] Redman adds, "One trend in worship which increasingly worries me is the whole performance thing. . . . Praise is a contradiction of pride. Pride says, 'Look at me,' but praise longs for people to see Jesus."[25]

Dependence on the Spirit comes from a life "undone" before God. He strips us, makes us "distinctly uncomfortable" because he is a holy King, insisting on a holy people.[26] Like the psalms of lament, true worship is never shallow, "shiny, happy." It comes from a heart broken before God. There is a time for abundant joy as well as a time for silence, ". . . just to know that God is God. A time to reflect on who he is and respond with the fewest of words and the simplest of songs."[27] Redman concludes, "In an age of informality and irreverence, true unveiled worshippers recognize the 'otherness' of God, and treasure the call to intimacy with Him. Transfixed by His glory and transformed in His presence, we become ever more like Him."[28] Here is Redman's "Heart of Worship":

> When the music fades,
> All is stripped away,
> And I simply come.
> Longing just to bring something that's of worth
> That will bless Your heart.
>
> I'll bring You more than a song
> For a song in itself
> Is not what You have required.
> You search much deeper within
> Through the way things appear
> You're looking into my heart.
>
> I'm coming back to the heart of worship,
> And it's all about You,
> All about You, Jesus.
> I'm sorry, Lord, for the thing I've made it
> When it's all about You,
> All about You, Jesus.[29]

CHALLENGE AND CRITIQUE

The older charismatic movement is a largely spent force. Rather than renewing mainline denominations, it has been marginalized by them. Most charismatic ministries are not expressed in Sunday services. They are relegated to prayer groups, off-night healing services, and special renewal conferences and have small, aging representations in major denominations. Many affected by the charismatic renewal have drifted to independent charismatic churches, Calvary Chapels, or Vineyards or to the older Pentecostal churches, such as the Assemblies of God or the International Church of the Foursquare Gospel. The Jesus Movement lasted for less than a decade. Yet it is estimated that three million new converts came to Christ through that period. Where it was institutionalized as organized churches, its impact endures. Some of the more radical 1960s churches, such as Calvary Chapels, have tended to revert to mainline evangelicalism in their practices, dropping the charismatic element from public worship.

Along with historic Pentecostalism, Third Wave churches continue the charismatic theme with a large spectrum of practices. The phenomena of singing with arms raised, singing in the Spirit, releasing spiritual gifts such as prophecy, and physical manifestations of the Spirit's power such as shaking or falling vary from church to church. Prayer ministry at the latter part of the service is common.

The heart of Third Wave churches is corporate worship. In this context there is a growing concern for an accompanying theology of worship that is solidly biblical. This includes the elements of high praise, surrender (*shachah*, literally, "to fall down," Psalm 95:6), sacrificial giving, intercession, prophetic words, and songs of intimacy with God. As this develops, lyrics are becoming more theologically responsible. The holiness of God as the divine King balances intimacy with God as the embracing Father. The love of Christ balances love for Christ. Personal salvation balances incorporation into community. Spiritual growth balances sacramental expression. Personal morality balances social responsibility. A passion for holiness balances a passion for justice. Earthly discipleship balances heavenly destiny.

God's self-disclosure in his Son will affect our own self-disclosure. Brenton Brown, worship leader for the Vineyard in the United Kingdom, writes in an email, "I think our honesty about personal problems culturally (versus the preceding recent generations) has freed us to return to a more biblical model of worship that is unashamedly petitionary. Davidic worship is nothing if not need oriented, even though God centered ('O Lord, have mercy on me and heal me')." Like the psalms of lament, this new worship will hold the balance between God and us. As the congregation becomes the choir, worship will also be less focused on the charismatic leader and the band's musicianship.

Critics of charismatic worship argue that what is new is not what is best. In fact, the proliferation of new music that is culturally current severs this generation from the preceding experience of the church in worship, the richness of its tradition, and the depth of its theology mirrored in the great hymns of the faith. In response to this, it is important to note that many charismatic services include historic hymns and gospel songs in their worship diet. John Wimber's memorial service, with over four thousand people in attendance, included many of his contemporary Jesus songs. The climax, however, came in a slow singing of "Blessed Assurance." Every line seemed to reference Wimber himself that night.

Each generation finds its own musical identity and then tends to recover the best of the past. This is true for much charismatic worship as well. At the same time, every revival births new music. This is one of its authentic signs. To bemoan this is to bemoan a central expression and instrument of the church's renewal.[30] No one can stop this wave from rising and carrying a generation with it.

Critics also fear that charismatic worship is excessively subjective, reflecting our current narcissism, centering on us rather than on the God we worship. As we noted above, the best of charismatic worship holds the tension between who we are and who God is. For example, Brenton Brown writes this:

Thank You for the Cross

Even when we turned our backs on You,
In wickedness and lies suppressed Your truth.
Even then You showed Your love for us,
Giving up Your life upon the cross.

Jesus, thank You for the Cross
For the blood that sets us free
The crimson stain of all our sin
Washed away in Your mercy.[31]

Evangelical piety and self-disclosure have always bothered formal religion. As George Whitefield, the eighteenth-century evangelist, put it to his clerical detractors, "You preach Christ without; we preach Christ within." "Christ within" necessarily demands subjective, experiential responses. The very power of charismatic worship, however, carries the danger of losing its grace base, throwing us back upon ourselves, subtly manipulating God's responses through our worship effort. But all is in him and what he evokes in us.

The best of charismatic worship includes cries for justice, confronting our social ills. As Brenton Brown and Tom Slater write:

Let My Life Be like a Love Song

And now I want to give just as I've received,
To live a life that shines Your love to those in need.
. . . .
Let my life be like a love song
To Your heart. . . .

So let justice roll like an endless stream,
Flowing through my life to the poor and weak.
Let the things I do and the words I speak
Reveal the awesome love You have shown to me.[32]

Likewise, Matt Redman sings:

Justice and Mercy

You've put a new song in my mouth,
It is a hymn of praise to you.
Justice and mercy are its theme,
And I will live it back to You.
The kind of fast you've chosen, Lord,
It must reach out
To broken lives and to the poor,
So change me, Lord.

I know You are the orphan's hope,
I know You are the widow's song,
O Lord, You're showing me what's on your heart,
Lord, I won't bring an empty song.
It's meaningless
Without compassion in my life and holiness.[33]

Finally, critics worry that charismatic worship tends to be sentimental, catchy, or cute. To this Brown responds (via email),

> [We must not] run the risk of negating the positive aspects of culturally contagious songwriting by even slightly dismissing songs that are "catchy" (cf. the Wesleyan approach to corporate worship).... I don't have a problem with catchy worship songs, or even sentimental worship songs (didn't God give us emotion and sentiment to enjoy?). We need these songs.

This is not only true for spiritual health (and healing); it is also true if we are to reach up to God as well as out to our world. We are called to those who are distant ideologically and culturally from the traditional church, longing for a deeper experience than the sensuality of pounding lust and chemical highs. Songwriters such as Martin Smith of *Delirious?* are uncompromisingly confronting a new generation with the gospel in its own idiom.

Worship ultimately calls us out of ourselves into the presence of the living God. Here we find our true selves. As in John's visions in the book of Revelation, worship purges our imagination of the idols of our age and replaces them with the sights and sounds of heaven itself. There, praise before the throne of God and the Lamb is unceasing, vital, and filled with shouting and songs of victory. As John undermined the pretensions of Rome and the satanic powers that enthralled her with the truth and glory of God, so our worship today must be just as subversive. The blood of the Lamb and the testimony of the saints will bring down the powers of this age as we glorify God in Spirit-led and Spirit-empowered worship.

A LITURGICAL WORSHIP RESPONSE

Paul Zahl

This is an informative and enlightening chapter, for it gives the history of charismatic or neo-Pentecostal worship over the last fifty years or so. I have lived through it, have experienced much of it, and have been helped by it. Don Williams is particularly good on the John Wimber phenomenon, without mentioning, however, that Wimber's death came against the "signs" and discouraged many in the charismatic world that he had himself done so much to shape. The English charismatics are very well respected in this piece, especially the persuasive and gifted Matt Redman from the United Kingdom.

I like this paragraph immensely, which draws from Redman's book *The Unquenchable Worshipper:*

> Dependence on the Spirit comes from a life "undone" before God. He strips us, makes us "distinctly uncomfortable" because he is a holy King, insisting on a holy people. Like the psalms of lament, true worship is never shallow, "shiny, happy." It comes from a heart broken before God.[34]

Williams acknowledges the painful fact that the charismatic movement of the 1970s has become a spent force, empirically speaking. It is marginalized throughout the mainline and in Roman Catholicism and now exists in institutional form within Calvary Chapels, Vineyard Fellowships, and nondenominational "cathedrals of praise." It makes me ask the haunting question found in an early Renaissance poem: *Où sont les neiges de hier?* ("Where are the snows of yesterday?")

153

I am not sure Williams has lanced the wound, however. The core problem with the charismatic renewal movement, from Van Nuys to Toronto, from Malmesbury to Antwerp, was its emphasis on victory rather than on the dereliction of the Cross, on sanctification rather than on redemption, on victorious living rather than on *simul iustus et peccator* ("justified and sinful at the same time"). The charismatic movement blew it because it wanted to pole-vault over Calvary on the way to Pentecost. (Who does not?) It flew right over the unevangelized dark continents of the Christian heart. It underestimated the awesome devastating force of inherited and continuing sin.

For me, although I gladly identify myself with the charismatic movement of the late twentieth century, the problem was the anthropology. In its rush to blessing, it blew right by the truth of original sin. Yet, do you not still crave that blessing?

A TRADITIONAL WORSHIP RESPONSE

Harold Best

What a splendid chapter to read, digest, contend with, and pray along with! I am not a charismatic in many of the delimiting ways charismatic worship is popularly described. But I must confess something. As much as I am drawn to the combined mysteries and elegance of liturgical worship, and as much as I long for a polystylistic approach to all worship, there is something within me that always wonders if, in my spiritual sojourn, I am missing something or if something has missed me. Part of this is due, I am sure, to my Christian and Missionary Alliance background and the overemphasis, at that time in my life, on the possibility of missing God's best and ending up with second best.

In all of my ups and downs since, and in these blessed later years of a biblically based blessed assurance, there is still the longing, the wondering, even the lingering confusion that comes of hearing people talk about what this worship model accomplishes that another one does not. And when it comes down to the phenomenal, the overtly noticeable, the out-of-the-ordinary, I wonder again and again if I am missing out on something. So my prayers are fraught with openness and hunger, but guided by old Eli's words in 1 Samuel 3:18: "It is the LORD; let him do what seems good to him" (NRSV). I pray this as I observe all forms of worship.

I say this also even as I ponder the legitimate psycho-sociological differences that exist among people—some very private and quiet, others overt and loquacious; some literalists, others imaginers; some hearing within the whirlwind, and others in the still, small voice. And do you know what? Jesus is in all of these folks, both willing and working toward his good pleasure. I am more convinced than ever before that he, not us, has made provision for the near plethora of worship styles, none of which is superior, each of which accommodates and inhabits the complexities of the hungering, thirsting race of humankind. If genuine charismatic worship has done one thing for me, it is to make me long for anything the Lord, through his Spirit, is willing to bestow on me, even if it takes the form of a smoking flax or a bruised reed (Isaiah 42:3 KJV). In this I take my rest, even as I continue to pray, "It is the LORD; let him do what seems good to him."

Now I can return to Don Williams's wonderful writing. I thank him for his scholarship, clarity, and humility and the architectural finesse with which he has made the case. I thank him for his teacherly approach shown, for me, in what I learned from his writing. I thank him for writing about charismatic worship on its own terms, rather than positing it as an (or the) alternative to the perceived failures, weakness, or belatedness of other models. This is the way to talk about the work of the Lord—that is, to talk about the Lord's terms of reference and to acknowledge that for him, a thousand tongues will never suffice and a thousand flowers are free to bloom as long as they are informed by the only Word and tended by the only Gardener.

I have some questions. How do charismatics behave during the week? Are they that different from other Christ-centered Christians, or does the overt nature of charismatic worship spill over into carpentry, sewing up wounds, exercising the intellect, making art, and having babies? In other words, is there a charismatic life that sets itself apart from a sanctified life or a liturgically framed life? This, I must confess, is more important to me than the weekly times of charismatic worship.

Or are there personality types that behave accordingly? I have friends and relatives who are charismatics, and while there may be an abundance of "God talk" (I mean this reverently) and an emphasis on "God told me to do this or that" (I also mean this reverently), I find an absence of ideas or speculative thought or creative spontaneity. I see all too often a split worldview in which heart blocks out mind, flesh has little to do with spirit, and worldliness has more to do with things or acts than with having a worldview.

Now, it is Williams's scholarship along with that of others, especially Edith Blumhofer, that helps me a bit, but I do wonder about a deep theological model that goes beyond the worship mode and into the workplace—a model of such extent that it can counter, or at least dialogue with, the several elegant articulations issuing out of Reformed theology (both Genevan and Lutheran) as well as out of the Anglo-Catholic traditions.

There are other questions. In reference to Wimber's idea that "worship draws the heart of God to his people"—is that not a bit backwards, a mite too free-willish, and does it not make the action of God contingent on ours? I realize the scriptural importance of drawing nigh to God so that he will draw nigh to us (James 4:8 KJV), but is that not about all of life, and is not all of life about worship? Then, a bit further, I hear Wimber talking about worship as singing, the Word as preaching, and prayer and laying on of hands as ministry. The idea of "worship as" separated away from other acts of worship bothers me greatly, especially when (as in so many other contemporary practices) this human artifact, this emotional drip-drier called music, becomes the central fact in worship sets as well as a predetermined sequence for achieving intimacy. I worry greatly about the use of music as a behavioral tool, as evidenced in the various worship curves or progressions that depend on harmony, rhythm, texture, and tempo: classic, earthquake, mild, and the like.[35]

Two related questions come to mind. First, how can worship be so easily broken down into parts, and how do we end up with intimacy when intimacy has been initiated and set in immediate and perpetual motion by the blood of the Cross and by the new birth? Further, if spontaneity is of the essence in charismatic worship, why is the fivefold model so deterministic in its gradations? As for individual worshipers, if there is any trace of introspection or doubt in them, is there not the possible fear that they may be missing out—not quite realizing some detail to the full—as the stages are gone through? What if intimacy or exaltation turns flat—will the rest stay sharp despite this? I realize that the overall question "Am I worshiping or not?" can dog any believer in any setting, but in Wimber's model this fear could be especially real.

Williams does spend time on the theology of charismatic worship in general, and there is much to commend it. There is, however, a bit of ambiguity as to whether charismatic worship rests in a Pneumocentric Christology or a Christocentric Pneumatology. In the body of his comments concerning the work of the Spirit, both in restoring him to worship and understanding his role in bearing witness to Christ, the centeredness is on the Holy Spirit, whereas in note 13, Williams says that charismatic worship is also Christocentric. I do not doubt the latter for a moment as a specific tenet, but if the role of the Spirit is to bear witness to the Son and to bring him forcefully, continually, and pedagogically into our fullest spiritual purview, then it becomes critically important for us to keep our attention on the Christ.

My memory is shaky here, and I have no way to verify the source, but was it Martin Luther who told of a time when he was focused intently on the person and work of Christ? The Holy Spirit was there as if in the form of a dove, gently alight on his shoulder, and when Luther turned his attention to the Spirit and away from Christ, the dove flew away. This story may go too far in the other direction, but I believe it contains at least a modest lesson for all of our worship. We need this balance continually: "Christ in you, the hope of glory" made powerfully real by the Spirit, and being filled with the Spirit in order that the finished work of Christ will drive us to the ends of the earth with Good News. It is in this sense that witness is overheard worship.

Nonetheless, Williams goes on in the next few paragraphs to recount for us the full work of the Spirit and the Savior together. They are wonderful words, concisely put and heartwarming. I almost wish I had not raised any question in the previous paragraph except for the practitional imbalances that can so easily occur when charismatics attribute nearly everything happening to the work of the Spirit.

For Williams, in the section "Future Direction," to center in on the work of Matt Redman is to bring history, theology, and futures down to exactly the right person. I hope someday to meet Matt Redman and allow some of his sun to shine in on me. It seems that Redman is a humble part of the Lord's answer to all worshipers, not just the charismatics. His thinking and devotion are purified by truth. Every reader of this book should spend significant time with Williams's summary of Redman's work.

Finally, the growing eclecticism and attention to social issues of charismatic worship are most refreshing. Listen to

Williams: "In fact, the proliferation of new music that is culturally current severs this generation from the preceding experience of the church in worship, the richness of its tradition, and the depth of its theology mirrored in the great hymns of the faith." Further on, he quotes from lyrics by Brenton Brown and Tom Slater illustrating this.

Thank you, sir, for helping me out in your chapter and for persuading me just that much more that there is a deep structure behind all worship which, if sought out and attested to, will gladly lend a hand in shaping these many spiritual dialects that we freely call "worship."

A CONTEMPORARY WORSHIP RESPONSE

Joe Horness

Don Williams has wonderfully described the emergence of charismatic and contemporary worship through the Jesus Movement and John Wimber. The formation of Willow Creek Community Church is just one example of the profound impact of that movement. Contemporary worship has arisen from the same roots and shares the same longings as the charismatic worship movement. The primary difference lies in how the gifts of the Spirit are viewed or incorporated.

At the heart of charismatic worship is the belief that worship was designed by God to be a place where he and his people interact and where the Holy Spirit is set free to move and to speak as God is lifted up. Those of us who lead in contemporary settings could not agree more. The mark of true contemporary worship is not just the use of culturally relevant instruments and modern songs. Like those in the charismatic movement, we who lead contemporary worship services are longing to create places where, as Williams states, the "worshipers become active participants." We believe that worship is meant to be "transformative," where the Holy Spirit is freed to change us and make us more like Jesus. The charismatic worship movement has influenced contemporary worship in the songs we sing, the instruments we use, the physical way we express ourselves, the time and energy we give to worship, the focus of our worship, and above all, in what our congregations long for worship to be. Though we love and affirm the hymns and cultural richness of our past and embrace them wherever we can, we come to worship today not just to sing about God, but to interact with him and to be changed by his Spirit.

Where the contemporary and charismatic worship movements differ is primarily over how the activity of the Holy Spirit is expressed during our times of worship. One of the major contributions of the charismatic worship movement has certainly been "functionally to restore the Holy Spirit to our services." As a result, we who lead contemporary worship have learned to seek the Holy Spirit's presence in our planning, our leading, and our service. We plan and prepare carefully and prayerfully, but then seek to be responsive to the Holy Spirit's promptings and activity while we lead. We come to worship believing the Holy Spirit will be present in that place and that our worship will free us to hear him and to sense his presence in powerful ways. We fully expect him to move—to comfort, to encourage, to convict, and to lead us to Jesus. But while both movements seek to encourage the activity of the Holy Spirit in our worship, the emphasis of the contemporary worship service would be primarily focused on the internal moving of the Spirit in the hearts of our people while the charismatic worship movement would embrace and encourage more outward signs of the Holy Spirit's presence as well.

You will find traces of charismatic worship in many contemporary worship settings. Things like the raising of hands, free-form singing in a church's given language, room for spontaneity and changes in the midst of the worship, and clapping or "shouting" to the Lord may be parts of a contemporary worship service and are influenced directly by practices of the charismatic church. But in most contemporary worship services you will not find an emphasis on speaking in tongues, singing in the Spirit, healings, or prophetic words. In some cases it is because the churches involved have markedly different views on how the Holy Spirit expresses himself today. They may even believe that these outward gifts of the Spirit were given for the early church but are no longer accessible to the church today, a premise our charismatic friends would certainly differ with! In other churches these manifestations of the Spirit are affirmed, if not always embraced, but approached as gifts that are meant for edification in private or under the careful supervision of the elders and the leadership of the church. In such cases, expression of these gifts in a corporate setting would not be seen as appropriate and therefore would not be a part of the church's corporate worship experience. Thus the Holy Spirit, while acknowledged, surrendered to, and invited, expresses his presence in less outward ways. Contemporary worship leaders draw powerfully on the influence and the heart of the charismatic worship movement but apply what is applicable within their theological setting. The challenge for contemporary churches, as Williams correctly points out, is not to neglect the presence of the Holy Spirit in our services out of overreaction or fear regarding the outward expressions of his gifts.

To that end, I love Williams's exhortation, via Matt Redman, for worshipers to walk in the presence of the Holy Spirit day to day: "If we truly want to be led by the Holy Spirit, we need to make sure we're keeping in step with Him in our everyday lives." If we are not to mishandle the Spirit, either by an overemphasis on signs and wonders or by simple neglect, then we need to be people, and worship leaders in particular, who learn to sense his quiet leadings moment by moment and day by day. Only then will we learn to recognize when it is his voice that is speaking and prompting, regardless of the theological grid we start from. When we come before God in humility, undone, broken before him, and focused not on ourselves but on the offering we come to bring to God, then his Spirit will be free to move, inwardly or outwardly, in quietness or in overwhelming power.

A BLENDED WORSHIP RESPONSE

Robert Webber

I always admire the writings of those who are able to bring Scripture, history, and contemporary relevance together in a clear synthesis of thought. Don Williams has done just that in this excellent chapter on charismatic worship.

I appreciate his concern to recover the charismatic aspects of New Testament worship that are often neglected by the liturgical, traditional, and even contemporary worshiping communities. I deeply appreciate his attention to the cultural setting of the rise of charismatic worship out of the Pentecostal Movement through the Jesus Movement and into the signs and wonders movement led by John Wimber. Furthermore, his concern that worship now and into the future should be Trinitarian, ordered, organized, free, surprising, and Spirit-led is equally welcome, as is his call for balanced worship.

But I do have one major question to ask Don Williams: Why, after touching on nearly every aspect of worship, is there not one single word or reference to the Eucharist? Consider the attention given to the Eucharist in the New Testament and throughout history.

The New Testament has a great deal to say about worship at bread and wine. Jesus taught by both word and action, "There is a way to remember me." One of the most powerful stories of the Gospels is the account of Cleopas and his companion knowing Jesus at bread and wine; Paul says that in the celebration of bread and wine we are to remember him until he comes again (worship is both memory and anticipation); the book of Revelation sees the ultimate downfall of Satan and all the powers of evil celebrated in the great supper of the Lamb. Furthermore, the Eucharist is everywhere attested to in the liturgies of the early church. Ancient Christians not only told the story of God's mission in Jesus Christ to save the world; they also enacted story in the Eucharist.

The earliest evidence of Eucharistic liturgies indicates that they were Trinitarian in structure (Williams reminds us that worship is Trinitarian). The Eucharistic liturgy calls us to enter into the heavens with the angels and archangels who forever sing, "Holy, holy, holy" (praise to the Father). Then a great prayer of thanksgiving for the work of the Son sweeps from Creation to re-creation to tell how God in Jesus came from heaven to be born of a virgin, to be a voluntary sacrifice for our sin, to destroy death and the powers of evil, to be resurrected to new life, and to bring into being the church, the people called to witness in their worship to the accomplished mission of God in Jesus. And then the prayer calls upon the Holy Spirit to make this people one and to confirm the truth in our hearts.

While the Eucharist was corrupted in the late medieval period, the Reformers called the church back to Word and Sacrament. But Protestants for the most part have neglected the biblical roots, the early historic development, and the call of the Reformers to return to the biblical and ancient practice of telling and enacting the gospel at the table of the Lord.

Charismatics want to be known as those who rediscover the fullness of biblical worship. So I ask, why do you neglect the Eucharist?

AN EMERGING WORSHIP RESPONSE

Sally Morgenthaler

THIRD WORLD ATTRACTION AND NORTH AMERICAN BARRIERS

Charismatic-Pentecostal worship forms are the least understood yet most practiced of all worship expressions worldwide. Regardless of what we think of its theological foundations and emphases, worship that emphasizes the outward manifestations of the Holy Spirit (characterized in 1 Corinthians 14) is the fastest-growing worship model in the world. When LaMar Boschman and friends host their annual Worship Institute in Dallas each year, over a third of its three-thousand-plus attendees are from churches outside the United States. Each July, worshipers, worship leaders, and pastors stream in from places as faraway as Indonesia, Australia, Bolivia, Guatemala, Kenya, South Africa, Haiti, Thailand, South Korea, the United Kingdom, and Eastern Europe. They bring with them incredible stories of God's movement among their people—fresh narratives of evangelism, commitment, healing, and deliverance, both inside and outside their worship settings. The Charismatic-Pentecostal God is not a tame or sleeping God.

Cultural acceptance has come significantly slower in North America. Even in today's neo-spiritual climate, evangelical Christian supernaturalism is held suspect. Never mind that we watch the television program "Crossing Over" with medium Jonathan Edwards, absolutely convinced that he is connecting the audience to their deceased loved ones. Never mind that we sit—spellbound—as psychic Uri Gellar bends spoons with his thoughts on "Connie Chung." Never mind that a photographer captured a demon's face in the World Trade Center smoke, and the photo appeared for several nights on national news. In North America the supernatural only gets the cultural "thumbs up" if it does not involve big hair, singing to God in weird languages, or specific references to Jesus Christ.

BRIDGING THE DISCONNECT

Jesus Christ is a nonnegotiable. Big hair may not be advisable. But uninterpreted weird language is a problem. It seems to be the exceptional charismatic service where the speaking-in-tongues discipline—so intricately laid out in 1 Corinthians 14—is actually followed. No wonder outsiders think we are nuts! (Read 1 Corinthians 14: 23.) Don Williams acknowledges that there is a scriptural ideal for order in worship: "Since the gifts of the Spirit are biblically grounded, charismatic worship welcomes their manifestation or release. When they are exercised in an orderly way, the whole church is built up." But he does not acknowledge the prevalence of charismatic churches that weekly disregard this passage. When it comes to speaking in tongues, Scripture seems fairly clear: "If anyone speaks in a tongue, two—or at most three—should speak, one at a time, and someone must interpret. If there is no interpreter, the speaker should keep quiet in the church and speak to himself and God" (1 Corinthians 14:27–28).

That being said, the charismatic church's lag in impacting North American culture (in comparison to its success in the rest of the world) cannot be explained solely in terms of its worship practices. Williams referenced an inherent isolationism found in earlier charismatic traditions: "the [earlier] charismatic renewal ... tended ... not to impact evangelism, issues of social justice, or world missions."

In many ways, charismatic/Pentecostal churches in North America still tend to be bound up in their religious subcultures, cut off from the aesthetic, intellectual, and social contexts of the larger culture. Increasingly there are exceptions to this pattern, but they are intentional: hard fought and hard won. Here are just a few examples:

- The Cincinnati Vineyard is known for its servant evangelism throughout the city, including houses renovated for the poor, soup kitchens, and free car repairs.
- New Life Church in Colorado Springs has developed a burgeoning discipleship network based on affinity groups. They find out what unchurched people are passionate about and get them together with Christians who have that same interest.
- New Community Church in Muskogee, Oklahoma, is a refuge for the emotionally scarred, and especially a place of healing and renewal for those wanting to leave the homosexual lifestyle.

I predict that the most effective Third Wave churches in the U.S. will not simply be made up of churches with a more comprehensible, culturally sensitive worship experience. They will be composed of Spirit-filled churches that take Romans 12:1 "worship as a life" out into their streets and homes; they will be gatherings of the faithful who are driven not simply by Acts 2 (Pentecost), but also by Acts 17 (Mars Hill).

INTIMACY AND INTERACTION

Williams describes John Wimber's view of worship as "worship [that] draws the heart of God to his people." Indeed, Wimber's quest for God-intimacy in worship seems to be the primary focus of his worship theology and practice. His preference for songs sung *to* God over those *about* God resulted in one of his greatest contributions to the body of Christ around the world: permission to love God intensely and to express that love unabashedly. The contemporary praise choruses of Wimber's time still retained a certain stylized distance from God.

According to Williams, "Eighty percent of all white Protestant churches in the United States include Vineyard songs in their public worship." Aside from the widely encompassing, generic label "contemporary," I doubt that any other single tradition of worship music can claim such a broad representation in our nation's churches. And because of that, we need to take serious note. There is a reason that people of all ages—and especially our youth—are clamoring for radically expressive, unrestrained worship music. Whether he realized it or not, Wimber was helping to correct the preponderance of cerebral, impassive worship music within certain sectors of Protestantism. In an increasingly expressive, post-rationalistic culture, this shift toward intimate, "in the moment" spirituality not only made relational sense; it made sense culturally.

Wimber's emphasis on worship as interactive and deeply responsive was yet another shift: away from passive, leader-focused services to the full and, for the most part, unscripted participation of God's people. Conversions, healings, deliverance, prophecy, visions, evangelism, ministry time, waiting on the Lord, hearing from the Lord—these all speak of God in the immediate: living, acting, and responding to people in their midst. This is not a God in a galaxy far, far away or a God residing in a dusty prayer book or Bible lesson. Worship is our response to revelation: who God is and what God has done. It is no small thing that in the decades preceding the interactive age, Wimber took interaction (specifically, unscripted response to God and ministry time) to unprecedented levels.

CONCERNS

I express my concerns cautiously and with great respect for the charismatic-Pentecostal tradition Williams describes in this chapter. Having grown up in one of the over-restrained, cerebral sectors of Protestantism, I have personally experienced most charismatic worship services as deepening, refreshing, and—when drawn to Jesus Christ in the midst of it all (as Williams duly reminds us, the Spirit is meant to do)—transforming.

My concern is that too often what Williams outlines on paper as Trinitarian worship is actually unitarian in practice. Theologian Harold O. J. Brown once expressed to me that, left unchecked, most religious movements gravitate toward one form of unitarianism or another. I have always remembered that statement.

Williams claims, "Charismatic worship, like all historic Christian worship, is Trinitarian: worship directed to the Father, through the Son, in the Spirit." He also makes a case for charismatic worship as Christ-centered: "True charismatic worship is not human-centered or emotion-centered. The Spirit comes to bear witness to Christ (John 15:26)."

But in a recent study of two hundred songs regularly used in charismatic worship services, only thirteen focused on the person or work of Christ. Certainly this does not address the content of the preaching, prayers, or other worship elements present. Yet charismatic worship services are largely made up of singing. Just what are people singing about? If, as Scripture says, the Spirit comes to bear witness to Christ, then this deletion is a serious problem. Ultimately our intimacy with God is not achieved by navigating through five levels of phases, but by the Son of God himself, through whose blood "we have confidence to enter the Most Holy Place" and by whose priestly act—his death—we are able to "draw near to God with a sincere heart in full assurance of faith, having our hearts sprinkled to cleanse us from a guilty conscience and having our bodies washed with pure water" (Hebrews 10:19–22).

We may need five phases to get us from the parking lot to the point where we can reacknowledge and realign ourselves to the unfathomable truth of our redemption in Jesus. But as we go through those phases, we need to affirm that it is God himself who has made possible the unfettered, unrestricted intimacy we seek. Our closeness with God is not of our own doing. It is not a result of how excellent, how passionate, how demonstrative, or how long our song sets are. That is clear. Third Wave churches that seriously refocus on the person and work of God the Son—revealed by the power of the Holy Spirit—will give postmodern North America and a waiting world a glimpse of Revelation 5. If, as Williams says, "The gift of 'charismatic worship' to the church has been functionally to restore the Holy Spirit to our services," then it is for the purpose of lifting up the Lamb of God—and that purpose alone.

Chapter 4: Charismatic Worship Notes

Proposal: Don Williams

[1]See Paul Basden, *The Worship Maze: Finding a Style to Fit Your Church* (Downers Grove, IL: InterVarsity Press, 1999), chap. 1, especially p. 19. Scholars use "charismatic" in the larger sense of free, spontaneous worship. For example, Horton Davies writes of "the traditional and charismatic" merging in eighteenth-century Anglican evangelicalism in *Worship and Theology in England: From Watts and Wesley to Martineau, 1690–1900* (Princeton, NJ: Princeton University Press, 1961), 210.

[2]See Frank Bartleman, *Another Wave of Revival* (Springdale, PA: Whitaker House, 1982); Edith Blumhofer, "Restoration as Revival: Early American Pentecostalism," in Edith Blumhofer and Randall Balmer, eds., *Modern Christian Revivals* (Urbana and Chicago: University of Illinois Press, 1993); Harvey Cox, *Fire from Heaven* (Reading, MA: Addison-Wesley, 1995); and Alister McGrath, *The Future of Christianity* (Oxford, UK: Blackwell, 2002), 106ff.

[3]See Dennis Bennett, *Nine O'clock in the Morning* (South Plainfield, NJ: Bridge, 1970); Dennis and Rita Bennett, *The Holy Spirit and You* (South Plainfield, NJ: Bridge, 1971); and Dennis Bennett, *How to Pray for the Release of the Holy Spirit* (South Plainfield, NJ: Bridge, 1985).

[4]See Francis MacNutt, *Healing* (Notre Dame, IN: Ave Maria Press, 1977); reprint: *Healing* (Altamonte Springs, FL: Creation House, 1988), 13–19.

[5]Laurie Klein, "I Love You, Lord" (1978), in *Maranatha! Music Praise Chorus Book*, 2d ed. (Maranatha! Music, 1990), Song 84. Used by permission.

[6]Much to the dismay of traditionalists such as Marva Dawn, *Reaching Out without Dumbing Down: A Theology of Worship for the Turn-of-the-Century Culture* (Grand Rapids: Eerdmans, 1995). For a balanced critique of Dawn's position, see John Frame, *Contemporary Worship Music: A Biblical Defense* (Phillipsburg, NJ: Presbyterian and Reformed, 1997), 155–74.

[7]Kevin Springer, ed., *Riding the Third Wave* (Hankt, UK: Marshall Pickering, 1987), especially John Wimber, "Introduction," 30ff., and C. Peter Wagner, "God Wasn't Pulling My Leg," 48ff.

[8]Wimber writes, "About this time (1977) I began asking our music leader why some songs seemed to spark something in us and others didn't. As we talked about worship, we realized that often we would sing about worship yet we never actually worshiped.... Thus we began to see a difference between songs about Jesus and songs to Jesus." See John Wimber, "Worship: Intimacy with God," in John Wimber, ed., *Thoughts on Worship* (Anaheim, CA: Vineyard Music Group, 1996), 2.

[9]Matt Redman, "Worshipper and Musician," in David Pytches, ed., *John Wimber: His Influence and Legacy* (Guildford, Surrey, UK: Eagle, 1998), 69.

[10]Wimber, "Worship: Intimacy with God," 4–6; see also Redman, "Worshipper and Musician," 65f.

[11]See "Britain," in Stanley Burgess, ed., *The New International Dictionary of Pentecostal and Charismatic Movements*, rev. ed. (Grand Rapids: Zondervan, 2002), 42–46.

[12]Carol Wimber, *John Wimber: The Way It Was* (London: Hodder and Stoughton, 1999), 143. Used by permission.

[13]It is also Christocentric. James Torrance writes, "Christian worship is ... our participation through the Spirit in the Son's communion with the Father, in his vicarious life of worship and intercession." See James Torrance, *Worship, Community, and the Triune God of Grace* (Downers Grove, IL: InterVarsity Press, 1996), 15.

[14]*A Treasury of A. W. Tozer* (Harrisburg, PA: Christian Publications, 1980), 40.

[15]Tom Wright, *Bringing the Church to the World* (Minneapolis: Bethany House, 1992), 51.

[16]Tim Hughes, "Fill Us Up, Send Us Out," in *New Wine* 19 (Summer 2002), 17.

[17]Matt Redman, *The Unquenchable Worshipper* (Eastbourne, UK: Kingsway, 2001; Ventura, CA: Regal, 2002), 11.

[18]Ibid., 16.
[19]Ibid., 36.
[20]Ibid., 38.
[21]Ibid., 29.
[22]Ibid., 42.
[23]Ibid., 43.
[24]Ibid., 65.
[25]Ibid., 66.
[26]Ibid., 22.
[27]Ibid., 51.
[28]Ibid., 53.
[29]Ibid., 78. Used by permission.

[30]Horton Davies writes of the Evangelical Awakening in England, "It had become clear by 1779 that a great deal of the popular appeal of Methodism was due to its remarkable hymns" (*Worship and Theology in England,* 203).

[31]*Holy* (UK: Vineyard Music, 2002), #1. Used by permission.

[32]Ibid., #12. Used by permission.

[33]*The Father's Song* (UK: Kingsway Thankyou Music, 2000), #4. Used by permission.

Response: Paul Zahl

[34]Redman, *The Unquenchable Worshipper*, 22.

Response: Harold Best

[35]See Andy Park, *To Know You More: Cultivating the Heart of a Worship Leader* (Downers Grove, IL: InterVarsity Press, 2003), 163–67.

Chapter Five

BLENDED WORSHIP

BLENDED WORSHIP

Robert Webber

"Blended worship simply doesn't work."

"Blended worship is blah, vanilla, nothing!"

"There's something in blended worship to offend everyone."

I need not go on. We have all heard these statements over and over again. They have been spoken to us, written to us, and drummed into our minds. But are these statements true? In the way that the word "blended" is generally used, these criticisms are true. What most people usually mean by blended worship is "sing hymns and choruses and you've got it—blended worship."

This simplistic view must be called into question. Therefore the purpose of this chapter is to provide a corrective, showing what blended worship is and is not, and to provide directions to those who wish to do it.

Here is what this chapter presents:

- The origin of blended worship
- The distinguishing features of blended worship
- What problems blended worship overcomes
- What blended worship looks like

THE ORIGIN OF BLENDED WORSHIP

In brief, blended worship is a synthesis of the liturgical and contemporary worship renewal movements of the twentieth century.

These historical roots are very complex and deserving of a doctoral dissertation. The most we can do here is provide a brief introduction to the major events and themes of both the liturgical and contemporary movements from which blended worship springs.

The Liturgical Renewal of the Twentieth Century

Let's start by looking at traditional worship. In the first sixty years of the twentieth century, traditional Protestant worship had settled into eight major traditions:

- Liturgical tradition—emphasis on beauty
- Reformed tradition—emphasis on the centrality of the Word
- Anabaptist tradition—concern for community and discipleship within worship
- Restorationist tradition—commitment to weekly Communion
- Revivalist tradition (Baptists, Methodists, evangelicals)—concern to move toward the invitation and call sinners to repentance
- Quaker tradition—call to silence and waiting for God to speak
- Holiness tradition—emphasis on the need to break through and achieve sanctification in worship
- African-American tradition—emphasis on soul worship

Three things characterize these traditions. First, for the most part they are tied into a print form of communication that traces back to the invention of the Gutenberg printing press. Each tradition has a prayer book, a hymnbook, or bulletins; is primarily verbal; and is given to one-way communication. Second, traditional worship is predictable. For example, a Baptist living on the East Coast in the fifties will experience the same form and style of worship on a West Coast visit because the same can be said for every denomination and fellowship. Third, traditionalists are also worship isolationists. They seldom worship outside of their own tradition because they are denominational loyalists. When taking a vacation, these traditionalists look in the Yellow Pages for a church of their own denomination. The result? Worship never changed. It looked and felt the same everywhere and at all times before 1960. It was a comfortable, never-to-be-questioned security.

Then came the liturgical renewal in the sixties and seventies that burst out of the Roman Catholic reforms of Vatican II, 1963–1965. The first document off the press was *The Constitution of the Sacred Liturgy,* 1963.[1] This document called the Catholic Church to return to its biblical and historical roots in worship. It revolutionized Catholic worship in that it put it into the language of the people; simplified it; restored preaching, congregational participation, and singing; and focused on the renewal of every aspect of worship, including its theology, structure, style, architecture, and environment.

This was a momentous movement that created sweeping reforms. Consequently, it caught the attention of scholars and leaders in Protestant traditional denominations. Soon, movements within these denominations called for change. They too wanted to return to the biblical and historical roots of worship. Subsequently, every major denomination produced new books and resources in worship renewal. There were at least six movements emerging in different degrees among traditional churches that included the following new interests: (1) concern to restore the theology of worship, (2) new attention to the historic fourfold pattern of worship, (3) a rethinking of the Eucharist, (4) a restoration of the Christian year, (5) new questions about the role of music and the arts in worship, and (6) concerns about how to intensify the participation of the congregation. Enormous changes were made in every tradition. But something was missing.

Contemporary Worship Renewal in the Twentieth Century

During the twentieth century three worship renewal movements fed into the broader contemporary renewal of worship. The first of these, the Pentecostal Movement, began at the famous Azusa Street Revival in Los Angeles in 1906. These people experienced a new outpouring of the Holy Spirit manifested in the gift of tongues as its central characteristic. This movement spread all over the world, creating new denominations such as the Assemblies of God. The second movement, the Latter Rain Movement, originated in Edmonton, Alberta, in the late 1940s and became manifest in Pentecostal churches in particular. It was known for its spontaneous worship. This became the charismatic renewal with its emphasis on the gifts of discernment, wisdom, prophecy, and knowledge.

The third movement—and the one with which the readers of this chapter may be most familiar—is the rise of the "chorus tradition." It has several sources. One is the music genre of Bill and Gloria Gaither and their choruses such as "There's a Sweet, Sweet Spirit in this Place." (Their songs also became popular in Pentecostal and charismatic circles.) Another source is found in the emergence of the Jesus People in the late 1960s and early 1970s. Many of these people, like Tommy Coombs, were secular musicians and bandleaders who, upon becoming Christian, used their talents to create the contemporary Christian music genre. They traveled the country with their new musical form, started churches that appropriated their new style, and caused many older churches, especially in the evangelical tradition, to adapt their style. Adaptations were made by the megachurch seeker tradition (with a different origin), and new movements were founded on the new musical style (e.g., the Vineyard Movement). Both the strength of each of these three movements and the thing they all held in common was experience. They wanted a real, vital encounter with God to happen in worship. It did. But something was missing.

The Blending of Liturgical and Contemporary Worship

Something was missing in both the traditional and contemporary worship renewal. What was missing in one was the strength in the other. The traditional church was missing the sense of a real and vital experience with God. The contemporary movement was missing substance. Blended worship brought the content of the liturgical movement and the experience of the contemporary movement together.

The blending of traditional and contemporary worship began in 1987. I was working part time for Maranatha! Music in the area of research and development. Chuck Fromm, the CEO of Maranatha!, and I began brainstorming about the future of worship. We were both convinced that wherever there is a thesis and antithesis, the likelihood is that a synthesis between the two will occur. We determined to experiment with a blending of contemporary and traditional worship.

Consequently, Maranatha! sponsored a national workshop that met in Irvine, California, for the specific purpose of bringing together leaders of the liturgical movement and leaders of the contemporary movement. In that three-day conference, blended worship was born, but the history of the movement is extremely difficult to unravel. On one side of the movement, it meant little more than the blending of hymns and choruses. On the other side, it meant the converging of the six concerns of the liturgical renewal with the contemporary concern for the immediacy of the Spirit and a genuine experience with God. In this chapter I propose that true blended worship is the fullness of the liturgical renewal blended together with the concern for the immediacy of the Spirit. Blended worship at its best is substance and relevance, truth and experience, divine and human.

DISTINGUISHING FEATURES OF BLENDED WORSHIP

What, then, are the distinguishing features or marks of blended worship? These marks can be arranged under three headings—content, structure, and style.

Content

We see a great deal of confusion regarding the content of worship—even among those who are committed to worship renewal.

The most frequent statement heard today is that worship is "for God." But when asked, "What does that kind of worship look like?" the most common answer is "thematic worship. Pick a theme about God—his love, his mercy, his faithfulness—and build your entire service around it. Sing it, read it, preach it, pray it." The thematic view of worship needs to be called into question.

Blended worship is about the triune God. We worship God the Father in the language of mystery, God the Son in the language of story, and God the Spirit in the language of symbol. Let me explain.

Language of mystery. Worship needs to acknowledge the unknowable nature of God, who is transcendent and other and dwells in eternal mystery. We see, as Paul states in 1 Corinthians 13:12 (KJV), "through a glass, darkly." God cannot be understood by our finite minds nor grasped by our earthly thoughts or language. This mystery, what Rudolph Otto calls the *mysterium tremendum* or the numinous, is acknowledged in our use of space, in the beauty of the arts, in gesture, and in words of praise such as the *Sanctus*, the *Gloria in Excelsis Deo*, and the *Kyrie*.

Language of story. While the essence of God is unknowable, God's actions in history are known. God has been revealed in history, in Israel, and in Jesus, and this revelation of his speech to humanity and his involvement in the history of the world, especially his incarnation in Jesus Christ, is intelligible. We can talk about it. We can think it, understand it, interpret it, study it, and communicate it. The content of God's involvement in history is the *missio Dei*. This mission of God is his purpose to rescue the fallen world. God's mission begins with Abraham and then extends to Israel, to the Exodus, and to the founding of a people with whom he enters into covenant to bring them to the Promised Land. In these Old Testament types and shadows we see what is fulfilled in the New Testament. God has become incarnate in our world in Jesus. He has died for our sins. He is resurrected from the dead, he inaugurates his kingdom, and he sends the Holy Spirit to create the church as the witness to his present rule in the world and to prepare his people for his ultimate destruction of the powers of evil at the end of history and his eternal rule over all creation forever.

Here we have a story—the story of the meaning of the universe. This story, told in the Bible, is the story from which all worship derives. Daily worship tells the story of creation from the dawning of the day to the setting of the sun. God is worshiped as the Creator and the Finisher of life. He is the reason for the morning when we wake to begin a new day. And he is the one who has brought us through the day and now watches over us as we sleep through the night and ready ourselves for another day.

This story is also the story of our Sunday worship. We gather in God's presence to read and tell the story through the Word and to sing it and enact it as we gather around bread and wine.

The Christian year also proclaims and enacts the story. Christian time recalls the mighty acts of God's salvation. Advent anticipates the coming of the Messiah; Christmas announces his arrival; Epiphany proclaims that the Messiah is for the whole world, not the Jews alone; Lent travels toward the death of Jesus; Holy Week remembers the saving events; Easter proclaims the resurrection; and Pentecost celebrates the coming of the Holy Spirit and the birth of the church.

Daily worship, Sunday worship, yearly worship all proclaim in a 24/7/365 way the story that tells the meaning of human existence. How can the world know this story about itself unless we practice it in our public worship and in the routine of our daily lives?

Language of symbol. Symbol is how we experience the worship of the Holy Spirit. The Spirit has always been associated with God's presence in the world. For example, the Spirit hovered over the waters in Creation; the Spirit led Abraham out of the land of Ur; the Spirit led the people of Israel through the Red Sea to Mount Sinai, where they entered into covenant with God; the Spirit dwelt in the tabernacle and the temple in the Holy of Holies; the Spirit inspired the prophets and the writing of Scripture; by the Spirit, Jesus was conceived in the womb of the virgin Mary; the Spirit led Jesus into the wilderness and fortified him in his temptation; the Spirit came upon Jesus at his baptism, empowered his ministry, and raised him from the dead; the Spirit came at Pentecost to provide the disciples with new understanding, to dwell personally in all the children of God, to empower the mission of the church, and to attend to the events that will surround the coming again of Jesus in history to set up his kingdom forever.

Now the Spirit gathers us for worship, is present in every believer, shines through the function of ministry, attends the reading and preaching of the Word, and is released through the signs of bread and wine. Through the Spirit we enter into the Holy of Holies, into the very dwelling of God, and with the angels and archangels we join in the heavenly song, singing, "Holy, holy, holy, the whole earth is full of his glory."

Here, then, is what worship does. It acknowledges the transcendence, the great glory and incomprehensible nature of God the Father. It tells the story from beginning to end of how God created, how the world fell away from him, how he became involved in the history of the world in Israel and in his incarnation in Jesus to rescue the world through his death, resurrection, and coming in glory to reign as Lord over all creation. And it unleashes the power and presence of the Holy Spirit in the assembled people, in ministry, in Word and Sacrament, and it connects God and people in a relational encounter.

Structure

The content of worship is inseparable from its structure or order. The structure of worship is not a program or a presentation of the Christian story, nor is it the manipulation of emotions into a fleeting experience of feeling good. It is instead a communal rehearsal of our relationship with God—Father, Son, and Holy Spirit. The biblical order of worship itself brings us into the presence of the transcendent God, draws our lives into the story (this is what I mean by the word "rehearsal"—it is a real, authentic involvement in God's story, not a preparation for it, but an experience of the real thing), and unleashes the power and presence of the Holy Spirit in our lives here and now in public worship, and then in the worship of our whole life in all that we do.

This structure or order of worship is called the fourfold pattern because it does four things: (1) it gathers the people in God's presence; (2) it tells and proclaims the story in song, in Scripture, in preaching, in prayer, and in the kiss of peace; (3) it enacts the story in water, bread, wine, oil (the symbols speak and act); and (4) it sends God's people forth into the world to love and serve the Lord. This fourfold pattern is rooted in Scripture and attested in history.

For example, the first description of public worship is recorded in Exodus 24:1–11. Here God calls Moses and the people to gather at the foot of the mountain; the book of the covenant is read to the people and they agree to keep it; a sacrificial act ratifying the covenant between God and Israel is made; a celebratory meal is eaten before God; and the people go forth to love and serve the Lord.

This fourfold pattern is repeated in every covenant of the Old Testament; it is the pattern of New Testament worship described in Acts 2:42; it is the pattern of worship of all early Christian liturgies; and it is the order advocated by Luther, Calvin, and some leading Anabaptists. However, during the modern period of Protestant history the fourfold pattern of worship was lost, especially as revivalism emerged in the nineteenth and twentieth centuries. Revivalism practices a threefold pattern: preliminaries, sermon, and invitation. This threefold pattern has been modified in what is now considered traditional worship and in contemporary worship as well. What is now considered traditional worship is an interplay between music (often choir and hymn driven) and sermon. Contemporary worship, in its structure, is not much different: it is an interplay between music (band and chorus driven) and sermon.

The blended worship that I advocate calls for the return to this biblical and historical order of worship. It recognizes that four different worship acts underlie the Sunday celebration: *Gathering* is a spiritual act of centering before the almighty transcendent God; the *Word* is a spiritual hearing of God's story and a resolve to live by God's instruction; and *Table* worship is a participation of heart, mind, and will in the remembrance of God's great saving action in Jesus Christ, in his present eternal intercessory prayer for the world, and in an anticipation of his coming to destroy the powers of evil and to rule justly as the Lord of all creation. Finally, the *sending forth*, brief as it is, is a blessing from God, who promises to go forth with his people as they work and serve him in all of life.

One can see how this structure of worship is related to the theology of worship. While there is a Trinitarian consciousness to all four parts of worship, we emphasize God's transcendence in the gathering, a retelling of the work of the Son in the service of the Word, and an unleashing of the power of the Holy Spirit in the symbol of bread and wine. The culminating act of sending is always in the name of the Father, the Son, and the Holy Spirit.

Style

We turn now to the third issue in the trilogy of content, structure, and style—and we ask, "Is there a God-ordained style?"

To answer this question we must turn to history and culture. Throughout the various paradigms of history—ancient, medieval, Reformation, modern, and now postmodern—we discern a variety of styles. Broadly speaking, the style of worship reflects culture. In the first three centuries, Christian worship was simple and uncluttered. If anything, it was countercultural to the more elaborate styles of the Roman cults. Worship during the medieval era reflected the Christianization of culture and, in fact, became synonymous with culture. During this period of oral communication, worship became highly visual and spectacular. It was something to watch, not to do. The Reformers rightly simplified worship and, most important, returned it to the people by translating the liturgy into the language of the people and providing opportunities for participation. During the modern era, worship became influenced by the culture of reason on the one hand and the culture of experience on the other hand. Traditional worship has been primarily oriented around reason, whereas revivalistic worship and its daughter, contemporary worship, have been primarily shaped by experience (the experiential invitation in revivalism and the emotional music of contemporary worship). But the most serious problem with both traditional and contemporary worship (with some exceptions) is that they are nonparticipatory. In sermon-driven, choir-driven, and band-driven worship, worship is done *to* the people and *for* the people, but seldom *by* the people.

Fortunately, there is a trend today, particularly among the next generation of leaders, to return worship to the people. Worship in the postmodern era, like worship during the early church and somewhat like the worship of the Reformers, will be countercultural and more participatory.

So, then, is there one style of worship that is more Christian than another? This is probably not the right question. Perhaps it would be better to ask, are there biblical principles that should affect the style of worship in every age and every geographical area? Theologically, the first guideline for this question is found in the Incarnation and the Christological thinking of the church. In the Incarnation, the Scripture teaches that the Word became flesh (John 1:14). In the Christological thinking of the church (Chalcedon Creed, 451) we confess that the union of God and man is "without confusion, without change, without division, without separation."

This recognition of the full divinity and the full humanity of our Lord united in one person is not incidental to the issue of style in worship. Worship is both divine and human—fully divine, fully human. When worship comes only from above, it denies the humanity of our worship. When worship comes only from below, it denies the divinity of our worship. True worship is divine because it is the work of God. True worship is human because it is the work of the people. Consequently, the fundamental issue of worship style is that worship must be participatory. Worship is a synergism of divine and human activity; it is dialogic. Worship that is a monologue, either of God or of the people, fails to meet the criteria of the divine-human relationship modeled by God's Incarnation and the church's theological reflection.

A second theological source for thinking about style is the theology of Creation. Christian theology acknowledges God's act of creation to be good. Because this is God's world, matter is the means through which the invisible God is made visible. This theme is heightened by both the Incarnation, seeing that God became matter, and by eschatology, seeing that God will free matter from the power of evil, which has brought creation into "bondage to decay" (see Romans 8:18–22). Salvation is the rescue not only of people, but of the whole creation. This conviction of Scripture is the basis for the arts in worship.

Broadly speaking, then, style, at its very least, from a biblical view demands the participation of the people and the freedom of the artist to release creation through the use of the arts to proclaim God's redemption of the entire creation to the praise of God.

WHAT PROBLEMS DOES
BLENDED WORSHIP OVERCOME?

How does this persuasion about content, structure, and style relate to the two very crucial problems of traditional and contemporary worship—instrumental and presentational worship?

Instrumental Worship

Instrumental worship always asks, "What will this worship accomplish?" Nearly every worship-planning group asks this question. Picture the setting: The planners have gathered and are discussing their worship plan for next Sunday. Somebody says, "Hold on! We need to ask, 'What will this worship accomplish?'" Everyone thinks that's a good question.

"Evangelism," says one. So off they go, planning a worship that will be directed toward the unconverted. Some churches may follow a revivalistic order ending in an invitation. In others, it may be a seeker-sensitive service, taking into consideration the needs, feelings, and situation of the seeker.

At another time someone will cry out, "Isn't worship for the believer?" Convinced this is true, the planners develop a service directed toward the believer with the purpose of edification. Perhaps a theme will appear: "People need to hear about the faithfulness of God." So the plan will be to emphasize God's faithfulness through music, sermon, prayers, songs, and response of the people.

In a third instance someone is apt to say, "Think of all the brokenhearted people who will be here." Convinced of the pastoral wisdom of this statement, planners will quickly move to therapeutic worship. Consider the songs, the sermon, the time of ministry. How will we offer comfort and healing to the hurts of the worshiper?

"What is wrong with this?" you ask. Do we not want people to be saved, to be edified, and to be healed in worship? "Yes, of course," but those goals are not the point of worship.

The question is not "What does worship accomplish?" but "What does worship signify?" To go back to our theology of worship, worship signifies God and God's mission to rescue the world. Therefore we must ask, does worship tell and enact God's story? Does worship draw us into a participatory relationship with God? When the answer to these questions is yes, guess what happens? The unconverted will be converted. The saints will be edified. The brokenhearted will find healing.

Presentational Worship

The second major problem is presentational worship. The attempt to present God or present salvation will always follow the pattern of a program. People even speak of worship as a "program." Programs range from sloppy ("Let's sing a couple of songs, have a prayer, collect the money, give the announcements, hear a solo, listen to the sermon, sing another song, and go home") to perfectionistic ("We must be concerned about excellence in everything we do. It has to be good music, good art, and good drama—so the people are really engaged and even entertained in the best sense of the word. Remember: Our God is attractive, so our worship presentation needs to be attractive and compelling").

"So," you ask, "what is wrong with that?" Primarily this: Such worship, which can be a traditional choir-driven style or a band-driven contemporary style, follows the broadcast theory of communication. It sends out the message and seeks to do so by copying the style of television communication (at least in principle). The larger megachurches have the money and talent to compete, while the smaller churches may try, but end up doing a program that is inferior to those of their bigger sisters.

Consider two problems in broadcast worship. First, worship so styled becomes co-opted by culture. Second, presentational worship ultimately becomes a program, a spectacle, and a show.

It is interesting to note that the presentational approach to worship repeats the problem faced by the Reformers. Medieval worship was a show to be watched. And a grand show it was! Every movement of the priest, the altar boys, and the choir was choreographed.

But the Reformers saw that worship must be returned to the people. And today's Reformers, particularly the younger evangelicals (the next generation of leaders), are intent on returning worship to the people.

On the human side, worship is not something merely seen and heard (although it is that), as if the worshiper is merely acted upon. No, worship on the human side is a prayer. Worshipers pray in response to God's action of gathering, prayerfully hear God's Word, prayerfully enter into relationship with God at the Table, and go forth to offer all of life as prayerful service (worship) to God.

A BRIEF DESCRIPTION OF BLENDED WORSHIP

We are now ready to bring all of this together in a brief description of blended worship. What does worship look like when it reflects the best of the liturgical and contemporary worship renewals of the twentieth century? What does worship look like that expresses the content of the biblical story of the triune God? What does worship look like that is modeled on the biblical, fourfold pattern? What does worship look like that is not instrumental, not a program, but a participatory, interactive prayer?

Perhaps we should begin with the environment. The theology of the church—Creation, Incarnation, and re-creation—may be reflected in the environment. The assertion that the place of meeting should look like a corporate building is a denial of the Christian worldview, a capitulation to secularization, a fear of truth. Younger evangelicals who have turned their backs on the pragmatic Christianity of baby boomers pay attention to their space of meeting. Generally, the new generation sits relationally in a space that speaks of transcendence. They may use a large cross, numerous flickering candles, and icons and stained glass flashed on the walls—all of this centered on the pulpit, the Table, and perhaps the water of baptism. The faith is visualized.

Next, the community may engage in some pre-gathering rites. A welcome may be extended, guests introduced (depending on the size of the congregation), and announcements made. Something that will be done in worship may be explained, perhaps practiced. A rite of friendship may be extended. In all this, a sense of community has been created. And the announcements having been given, the worship is free to unfold without interruption.

Now we come to the gathering. People are already convened. But the events about to unfold gather them in a centering prayer into the presence of God. Acts of worship bring the community to the praise of God, to confession, and to a time of lingering in the presence of God. Hearts are open to God, who is invited into one's life either in acts of conversion (in the case of seekers) or in acts of renewal or cleansing and revitalization (in the case of believers). Worship and spirituality have been brought together. God has been met. The people have responded. And the style? The style should be indigenous to the community, sensitive to the demographics of the area. It does not really matter if it is traditional, contemporary, or blended. Did these people from this neighborhood meet and respond to God? Did they center in prayer? Did the gathering do what a gathering is supposed to do—gather the people in the presence of God and ready them to hear the Word of God?

Next is the Word. The purpose of the Word is to hear God's story, to hear what God is calling his people to be. In the Word, worship and discipleship are brought together. It may be done formally with the three Scripture readings, a Psalm, and a gradual. It may be done informally with a Scripture reading and a sermon. Or it may be done interactively, as is practiced now in many communities given to worship in a postmodern setting.

The sermon may begin or end with a question. Discussion may follow. What do you hear God saying to you in the Scripture? How will you fulfill this teaching and admonition? The issue of traditional versus contemporary is irrelevant. The questions become "Did God's Word take up residence within you?" and "How will you live this out?"

And then comes the Eucharist, which brings worship and spirituality together. In the Eucharist the congregation encounters the death and resurrection of Jesus and is called to live in that pattern. How do we respond? How do we learn to die to sin, to be resurrected to the Spirit? Historically, some guidelines govern this aspect of worship. It is to be triune. We begin by praising the Father in the "Holy, holy, holy" *(Sanctus)*. We continue by remembering the story of God's involvement in history, culminating in the work of Jesus, and moving to the words of institution. Worship continues as the Holy Spirit is called upon to gather the church into one and confirm our faith in truth. Then the people come forward to receive the bread and wine. The community sings songs of death, of resurrection, of intimacy with God, of thanksgiving. Anointing prayers may be said at the same time.

In these acts, the whole triune Godhead is proclaimed in the fullness of his saving work. The people respond in prayer. They offer prayers of adoration, intimate relationship, intercession, and thankfulness. The music may be the great hymns of the church or choruses or both. This may be determined out of an understanding of the indigenous nature of the congregation. The important issue here is that we have deepened our relationship with God. Table worship is not running through the motions, but doing what Table worship does—enact the story of God and enter into an intimate nurturing and healing interactive relationship with God, the Creator, Redeemer, and Sustainer of our lives.

Last comes the dismissal. We go forth into the world, sent by God to do his will and purposes. And God, in this act of worship, promises to go before us and accompany us in all we do. On our part, we resolve to do his will, to be his person in the circumstances of life. Again, the issue of doing this in a traditional or contemporary manner is not the real point. The dismissal sends the congregation forth with a sense that God goes before them, with their response of the will determined to live in God's way, doing God's will.

CONCLUSION

I began this chapter by referring to the common negative response to blended worship. I still agree with the critics: Blended worship that accents style is doomed to failure. With some exceptions, this kind of blended worship does not work, comes off as "blah," and offends most people. I have not defended and will not defend this popular notion of blended worship.

I have asked you to consider another kind of blended worship, a worship that blends the fruit of the liturgical scholarship of the twentieth century and the concern for the immediacy of the Spirit called for in the best of contemporary worship.

This worship is biblically and theologically sound. It represents the story of the triune God whose mission is to save the world; it stands in continuity with the worship of the early church and the Reformers; and it is pertinent to our culture, not because it looks like our culture, but because of its countercultural message and its calling to the church to be a distinct people of God, a witness to the lordship of Christ over all creation. The style proposed by this kind of blended worship gets beyond the triviality of the present war between traditional and contemporary. It affirms both hymns and choruses, but asks the church to be sensitive to the setting in which it serves. Furthermore, it puts the style issue where it belongs—in worship as a participatory prayer.

How can this kind of worship take root? It is not going to happen in a day or two, in a month, or in a year. We Protestants have neglected biblical, theological, historical, and cultural reflection on worship. The issue runs deep. Seminaries neglect the subject. Pastors push it off onto the music ministers. Music ministers are trained in music, but have no background in the disciplines needed to think Christianly about our worship.

How can we go forward when our leadership is neglectful, indifferent, and in some cases even hostile to thoughtful Christian reflection? The most hopeful sign for the future is that a number of musicians and worship leaders are now engaged in thoughtful reflection on the nature of worship. Moreover, the new generation of leaders (especially the twenty-somethings) are not comfortable with the current debate over traditional versus contemporary worship.[2]

We sense a new, widespread resolve to rediscover the nature of worship and see its relationship to evangelism, discipleship, and spiritual formation. Hopefully, the worship wars dividing our churches will be left behind as we rediscover how genuine worship becomes the path through which God connects with us and we with him, to his glory.

A LITURGICAL WORSHIP RESPONSE

Paul Zahl

This chapter is very good. It presents thoughtfully, theologically, and accessibly the principles behind the movement we hear so much about, known as "blended worship." The key affirming sentences are these:

> Here, then, is what worship does. It acknowledges the transcendence, the great glory and incomprehensible nature of God the Father. It tells the story from beginning to end of how God created, how the world fell away from him, how he became involved in the history of the world in Israel and in his incarnation in Jesus to rescue the world through his death, resurrection, and coming in glory to reign as Lord over all creation. And it unleashes the power and presence of the Holy Spirit in the assembled people, in ministry, in Word and Sacrament, and it connects God and people in a relational encounter.

Blended worship consists in story and word, praise and gathering, Eucharist or Table fellowship, and sending out. It blends verticality with participation and thus embodies the fourfold New Testament pattern. So far so good.

Robert Webber also gives a crucial caveat for all who aspire to create gripping experiences of such blendedness: "I still agree with the critics: Blended worship that accents style is doomed to failure." I believe we know this now. We have experienced it. When you focus on style rather than substance, the style dates rapidly, its appeal fades, and the crowd begins to thin.

My problem with Webber's approach is his emphasis on incarnation and thus on the Communion or Eucharist. I am sensitive on this point simply because I live and breathe within a denomination, the Episcopal Church, where the Eucharist has become everything. Most Episcopalians understand themselves to be incarnation-centered rather than atonement-centered Christians. This emphasis goes back to the Anglo-Catholics of 150 years ago, who reacted to their Anglican forebears' Evangelicalism. The result: a uniform focus on the "Holy Eucharist" that has become unintentionally clubby with a lot of in-house symbols and rituals. I call it "Christianity lite." It appeals to a section—a very small section—of church-going people. It is killing my church. Therefore I am sensitive on the point.

Where Webber himself is coming from, which I shall guess was originally free-church evangelicalism, the focus on incarnation may well appear salutary and restorative. From the experience of church I have known for fifty years, the focus needs to be redirected in exactly the opposite direction.

A TRADITIONAL WORSHIP RESPONSE

Harold Best

Robert Webber has spent many years producing a bevy of materials that narrate, historicize, and reason their way toward his present (are they final?) conclusions. I want to begin with the latter two-thirds of his chapter before dealing with some matters in the first third. Above all, I want all my comments and questions to underscore, not cut down, the worth of the blended worship model. If the model were a hodgepodge, a personal whimsy, or a liturgical setup for guruism, it could be dismissed out of hand and any one of the other models in this book faithfully used, for each has considerable value.

The blended model that Webber encourages is, in ever so many ways, a wonderful and good model to the degree that it remains free at its deepest roots from culture creep. By this I certainly do not mean that culture is irrelevant or even secondary, but that the body of Christ has the enormous responsibility to engage with culture in a completely different way, one that believes that cultural action is symptomatic rather than causal. The church, then, has the celebrative task of beating culture at its own game. In reference to Webber's model, this is what I mean. On the surface, the model looks more Euro-American than global, more neotraditional than New Testamental, and more establishmentarian than indigenous. But if under the surface there is ample theological and biblical underpinning to grant this style both a culturally sensitive and culture-informing force, the cultural matters will be properly addressed. The secret is to make sure that its depth takes continual precedence over its surface. "Does this model work?" is less important than "Is it right?" Allow me to explain a couple of surface concerns.

This model looks to be more Euro-American than global because I am not sure how Christians in the eastern highlands of Papua New Guinea or, for that matter, a black congregation in Chicago's Southside would accommodate the sequential and explicitly modular nature of the model. And does the gathering to worship mean "to worship" or "to corporate worship," as if the former were initiated only by the gathering? And why does the dismissal stress going out to serve when the concept of worship as service is so clear throughout the Bible?

The model looks to be more neotraditional than New Testamental because there is little evidence in the New Testament that Christians gathered together to undertake all of the things—among them, gathering "to worship"—that Webber suggests. I am fascinated by the continual need of worship thinkers to go back to the Old Testament for sequential categories without going forward to the New Testament to examine how these might have been Christocentrically fulfilled or transcended in entirely new and organic ways. Thus the blended worship model is little more than a simplified dialect of historical-liturgical worship, much of which is tradition-bound.

In short, how many kinds of traditionalism are there? What does "contemporary" mean in light of the fact that the current ecclesiastical concept of contemporaneity depends on people already being so used to a style or styles that they find themselves idiomatically at home in the gathered assembly? Put in the form of a statement, stylistic familiarity is of the essence in all forms of public worship; otherwise communication is out the window.

Likewise, the model is more establishmentarian than indigenous in that it does exactly what all other universalized models tend eventually to do, including what Webber objects to in his Yellow Pages critique of denominational worship: It encourages sameness from parish to parish and, if treated carelessly, produces a liturgical "McDonald's"—it tastes the same wherever you go.

By contrast, if the blended template, or any other possible one, were to contain such biblical completeness in each of its parts, to the extent that each part takes responsibility for the full story rather than being a module within it, then the model will work, as will any number of alternatives. What I am driving at is that worship in the fullness of Spirit and in the fullest reaches of truth is atypological and therefore is inherently blended. Thus, any of the approaches that Bob questions as being one-dimensional are potentially valid as long as they seek out the theological fullness and stylistic fullness with which all worship is to be clothed.

So a burning question remains: Is there a deep structure to worship that defies or transcends the surface protocols and dialects, of which Webber's model is but one? I believe there is, for I am not sure that I need a fourfold breakout to get at the whole story, any more than I need a four-or-five-course meal to get the right amount of protein, carbohydrates, and other nutriments for my body. I simply need a steady, balanced, and integrated diet. For that matter, if the entire story rests on a four-part taxonomy, why are two of its parts, the gathering and sending forth, so liturgically foreshortened compared to the glory and saturated weight of the Word—systematically read, thoroughly preached, and knowingly sung—and the Eucharist? Let me try an analogy.

Think of a balloon, of all things. Blow it up to the full. The shape is virtually symmetrical; the seamless space inhabited equally throughout by air, no place having more air than any other, the air of the same quality and consistency throughout. Think of this full balloon as the biblical fullness of worship, consistent in all its parts and all parts consistently filling the balloon. Then, as street vendors often so skillfully do, twist any kind of shape out of the balloon—an emphasis here, a turn there, a massive contour here, and minutiae elsewhere. The important thing is that you have created a unique shape out of the symmetrical and organic whole. This new shape is a singular shape, a local shape, and an evidence of someone's ability to coax variety out of unity without compromising either one. All along, the same air in the same quantity and overall homogeneity remains in the new shape as was originally in the beginning whole. This originating wholeness could be called "deep structure" and the eventual shape "surface structure."

There are two crucial questions to be asked of the balloon people as of the worship people: (1) To begin with, is the balloon full or barely inflated? If the latter, something is fundamentally wrong from the beginning—no shapes are possible, the equivalent of lifeless and uncentered and probably Laodicean worship, no matter the style; and (2) do the shapers keep the fullness of the balloon constantly in mind as they decide on a shape or do they think that each part of the shape is independent of the rest? If the latter, then we have the kinds of worship to which Webber objects, including the same potential in the one that he encourages. That is, any kind of worship—even the most ideally blended or synthesized—runs the risk of failure if the fullness of worship does not inhabit each of its parts and if the theological fullness of each of the parts somehow becomes unattached from that of the others.

Given the assumption that Webber's or a local assembly's balloon is filled to the full even before its shape emerges, the appeal of blended worship—O for a better name for it!—lies in its potential for stylistic flexibility, stylistic pluralism, and God helping us all, brazenly new stylistic leaps into new synergies. This will take faith long before it will demand creativity, for God only knows how many truly creative people are out there, standing, waiting at the fuzzy edges of what we so arrogantly call the "contemporary," longing for entrance, longing for a voice, longing to urge us back and forth from Genesis 1 to Resurrection, to Pentecost, and to a resounding engagement with an ideologically flatulent and darkened culture. If we but had the faith to hang on to the inertia-breaking centrifuge of Spirit-led worship—deep charisma—far beyond the worthy but usual notions of charismatic worship, we might find that labels disappear, even in the face of the wildest variety, all because worship is more than a verb. It is the whole of the sentence.

Now to the beginning of Webber's chapter. The history and origins parts are beyond my general ken and have less to do with the current relevance of blended worship than its present life and condition do. But even with my lack of a historical sense, I am troubled by some oversimplifications—among them, the short, almost toss-off descriptives for the eight traditions that Webber identifies early on. Since when or for what very limited constituency does the liturgical tradition emphasize just beauty rather than mystery, immanence, and transcendence, or Word and Sacrament? Why, for instance, is the revivalist tradition confined to moving toward an invitation when practically all such traditions have had a morning worship service that stressed singing, preaching, praising, praying, and Word, from which, then, evangelism or evangelistic services flow? And for that matter, is not all Good News a call to repentance? Is there any difference between an altar call in a revivalist service and the confession and absolution in a liturgical one? Or take the African-American descriptive: Is soul worship different from any other revivalist traditions except for differences in style and the culturally loaded word "soul"? The general reader needs more than these one-liners provide.

Also, I become a little confused by the interchange of "traditional" and "liturgical" when in other places Webber seems to distinguish more carefully between the two or contrasts "traditional" with "contemporary." Both with the descriptives mentioned above and these terminological confusions, it might have been better for Webber to talk about under- and over-emphases in all worship practices without using time or process labels to separate them. And I am not always sure what is meant by "contemporary." Is it a church-defined style, a cultural position, or a truly new, cutting-edge thing?

I very much appreciate Bob's criticism of theme-related worship. All too often, this kind of worship turns out to be overly managed, a mite deterministic, and too concerned with bold-print one-liners. Yet it is possible to have deeply structured theme-driven worship. The liturgical year is conspicuously theme-conscious, but at a much higher and more comprehensive level. The season of Advent, for instance, is an open invitation to contemplate all of the yearnings and hope for the several comings of Christ, just as Epiphany can stress all kinds of gospel-spreading from personal witness to missions, to apologetics and overt revivalism.

I offer this comment about Webber's emphasis on story. I realize that theology, preaching, and teaching as story are particularly *du jour*. I am comfortable with this only as long as it successfully integrates and balances narrative, metaphor, and proposition. Just because we are a culture of episodic and experiential narrative does not mean there is no room for the idea, the concept, and the proposition. Otherwise, where would scientific thought be, where would art be, where would the epistles to the Romans and Hebrews be—and for that matter, if story is so all-important, why is it defended propositionally instead of narratively?

But of all the schematic devices that Webber suggests, the one that troubles me most is this statement: "We worship God the Father in the language of mystery, God the Son in the language of story, and God the Spirit in the language of symbol." How can he dissect the Trinity and its typological/metaphorical relation to worship so disequally and compartmentally? What theological primer has he revised so as to create such a mixed-up triad, especially mixing the apples of mystery and story with the single orange of symbol? It would have been far more productive (and more balloon-like) to assign mystery, story, and symbol to each member of the Trinity. Knowing how orthodox Webber is in his basic theological thought, I am sure that his deep structure is solid, but I worry about the surface ways in which he is often led to express it. There is always a danger when true magnitude of any kind (worship is true magnitude) is made schematically simple and procedurally interlocked in such a way as to cloud the magnitude instead of essentializing it.

Even so, I thank Robert Webber for his overall work and this particular essay. I have personally benefited from his mind, his spirit, the sweep of his vision, his personhood, his energy, and his friendship.

A CONTEMPORARY WORSHIP RESPONSE

Joe Horness

This is a great chapter! Robert Webber never ceases to amaze me with his knowledge of Scripture, his understanding of church history, his passion for Jesus, and his understanding of how all of those fit together. It is an amazing combination that always moves and challenges me. He makes me think, he stretches my boundaries, and he always calls me to reach for something deeper in my worship of God. His teaching and writing have continued to inform and inspire me both in my worship leading and in my thinking about what that worship should look like. I am grateful for his influence on what contemporary worship looks like today.

Webber's teaching reflects a deep love for the historical structure of worship. Honestly, to my contemporary worship mind-set, the emphasis on structure usually leaves me a bit perplexed. It always feels a bit like creating a format on how I should tell my wife I love her. Do this, then tell her this, then the flowers, then the kiss. Now do it like that every time. Laying out a specific order of communication might help me express my love to her more effectively for a time or two, but after that the structure seems to get in the way of what I am trying to do. It seems to me that the heart can fairly quickly be overwhelmed by a strict adherence to form, and in worship the heart remains deeply important. As a contemporary worship practitioner I would argue that the form should serve the function. I want people to meet Jesus. How we get there will differ from week to week. Trying to lead people into his presence a certain way, simply because that is how they did it in the first century, is not a priority for me. Serving our congregation as they gather together, as they remember what God has done, and as they express their love to God is my highest goal.

Having said that, I want to emphasize my absolute and passionate agreement with Webber about the substance of worship. His chapter outlines essential elements that those of us who practice contemporary worship must apply if the worship we lead is to thrive or even survive.

In many ways, the contemporary worship movement shows signs of being in trouble. I watch as young worship leaders scramble from idea to idea, from style to style, and from CD to CD trying to find the next emotional fix for their congregation. "We unplugged the organ and bought a drum set, and that created momentum for a while. When it began to lag, we brought back the choir. Then we tried the new Hillsongs stuff, then stuff from the Passion movement. Next we're going to try liturgy and candles." In an absence of substance, we are doing our best to buoy up the sagging emotion, but everything is feeling a bit the same. The problem is that true worship cannot be sustained on emotion alone. The experience side of contemporary worship is inextricably tied to the liturgical content side that Webber so eloquently describes.

C. S. Lewis describes worship as a response to something we love. When we love something a lot, we respond in great ways. If we only like it a little, we respond in kind. For great worship to flourish, people must carry in their hearts a great picture of God. They have to learn to love him a lot! Great worship, rightly arrived at, is simply a great response to who he is. Webber describes a substance to worship here that is essential to leading people into worship that is an authentic response to God, not just a reaction to the newest fad on stage.

Webber begins his description of blended worship with the "gathering" of God's people. This is a crucial piece of effective contemporary worship as well. One of the practices of contemporary worship that drives me most crazy is the singing of worship songs to get people into the room. We use worship as "traveling, talking, get your coffee, and hand out the mints music," and in so doing we teach our people that worship is not really about engaging our hearts together in the presence of God.

Finding new ways to begin our service that communicate "we are gathering now and we are coming into the presence of our God" is essential. In a contemporary setting, this means finding another way to get people into the room. Then we may use a well-crafted call to worship or a reading of Scripture. We might use a video clip of nature, a special number, or simply a time of silence. But the key is that we want to focus people's hearts on Jesus before we sing. We want to declare to them, very clearly, "Now we come to express our praise. Here he is! Refocus your hearts and your minds on him and set aside the hurry of this day. Appreciate that we are together and he is here. Now, in response to the substance of what you have just heard or prayed or reflected upon, let's come before him." It is the gathering, the call to worship, that Webber described. It just may take a more contemporary or creative form.

The next essential element that Webber describes is "story," and once again I want to emphatically state that real worship cannot take place without a remembering of who God is and what he has done. For contemporary worship to thrive, we have to paint people a great picture of God. We have to tell some part of his story! In our setting, however, it most likely is not a set piece at a set time, as Webber seems to describe. In a contemporary setting the story may come through Scripture verses read at an appropriate time by members of the worship team, or they may be placed on the video screens to music. It might come through a testimony or from a time of reflection led by the worship leader. It might come through a beautiful video of creation, either placed to music or played during a song. It might come through dance. We often let the sermon tell the story, saving time to worship after the message in response to what we have just heard.

One of the major challenges for every contemporary worship leader should be to figure out how and where we introduce God's Word, God's character, and God's work into our worship times in an effective and meaningful way. Great worship rises and falls with our concept of God. Simply singing songs is not enough. Part of our job as worship leaders is to paint people a picture of God to which their hearts can respond. Then we can lead them in that response. We need to tell his story.

In his discussion of the element of participation Webber asserts that contemporary worship is nonparticipatory. While I fear that this may be a description of what happens in real life, this idea of nonparticipation in contemporary worship goes against everything that the contemporary worship leader should be striving for. If this is true of us, then our approach to worship is dead. As I assert in my chapter, the most basic question a contemporary worship leader should be asking is "How can we help our congregation engage their hearts in authentic worship during this time? How can we help them meet with, and draw near to, God?"

There are many contemporary worship performers out there who travel from church to church presenting worship songs and recording CDs. But the best contemporary worship leaders never do worship "to the people." They always begin with the participation of the congregation foremost in their mind. What will serve these people? How can I help them meet God? The best worship leaders leave time and space for people to pray to, listen to, and interact with God. At Willow Creek we may invite them to kneel, to turn and pray together, to stand and raise their hands, to leave their seats to bring an offering, or to receive Communion. We may invite them to get in the aisles and dance. And we lead songs in a way that invites and deepens their participation. We put songs in keys where people can sing them. We repeat them as many times as is meaningful to the congregation, not to the worship team. We are there to serve them.

I challenge our worship leaders to consider themselves worship facilitators, not worship performers. The very measure of an effective worship time is not whether we performed well. It is whether or not people engaged well. Did they meet with Jesus? Did they re-engage in the mystery and wonder of knowing God? If this is blended worship, then by all means start blending. Contemporary worship without participation is nothing more than a concert with spiritual words. It may be great music, but it is not great corporate worship.

Finally, Webber asserts that blended worship must include a "sending forth." In my mind, the simple word for that is "application." Authentic worship sets the Spirit of God free to move in our hearts and in our midst. The result is that authentic worship will always bring the potential for change if we will receive it and respond to it. Authentic worship may convict us, challenge us, encourage us, or simply remind us of the truth. But it will not just sit there. It will demand change. As worship leaders we should invite and encourage our people to respond to the moving of the Spirit that happens in worship. We do not gather and prepare simply to sing some songs. We have gathered to meet God, to remember his story, to participate with his Spirit, and to surrender and respond to his voice. This is real worship, in any name you choose to call it. We may differ in our ideas of form, but in the substance of worship we have a lot we need to learn from the synthesis of liturgical content and contemporary experience that Webber so beautifully describes.

A CHARISMATIC WORSHIP RESPONSE

Don Williams

In this chapter Robert Webber is calling for the blending of traditional worship—reinvigorated by the liturgical renewal—and contemporary worship—centered on experience. He is sensitive to both theology and history. He advocates a genuinely Trinitarian expression, patterned after the historic fourfold movement of the liturgy, open for a genuine encounter with God. This unites liturgy and the immediacy of the Spirit.

The triune God is expressed in liturgical worship: the Father in transcendent mystery (the arts help us here), the Son in biblical story (preaching helps us here), and the Spirit in symbol (sacraments help us here). We are also to experience this on the analogy of the Incarnation: God and mankind, joined together in dialogue.

When Webber discusses and defends liturgical content, he is at his best. He knows full well that liturgical churches need renewal as much as experiential churches need content. While making this case, Webber is also generous. He wants indigenous ministry, sensitive to demographics. Traditional, blended, or contemporary is not the issue. The issue is, as he puts it: "Did these people from this neighborhood meet and respond to God?"

While Webber clearly defines renewed liturgical worship, I miss what he means by contemporary worship. He writes of renewal movements, the chorus tradition, contemporary Christian music, and new style, but fails to notice the maturing of contemporary worship with a clear theological substructure. (See my comments on John Wimber in my chapter and my response to Joe Horness in the chapter on contemporary worship.) It seems that for Webber, contemporary worship is simply a shift in musical styles from Pentecostalism and revivalism to the Jesus Movement with a focus on the result: experience. This leaves me dissatisfied. When he blends worship, I am not sure what is going into his blender. The liturgy is in there, but what else? Do a few current choruses produce the experience sought by contemporary worshipers?

For Webber, the whole of worship is experiential, unleashing the Holy Spirit in ministry, Word, and Sacrament, resulting in a relational encounter with God. He focuses especially on the liturgical fourfold pattern. He claims that the content of worship is inseparable from its structure or order. This must contain (1) gathering us in God's presence; (2) proclaiming the story in song, Scripture, preaching, prayer, and the kiss of peace; (3) enacting the story in water, bread, wine, oil; and (4) sending us forth to love and serve the Lord. It is this structure that provides the proper content for worship. But is this so?

Do we find such a clear structure anywhere in the New Testament? Does it control the worship in Corinth as directed and corrected by Paul (see 1 Corinthians 11–14)? Does its absence in low-church worship, revivalistic worship, contemporary worship, or charismatic worship eliminate divine content and presence? Webber admits that in the first three centuries of the church "Christian worship was simple and uncluttered." Is God's power absent from simple and uncluttered worship today? With Webber insisting on his fourfold structure for proper worship, grace is gone. Webber has put us back under the law.

Webber sees experience not only dependent on the fourfold structure but also lodged in the sacraments. He promises an "unleashing" of the Spirit's power in the "signs of bread and wine." I am disappointed, however, that he never tells us how this happens. Some anecdotes would help. Without them, Webber borders on magic. The "unleashing" happens through the symbols themselves, apart from faith, repentance, prayer, and waiting on the Spirit.

One value of blended worship is absent in Webber. It is the attempt to bridge the generations to meet a wider spectrum of cultural, musical, and emotional needs. In an increasingly pluralistic society, with the huge dislocation of the 1960s and the virtual loss of a generation from the mainline churches, blended worship attempts to hold the older, more traditional generation while welcoming the younger, more experiential generation so that they can learn from each other. Hats off to those who from sincere hearts have paid the price of congregational anger, fear of change, and late-night meetings for this kind of blended worship.

Webber sees blended worship as overcoming our preoccupation with function and presentation (or entertainment, the show up front). If this can happen, it is all to the good. After all, worship focuses on God, not the liturgist, symbols, preacher, worship leader, or even me as worshiper. If we can get this right, as Webber says, everything else will fall into place.

AN EMERGING WORSHIP RESPONSE

Sally Morgenthaler

BEYOND PALATABLE

I have never been a great fan of blended worship. The problem is, I have never been quite able to put a finger on the reason for my ho-hum response. As a result of Robert Webber's rich contribution in this chapter, I am beginning to decipher my ambivalence. The blended worship I have experienced has demonstrated very little of the depth, storied expanse, enchantment, and interaction of the worship Webber paints for us in his marvelous summary question:

What does worship look like . . .

- When it reflects the best of the liturgical and contemporary worship renewals of the twentieth century?
- That expresses the content of the biblical story of the triune God?
- That is modeled on the biblical, fourfold pattern?
- That is not instrumental, not a program, but a participatory, interactive prayer?

Such a vision makes the typical goal for blended services—musical palatability for the masses—seem paltry indeed. We think, "If we can just come up with that magic concoction of hymns and choruses; if we can please most of the people's musical tastes most of the time; if we can navigate through the worship-music battle zones without too many casualties," then we have done the best any church can do. We may not have worshiped well, necessarily. But at least we have not alienated the majority of our contributors!

Webber has nothing good to say about this reductionist, utilitarian view of worship: giving people at least one helping of their preferred musical style each week. Rather, he concludes the opposite: "Blended worship that accents style is doomed to failure." That is a pretty strong statement, and no doubt some will want to counter his assessment with data: ample attendance figures presumably tied to a blended approach.

Of course, worship failure is entirely relative to how one defines worship success. Many of us do consider attendance figures the unequivocal measure of worship achievement. Certainly numbers do say something. But that something is up for grabs. Perhaps we have simply managed to tap into the folks down the street who are disgruntled by their congregation's move to a high-decibel, screen-driven service. Still others of us measure success as a maintenance of the status quo. In highly polarized church situations, if we can just get through one more week without a nasty phone call or note, then we feel we must have hit the mark.

FROM SUCCESSFUL TO FAITHFUL

Webber, however, has a much loftier view of what makes worship successful.

> Here, then, is what worship does. It acknowledges the transcendence, the great glory and incomprehensible nature of God the Father. It tells the story from beginning to end of how God created, how the world fell away from him, how he became involved in the history of the world in Israel and in his incarnation in Jesus to rescue the world through his death, resurrection, and coming in glory to reign as Lord over all creation. And it unleashes the power and presence of the Holy Spirit in the assembled people, in ministry, in Word and Sacrament, and it connects God and people in a relational encounter.

According to Webber, faithful services wed the stuff of worship (the Grand Story or *missio Dei*) to experiences of God's presence. As Webber describes, the best worship is substance mixed with "a real and vital experience with God." It is a synthesis of what the liturgical church and contemporary church have been doing, respectively. Thus, Webber's new definition of "blended."

In many ways Webber's chapter is not so much a call for a new kind of blended model as it is an entreaty to radical worship faithfulness irrespective of model. If we are honest, most of our services fail to reveal more than a snippet of God's character and story. At worst, they reveal nothing at all about God, save God's benevolent interest in the featured felt need of the week.

J. B. Phillips once wrote a book entitled *Your God Is Too Small.* Webber could well be applying Phillips's perception to our services. Where is the fully-orbed God, cosmic, mysterious, and complex? Where is the Three-in-One Life Originator, Earth Refugee, Change Instigator? Faithful worship discloses a God bigger than our theme for the week, bigger than our felt needs, and most certainly, bigger than our musical forms. In disclosing this big God, faithful worship then gives worshipers a whole array of opportunities to interact and respond to the God disclosed. Webber's final litmus test is twofold: "Does worship tell and enact God's story?" and "Does worship draw us into a participatory relationship with God?" Faithful worship does both, and it draws upon the entire creation—all the arts, not just music—to do so.

THE FOURFOLD PATTERN IN A PANCHRONOLOGICAL WORLD

According to Webber, "The content of worship is inseparable from its structure or order." Or as Marshall McLuhan would say, "The medium is the message." We might cringe at the assertion that worship form and worship function are inseparable, but Webber makes an amazingly credible case for just that. "The biblical order of worship itself brings us into the presence of the transcendent God, draws our lives into the story . . . , and unleashes the power and presence of the Holy Spirit in our lives here and now in public worship, and then in the worship of our whole life in all that we do." He then brings the weight of Christian history to bear on the issue, describing this fourfold order as the pattern of Old and New Testament worship as well as the pattern of both early Christian and Reformed liturgies.

Webber takes his argument a step further. He contrasts the fourfold pattern with the threefold pattern adopted in Protestant modernity: preliminaries, sermon, and invitation—basically, the pattern upon which both nonliturgical traditional worship and most contemporary worship is built. "Traditional [Protestant, nonliturgical] worship is an interplay between music (often choir and hymn driven) and sermon. Contemporary worship, in its structure, is not much different: it is an interplay between music (band and chorus driven) and sermon." His inference is clear: Services that simply set up the sermon with preliminary music are not allowing people to fully interact with the person and ongoing activity of God. "The structure of worship is not a program or a presentation of the Christian story, nor is it the manipulation of emotions into a fleeting experience of feeling good. It is instead a communal rehearsal of our relationship with God—Father, Son, and Holy Spirit." This, I believe, is a prophetic statement, and we who craft worship each week would do well to examine our services in light of it.

A word of caution is in order, however. If it is true that the fourfold pattern (gathering, Word, Table, and sending) by nature enables this "communal rehearsal"; if it delivers Trinitarian, Grand Story substance more consistently than other forms—then why would any other worship structure ever be necessary? While Webber's argument linking the medium (fourfold worship pattern) with the message (worship substance) sounds logical—even compelling—the elevation of a single form to the level of God's preferred and necessarily only acceptable conduit has plenty of destructive precedent throughout church history. Ironically, Webber criticizes the adherents of style-based blended worship for their attachment to style (form) instead of a larger attachment to the triune God and God's continuing activity in and through creation.

Could it be that, as predominant as the fourfold pattern of worship has been in the history of the church, the issue at stake is still not this particular pattern, but the divine-human dialogic activity contained within it: interaction with God as transcendent Creator, incarnate Redeemer, and ever-present Re-Creator? In an increasingly nonlinear, discontinuous, post-cause/effect-Newtonian world, panchronological processing is on the increase. Just as elementary-age students begin their study of history with the American story and work backward to studying ancient history in high school; just as George Lucas begins the journey of the original Star Wars trilogy smack in the middle—so it is entirely conceivable that a worship service could start with the message of the Incarnation, or even an experience of re-creation, and work backward to Creation. Alternately, God the transcendent Creator might be revealed more intensely and clearly for some in the great Eucharistic prayer that precedes Communion than in a call to worship.

It is no accident that the postmodern art form of the pastiche (pasting elements of meaning together in new forms) is the *modus operandi* for expression, not only within popular culture, but within the fine arts as well. It emphasizes panchronicity—drawing from the resources available from all centuries—as well as a pangeography—drawing sounds, images, and styles from an entire planet. If worship is, as Webber says, a "synergism of divine and human activity," then it is already a pastiche of past, present, and future—God, who is outside of time and space, invades the now of our world and pulls us out of what we and our forbears have been into what we will become.

Deconstructing and reassembling the fourfold pattern may make for messier worship. But my sense is, it will give postmodern worship planners and artists much more room for creative freedom. They have the story. They understand Webber's essential juxtapositions of "substance and relevance, truth and experience, divine and human." They are past fixating on minithemes and past emphasizing just one part of the Godhead. Neither are they interested in going back to the 1980s: presenting a program or just manipulating feelings. They truly want to be faithful to what worship is and does. But here is the difference: They are far beyond linear—and too far beyond the lockstep liturgies of their parents and grandparents to be satisfied with tweaking an old structure.

Regardless of what eventually happens to the fourfold pattern, Robert Webber—with his incredible breadth and depth of understanding—has effectively given the church a theological launching pad for faithful, successful worship in the new millennium. I am not sure that what he has called us to is tame enough to be called "blended." "Fusion," maybe. Hang onto your seats.

Chapter Five: Blended Worship Notes

Proposal: Robert Webber

[1]See Mary Ann Simcoe, ed., *The Liturgy Documents* (Chicago: Liturgy Training, 1985).

[2]To be in contact with some musicians and worship leaders in the blended tradition, go to www.IWSFLA.org. More than a hundred students are engaged in worship study at the Institute for Worship Studies. If you are interested in the kind of worship described in this chapter, they would be pleased to interact with you.

Chapter Six

EMERGING WORSHIP

EMERGING WORSHIP

Sally Morgenthaler

THE EMERGING WORLD: MUSINGS ON A
MUCH-ALTERED LANDSCAPE

Worship leader Kirk McPherson has had a tough week. It's 5:30 on Friday afternoon, and things are only barely coming together for Sunday morning. If it wasn't one staff problem, it was another. He wonders what he might be able to pull out of his hat by Saturday night. *Hmmm . . . there are those worship sets from the retreat last fall.* He'll take a look at those tomorrow. Oh, yeah—John Tyler emailed him yesterday. *Wants some unchurched neighbor to talk about his spiritual experience. Something about a presence in his room, a light, something entering his body—no panic attacks or depression after that. Nice story, but what would people think? This guy isn't a Christian. Probably just a bunch of New Age garbage. Better not set a precedent. Maybe one of the teens in the youth group could give their testimony about accepting Christ at camp . . .*

Kirk wheels out of the church parking lot and begins his nightly reentry sequence. Three miles of taupe, stacked suburbia, and it's the exit to the interstate. He heads up the ramp only to find twenty other cars ahead of him, waiting their turn to merge. Start-stop, start-stop. He fumbles with his Palm Pilot, checks tomorrow's schedule, and logs on to his wireless email. "Hey, Brian, how about going to the game on Sunday?" He knows he'll be wasted after three services, but it's the semifinals, for Pete's sake.

He's third in line for takeoff now. Android-like, Kirk adjusts his headset and presses the auto-dial on his cell phone. *Hmmm, Amy must still be in her project meeting. Wonder if there's anything in the freezer worth cooking for dinner.* He dials his son's pager and leaves a message, then rings his daughter's cell phone. "Hey, it's Heather . . . I'm probably at Park Meadows, trying on army fatigues *(laughter)*. No, seriously, if you're cute, I really want to talk to you. So leave your number, okay? Byeee!" Kirk smiles for a moment, enjoying the sound of his thirteen-year-old's bell-like voice. *Hey, hadn't she promised to pay for that cell phone service six months ago? Not a red cent of babysitting money yet. She probably spends it all at The Gap.* When he was her age, he had a paper route. *Paid for a new basketball hoop, stereo, and a Rolling Stones concert in the first three months. Man, times have changed!*

A commercial for Taco Bell comes on the radio, and he's caught in "99-cent heart attack" land. Five minutes later he's inching his way down the off-ramp toward a fast-food appetizer. No Taco Bell, but he sees a sign for "Speedy Sushi." Why not? He steps up to the counter, where two Latino teens and a sixty-something Russian immigrant greet him with thick accents. The service is slow. One of the cash registers is broken. If there are apologies, they are unintelligible. He settles into the minimalist black stool at the back of the seating area (a stool too small for anyone over forty) and wonders whatever happened to booths, old-fashioned hamburgers, and people who can actually speak English.

He's back in the car again. Amy calls—her meeting got over late. *Sleepover? What sleepover?* Oh, yeah! Friday night, and it's his turn to take Heather to this weekend's preferred slumber party. *Not good.* As he pulls into the driveway, she is waiting. No, fuming. Not quite Brittney Spears risqué, but too close for comfort. Heather slumps into the car, incommunicado. Kirk sighs and prepares to pass her off to yet another single-mom-plus-boyfriend combo. "So, is this one of your more decent friends?" he queries dryly, revving out of the intersection. Heather is ready for him. "Sure, Dad. You mean decent, as in us? The last time Sarah was over at our house, you and Mom got into another one of your stupid fights and Mom ended up in the bedroom, drinking that stuff she thinks we can't smell."

Kirk drops her off and broods all the way back home. Yeah, he remembers the weekend. He'd had big plans to see a counselor the next week, but he never did it. *Too risky. What if the church found out?* He'd be history. But something had to happen. Five years of what seemed like the same fight, over and over. *Amy's late night trips to the liquor store. Sleeping on the couch. Kids more visitors than residents. But hey, no need to hang out your dirty laundry. God knows the world has enough of it, dangling like so many greasy rags on shows like Jerry Springer and Montel, flapping like torn, soiled sheets in the winds of every neighborhood:*

- The retarded girl next door, sobbing herself to sleep after another enforced lesson in lovelessness;
- The alternative crowd at the local Starbucks, brandishing tattoos, studded tongues, pierced eyebrows, and midriffs like so many weapons against emotional abandonment;
- Anglo Dad and Latino boyfriend-stepdad on the soccer field sidelines, exchanging more than a few "expletive deleted" verbal punches, plus racial epithets over why little Matthew's most perfected play is called "sitting the bench."

No, there's too much of this junk out there already. He wasn't going to add to the pile. *Better to look good and let people have their illusions. It's the way ministry gets done.* Besides, it's not his fault. Nobody bothered to prepare him for this new world, this new universe that, at some point in the last two decades, sped past every set of how-tos he'd ever owned; this motley collection of broken humanity, addictions, decimated families, unanswered questions, global fragmentation, self-constructed spiritualities, unprecedented immigration, ubiquitous technology, and mutating worldviews. Nobody told him that an alien dimension was headed this way. But it hit, somewhere between his first youth director job in 1984 and September 11, 2001. All he can do now is hang on, one Sunday at a time. And hope that someone, somewhere, is developing a formula that will make sense of it all.

THE EMERGING MIND-SET: WAKING UP
IN THE NEW MILLENNIUM

If you found yourself anywhere in Kirk's Friday afternoon, you are not alone. In reality, the majority of us ministry leaders are experiencing unprecedented disorientation. Some years ago we realized that our Bible college and seminary educations had not prepared us for an America past 1960. But now it's a stretch to get much past 1980. It is as if we have been asleep in entrepreneurial church land, waking up like religious Rip Van Winkles to an unrecognizable landscape.

Where exactly are the unchurched Harrys and Marys of targeting fame, those atheistic hordes lacking only logical, scientific arguments for God's existence, desperately seeking ten watertight proofs for the Resurrection? (They found God outside of church and are, as we speak, placing candles and icons at some street shrine in New York.) Where are all the two-income, successful families without debilitating addictions, pathologies, stepchildren, secrets, and other miscellaneous baggage? (They don't exist.) Where are the confirmed optimists, the pull-yourself-up-by-your-bootstraps Americans, pressing into our worship centers for their next how-to fix, those spiritualized lists that we tack at the end of our sermons? (They followed lists and rules for a decade and still hit the wall. As did their kids. So much for lists.) We look for the squeaky-clean, trendy church market of yore. When we find them, they are most likely inside our church systems already, cocooned in the subcultures we customized for them a few decades ago, reinforcing (unfortunately) our misconceptions of what the world outside our walls is and needs.

But the rest of America has moved on, and whether we choose to acknowledge it or not, the metamorphosis has been profound. When the temporary memorial to the World Trade Center victims is designed to evoke images of the Resurrection, when twenty-five percent of Internet users surf the web for some kind of spiritual content or experience,[1] rest assured, we have passed into new territory. (Atheists are getting difficult to find.) When the majority of the American adult population is not only single but also moving rapidly toward non-white, non-European origin, we are experiencing a brand-new demographics. Three in ten Americans identify themselves as something other than white alone.[2] (Dare we question our unwavering fixation on Caucasian, intact families?) And when the best-selling nonfiction titles are more about connection and collaboration than "doing it my way," more centered on spiritual process and journey than Spartan self-help, we are seriously reconsidering our identities.

THE EMERGING WORSHIP: CREATING SACRED SPACE IN A POST-HUMANIST WORLD

The emerging world may be fascinated with the supernatural and hungry for mystery. It may thrive on diversity and crave community (everything from antique gun clubs to eBay chat rooms). There is one characteristic, however, that overshadows the rest and, as such, needs to be the beginning point for any serious reworking of corporate worship in the new millennium: a profound recognition of personal and societal brokenness.

Surprise!—we are neither masters of our destinies nor masters of ourselves. We are not, as we imagined mere decades ago, one government program or one scientific discovery away from utopia. Despite our best attempts at dissecting, categorizing, understanding, and controlling life on this planet, we remain limited, biased, and severely flawed. Our knowledge is imperfect and our best motives, narcissistic. In postmodern nomenclature, we are imprisoned in our own narrow agendas, obsessed with and controlled by the pursuit of power. In biblical terms, we are depraved. One forty-something, formerly Catholic, unchurched male from Littleton, Colorado, sums it up this way: "Between Columbine, September 11, the Catholic priesthood crisis, my World.com stock, and my divorce, I've run out of people to trust. I'm a mess, the world's a mess, and we're all a mess. I'm either going to get an addiction, a big dose of God, or both."[3]

What is clear is that Americans no longer believe in their ability to construct a better tomorrow. Progress has moved into the realm of mythology, with the religion of human progress—humanism—functionally dead. For the first time in several hundred years, we realize that neither science nor government nor the best in Homo sapiens' efforts will be able to put Humpty Dumpty together again. William Langewiesche's statement in the wake of the 2001 attacks hits the nail on the head: "The dread that Americans felt during the weeks following the September 11 attacks stemmed less from the fear of death than from a collective loss of control—a sense of being dragged headlong into an apocalyptic future for which society seemed unprepared."[4] It is this loss of control, this long and sober stare into our limitations that has now replaced the utopian dream.

When will the church—and specifically worship—rise to meet this seismic reorientation? American culture had outgrown even our most progressive worship practices sometime in the early 1990s. (Worship attendance figures peaked in 1991, according to George Barna.)[5] But it was not until after September 11 that many of us sat up and took notice. Suddenly our enforced-happy, you-can-control-your-world services could no longer maintain the illusion of relevance. Easy-answer, religion-as-personal-project Christianity came up short—way short. Sure, we scrambled for our Theology 101 textbooks on September 12, went online to download somebody else's sermon on tragedy, dug through dusty hymnbooks. (Somehow, the feel-good choruses we'd been singing for the past decade and a half just were not going to fit very well with images of jetliners slamming into buildings.)

But we could not change years of theological and cultural inattention in a week. On September 16, 2001, hundreds of thousands of the confirmed irreligious packed into North American sanctuaries. Church attendance swelled to record numbers in the first two months after the crisis. Not six months later, it had dropped to pre–9/11 levels, and nine months later it was plummeting below early 2001 numbers. What were people looking for that they did not find? Certainly the American public is a fickle lot. Yet, when the church is handed such an unforeseen opportunity and fails to give people compelling, lasting experiences of God, something's wrong.

Truly, we know this. We know something is wrong. It is as if a giant searchlight has been switched on, revealing worship substance at millimeter depths; answers, embarrassingly ill begotten and ill applied; and a narcissistic focus rivaling a multilevel marketing convention. We recoil at what we are doing, but frankly do not know what else to do. Service themes that sounded profound just a few years ago now ring glib and hollow. Praise songs on the latest CD releases sound like so many distant sequels. And in our private moments, far from planning meetings and rehearsals—unspeakably bored with what we ourselves are putting out every Sunday—we are asking, "Where is the way forward?"

THE GIFT OF REALIGNMENT

For the handful of emerging worship ministries that began grappling with the post-humanistic, neo-supernatural shift in the mid-1990s, the way forward had much more to do with substance than with style. To the casual onlooker it seemed that their odd expressions (often dubbed "postmodern" for want of a better term) were all about dark and intentionally dingy worship spaces, candles, incense, digitalized Rembrandts, and unplugged, unsingable praise choruses. Yet for these fledgling congregations, here is what was and remains the core of worship: nothing short of a Romans 1 realignment of the human heart.

In the practical realm, realignment means reinstating Creator-referenced, God-focused expressions. Emerging worship leaders see much of contemporary worship as "self-referencing"—focused on human perceptions, needs, feelings, and desires. While not denying the importance of those elements, emerging worship services strive to engage worshipers primarily with the person and the continuing works of God through Jesus Christ. It is one of the tenets of emerging ministries that we are transformed through God's activity in and through us, not by what we think we need and certainly not by ruminating our way into better behavior.

Emerging worship experiences are anything but idealistic about the human spirit. They start with the assumption that our felt needs may indeed cause us to want something, but not necessarily the person and works of God. Thus an emerging worship experience begins in an entirely different place from most contemporary services: not with what people feel their needs to be, but with who God is, who they are, and who they were created to become. In the minds of emerging-ministry leaders, there is a huge difference between religious consumers (those simply seeking to get their felt needs met) and developing worshipers (those seeking to take an active part in the story and ongoing activity of God).

The understanding of worship as realignment has profound effects on worship planning. Scores of churches—from traditional to blended to contemporary—organize the worship hour to culminate in what is basically a sermonic punch line—that is, that moment when the attendee says, "Aha, this is what my problem is, and this is how I fix it." Other worship elements (and they are usually limited in variety) are supposed to function as logical stepping-stones to move people toward that realization. Despite the expected escort of music, situational drama, PowerPoint, film clips, and even emotionally touching moments, the dominant activity in most current worship models is mental.

Realignment in emerging models takes place not through carefully presented arguments, but in placing oneself inside the ongoing redemptive saga of God. There we recognize ourselves in the broken, limited God-followers of the biblical narrative. And in entering the drama of their stories, we engage with the person of God, not just the principles of God. In short, we know and are known.

Having shifted from "knowing-by-notion" to "knowing-by-narrative," realignment in emerging congregations is experiential more than mental, sensory more than read. It is a whole-person and whole-community immersion into the lived and living chronicles of God. And it necessarily involves movement first and foremost toward God so that the self can be seen clearly.

What does emerging realignment look like, sound like, feel like?

- It is the hushed tones of a gathering prayer—the drama of John 1:1–5 recaptured in poetry and set to a video loop of a swirling galaxy.
- It is the hymn "Let All Mortal Flesh Keep Silence" reconstituted in electronica and brought to life with a kaleidoscopic, digital backdrop.
- It is the mimed story of Jacob wrestling with God, followed by silent reflection and the option of "drawn" prayer ... worshipers sketching images of their God-conflicts on large sheets of butcher-block paper taped to the walls.
- It is reciting the Apostles' Creed together, each affirmation accompanied by scanned and projected "graffiti" art—children's spray-paint interpretations of Creation, Fall, Redemption, Revelation.
- It is any whole-person, experiential avenue of seeing God, seeing oneself, and being caught up in the unfolding miracle of divine grace.

A holy and necessary relocation—this is the result of worship that is fixed first upon the character and works of the One being worshiped.

THE GIFT OF CONTEXT

In a number of emerging ministries there is an increasing desire to craft weekly worship in an unabashedly liturgical shape: Creation, Fall, redemption in Christ, and fulfillment of the sons and daughters of God. Since the majority of emerging congregations have a Baptist or some other kind of frontier, evangelical heritage, such fascination with the elements of liturgy is an intriguing development. Emerging churches seem bent on righting what they see as a colossal imbalance in the American contemporary church experience: the almost wholesale rejection of anything older than we are.

It is hard to deny that the imbalance exists. How often in the past few decades have we as contemporary ministries pretended that we have no histories; that we are devoid of theological and ritualistic biases (as if any church can truly be theologically neutral)? Indeed, the coveted identity in the 1980s and 1990s was the "denominational runaway," the "intentional orphan," somehow untainted by the doctrinal melees of past decades and centuries. Under the microscope, our DNA may have been unmistakably Presbyterian, Lutheran, Baptist, Church of Christ, or Evangelical Free, but we chose not to own those chromosomes. Instead, we donned a nondescript wrapper: self-invented, streamlined Christianity of the late twentieth century, nondenominational "start-ups" stripped of ancestral records and the forms those records inevitably create.

In a culture of crisis, exponential change, and decimated hopes, emerging ministries understand that rootlessness is anything but an asset. It just may be our biggest liability. People are desperate for the strong, connective fibers of shared accounts, worldviews, experiences, and customs. Emerging congregations not only "get" this, but they instinctively understand that the most effective kind of remembering does not attempt to re-create or even imitate the past. To remember well is to recontext the past in the present, to fuse the best of yesterday with the best of today, and in the process, birth something entirely new.

This process goes way beyond most notions of ancient/future (adding praise choruses, PowerPoints, and occasional video clips to existing ancient liturgies). Essentially, it is wholesale deconstruction—the dismantling of a multiplicity of worship forms (both pre-Reformation and post-Reformation) followed by the postmodern art of pastiche: creating something unprecedented out of the pieces at hand. Add to that a strong penchant for paradox (the juxtaposition of seeming opposites) and eclecticism (the combination of seemingly distant and unrelated elements) and you get a palette of colors that is virtually endless. Sacred and secular, diverse geographies and ethnicities, past and present, celebration and lament, extreme participation and silence—these all combine and recombine in emerging worship services for the express purpose of exalting God.

Radical recontexting is the most noticeable difference between emerging worship and other forms, including those that are blended and convergence-type services. *In radical recontexting, the order of service may be more concurrent (several things happening at once) than homogeneous (everyone doing the same thing at a time).* For instance, instead of the normal three-point sermon on forgiveness, the story of Joseph may be experienced at various stations in the worship center. In one corner worshipers may view a patchwork, Technicolor coat with crumpled bits of parchment pinned to the fabric—the story of Joseph sold into slavery, read from shoulder to hem. In another corner there are short, taped interviews with several of Joseph's brothers. With their individual headsets, worshipers listen as each brother justifies his actions against Joseph, the favored son. Along one wall, worshipers may walk a labyrinth charting Joseph's journey from his homeland into slavery, on into the highest position of power under Pharaoh. At each point the worshiper gets to query, "What was Joseph's attitude toward God, toward his fellow human beings, and toward his brothers? What would I think, what would I do if I were Joseph?" Concurrency allows for a multiplicity of reactions, perspectives, and applications.

Radical recontexting also may mean borrowing elements of existing service orders, but repackaging them in an almost unrecognizable form. For example, the ancient liturgical act of "sending" might be used, but instead of enacted as priestly blessing, it is an openended, sending meditation—a visceral connection to the real world that one is about to reenter. Thus an emerging worship service might end with overlying quotes from second-century mystics on silent, rush-hour film footage—the only accompaniment a hushed drum loop. There are other borrowed liturgical elements that may also serve as fodder for recontexting. Scripture reading(s) might be morphed into a multisensory experience: an indigenous paraphrase of the famous praise psalm (150), recited in reader's theater format from the back of the sanctuary to ambient music; concurrently, worshipers making impressions of their uplifted, praising hands in walls of soft sculpting material. (Of course, the idea here is to save this afterward to become part of the worship space.)

The ancient practice of corporate confession might also be reconfigured. For instance, the story of Peter's denial of Jesus may be followed by a distribution of three smooth stones to each worshiper. Each worshiper then reflects upon his or her own experiences of denying Christ. As each chooses, he or she can then walk up to a central, darkened pool of water and toss the three stones in ... the sounds of Creed's "My Own Prison" echoing in the distance. Others might choose to glue their three "denial" stones into a newly constructed Communion table that the congregation will use from week to week. Communion itself may get a dramatic face-lift: the words of institution recast as poetry while a dancer enacts the events of the Last Supper. In another twist, a sculptor may carve the "body of Christ" into bread loaves as a video version of the Crucifixion unfolds. (Later, worshipers will feed each other pieces of this carved "body" as they celebrate the Lord's Table.)

THE GIFT OF PARTICULARITY

The contemporary, late-twentieth-century church developed prototype ministry into an art form. (Prototype ministry: ministry designed for a specific cultural profile or stereotype versus ministry designed for actual people.) We know prototype ministry best as church targeting, oriented to the dominant people group in an area (most usually, the people group most like the core leadership of a congregation). Based on the concept of affinity (grouping people according to lifestyle, economic status, age, and ethnicity), prototype ministry has proven helpful in jumpstarting communities where people need the initial safety of sameness.

Unfortunately, prototype ministry has severe limitations in establishing long-term, self-perpetuating communities (in sociological terms, those that are connective across a multiplicity of affinities). Historically, human beings are drawn beyond homogeneity to diversity, which is why long-standing, one-dimensional cultures are rare. Eventually, narrowly defined communities implode upon themselves. (Think about George Orwell's *Animal Farm*, and you get the picture.)

The incapability of the contemporary church to move from homogeneity to diversity is, frankly, its biggest hindrance as it wakes up to an exponentially diversifying culture. Nowhere is this self-imposed handicap more visible than in worship. There is a numbing uniformity to late-twentieth-century-styled services, a predictability and cultural incongruity rivaling any lockstep, mainline liturgy of the mid-twentieth century.

With only a few alterations in sequence, the contemporary liturgy (again, "contemporary" is not to be confused with "relevant") follows the same routine nationwide: walk-in music, an enforced-happy welcome, vaudevillian-styled announcements, a twenty-minute praise set, special music, message, prayer, offering/song, and a see-you-next-week dismissal. (If it is a service focused more on seekers, add a drama and cut the praise singing and prayer to bare minimum.) Mirroring the nondescript landscape of late-twentieth-century suburbia, the contemporary worship space is intentionally generic: off-white, bare walls; worship-team outfits; visually predominant technology (wires, screen, sound systems, monitors, speakers); standardized PowerPoint backgrounds; and an absence of all symbols save one—the ubiquitous church logo.

Contrast this weekly mantra of standardization with the 2002 Winter Olympics, and we begin to glimpse how far our cutting-edge churches actually are from the edge. The Salt Lake City experience was tribalism—a celebration of the oh-so-particular—on a grand scale. Ute Indian songs segued effortlessly into the strains of Sting, techno, and the ethereal intonations of a Russian choir. Meantime, the crowd became the locus of the action, wielding everything from multicolored sheets to flashlights and glow sticks. In the arena, skaters carved out visual prayer on ice, their lanterns and flowing costumes weaving a tapestry of transcendence and hope. This was anything but generic, as far from homogenous as a public event could possibly get. Yet these world celebrations were intensely communal and unifying, a veritable symphony of diversity played out night after night. Here were the stories of nations, and of nations within nations, being told—musically, dramatically, and visually—in all their glorious particularity. And to tell the truth, we relished the departure from the typical Hollywood, American fare.

If there is a call to the American contemporary church, it is a call back to particularity: the lost, tribal paradigm that Harrisonburg, Virginia, and Bend, Oregon, have seen carved out by distinct histories, narratives, songs, and shared rituals. Not only that, but each citizen of Harrisonburg and Bend has his or her own story, narrative, song, and life ritual. And finally, each congregation within Harrisonburg and Bend has a singular, unique voice, tuned and shaped by God. This is, at bottom, an incarnational perspective: God eternal came into our world at a specific juncture in time, as a member of a singular species, race, lineage, town, and gender. Jesus was not born as a prototype and did not minister to prototypes. Jesus came in human form and ministered to people in all their specificity: prostitutes, Pharisees, lepers, centurions, tax collectors, old and young, male and female, slave and free, rich and poor. How can we do any less? Ministry according to prototype is ministry stripped of personal journey, devoid of the very placedness and humble descent into the now that continues to characterize God's ministry to us. (See Philippians 2:5–11.)

The question must be asked, what would worship look like without the generic wrapper? What would happen if we truly let worship experiences emerge from the people themselves— if we stopped trying to hit targets, stopped trying to conform ourselves to a theoretical demography, and simply let lived and living stories speak? This would be a brave move, indeed. A move out of worship planned in cubicles to worship planned in community; an escape from worship as music (most often, whatever the worship-music industry is dictating this month) to worship as a whole-person, indigenous encounter with God: visual, aural, tactile, kinetic, emotional, and cerebral. If we welcomed a wild, untamable miscellany instead of a controllable facelessness, we would allow God to surprise us more often: an anonymous painting of the woman anointing Jesus' feet, wrapped in newspaper and set outside our office door; black and white candid photos of mothers and children at a homeless center; poetry of lament written in the wee hours at an emergency room; a fresh, twenty-something version of the Apostles' Creed penciled on a coffee-house napkin; a Redemption mosaic created out of glass shards from a local dump; an interactive video pairing "What Wondrous Love" with U2's "Walk On"—its creators a joint team of retirees and high-school tech junkies. Honestly, it might prove difficult to go back to five canned praise songs, church commercials, and a talking head.

At their core, emerging worship services are encounters with God born out of a dual passion for theological rootedness and a deeply transforming connection with a radically deconstructed culture. At best, they are balanced responses to the person and works of God on the one hand and the contexts of their individual, postmodern communities on the other. At worst, emerging worship services are experiences for experience' sake, replete with improvisation but devoid of the theme—the grand narrative of God in Jesus Christ—on which faithful improvisation depends. May what emerges be increasingly more about who it is we worship than about us who were created and called to worship.

A LITURGICAL WORSHIP RESPONSE

Paul Zahl

This may be the most important chapter in this book. It is creative, vivid, courageous, and stirring. While I disagree with some of the practical conclusions reached by Sally Morgenthaler, the way she gets there is gripping, even galvanizing.

The premise of the piece is that American culture has changed dramatically in recent years, September 11 being just a further, toppling expression of the change. Morgenthaler sees Americans as being more in touch with their brokenness now than before: "Surprise!—we are neither masters of our destinies nor masters of ourselves." She sees us as having become more pessimistic and less positivist. If she means that postmodern eclecticism and also real-world viewpoints have challenged otherwise well-established notions of control, she is probably on target. For me, I see the control mode of American self-understanding as still deeply and sinfully entrenched. I wonder if its hold will ever be broken.

In any event, Morgenthaler regards worship styles today as being under a giant searchlight that clarifies sin and substancelessness and narcissism. We need new forms of worship for new realities and also new wounds.

The practical burden laid on us by her idea, however, is considerable. In her changed universe, it is a make-it-up-as-you-go-along-Sunday-to-Sunday world for worship leaders. It makes me glad for Thomas Cranmer's old penitential liturgy! Unlike Morgenthaler, I do not wish every week to be "creating something unprecedented out of the pieces at hand." Better to have something good and true—the sound old prayer book, for example—on which to fall back.

Morgenthaler's chapter makes me tired. Is it not asking a lot to "repackage [existing service orders] in an almost unrecognizable form"?

What she seems not to realize is that planners and leaders always fall back on routine. It is part of human nature. Even classic Pentecostal worship, which trumpets its openness to the Spirit, is formulaic in almost every place that offers it. People who say they wish to make it up as they go along find themselves soon grasping at patterns and formats. So she is "tying burdens on men's backs too heavy to bear" (see Matthew 23:4; Luke 11:46). I know she does not mean to, but that will be the effect.

I also find her call to "particularity," which means adapting all prospective elements in worship to local givens, to be too diminutive. It is too contextualized. Are there not yet some universals at play in life, such as sin, paralysis, absolution, and deliverance? I am not convinced for a second that the drive to particularity will save the big and fair picture of the larger truths we serve, or better, the larger truth in the Person whom we serve.

Morgenthaler's chapter is fascinating. It is a page-turner. It carries reality. Everyone involved in shaping public worship needs to read it. But it prescribes an exhausting regimen of living absolutely in the moment.

A TRADITIONAL WORSHIP RESPONSE

Harold Best

I want to say at the very outset that I struggled hard and maybe failed to craft a useful response to this chapter. It could be that I missed the key, something central, to which I could attach my understanding. If I did, I apologize deeply, and I hope that the other responders will offer correction to both the reading public and me.

Given that every style described in this book rests on the importance of the adjectival (blended, contemporary, charismatic, emerging, liturgical, hymn-based), and in most cases gives less attention than is given to worship as noun, verb, and everything in between, I must ask this question: What is emerging worship emerging from and into? This question differs from asking how worship styles continue to change and even metamorphose. To me, "emerging" implies the appearance of something not yet fully seen from something that may or may not be related to it. This seems to be at odds with the biblical concept of "already realized, thus continuously and variously realizable." In this latter sense, change is based on the twin truths of reformed always reforming and wholeness staying whole as creative change brings ongoing nuance to it.

Nonetheless, Sally Morgenthaler defines emerging worship using statements that all worship leaders using all styles would identify with. Here is a sample: "Emerging worship services strive to engage worshipers primarily with the person and continuing works of God through Jesus Christ. . . . We are transformed through God's activity in and through us, not by what we think we need and certainly not by ruminating our way into better behavior."

So the key to emergence, then, rests in placing the worshiper "inside the ongoing redemptive saga of God" by entering the drama of the stories of the "limited God-followers of the biblical narrative," in order to find and engage with "the strong, connective fibers of shared accounts, worldviews, experiences, and customs." I infer that either worship emerges out of this engagement or it arises out of the enculturated means for seeking the engagement. There is value in this as far as it goes, but I am reminded of two things:

First, I recall Dorothy Sayers's idea that the drama is in the dogma. I keep looking for the full-orbed dogma in the variously dressed drama that Morgenthaler suggests. My sense is that dogma is at least partly lacking because of the emphasis on the narrative and artifactual to the apparent neglect of the conceptual and propositional. But Scripture is certainly more than narrative and truth is more than artifactual. The gospel finds unrivaled fullness in the conceptual/propositional creativity of John, Paul, the writer to the Hebrews and—bless God—in the seeing-ahead-and-longing constructs of the Prophets. Second, I find it difficult to understand how worship emerges at all. Does it not instead continue, having been washed clean by the blood of Christ only to persevere variously and consistently? Here are some thoughts that came to me as I read this chapter.

First, the "radical recontexting" that Morgenthaler suggests, in which concurrence replaces homogeneity, is in a sense less radical than traditional—more a matter of degree than kind—in that liturgical worship has been concurrencing for centuries. But what Morgenthaler suggests is an acceleration and enlargement of these to the point where the recontexting that she suggests risks eisegesis rather than exegesis. That is, much more can be personally or corporately read into a specific worship act than that act is capable of articulating on its own.

Second, I offer this comment on Morgenthaler's concern that the biggest hindrance to the contemporary church is its inability to wake up to "an exponentially diversifying culture." If she is correct about exponential diversification, then nobody could keep up, unless an ecclesiastical Esperanto is artificially created, which of course would speak *to* all cultures without speaking *from* them.

And we have close to an Esperanto in the commercial world. This whole diverse world turns out to be one huge Big Mac, with the postmodern idea of the global family having virtually tuned true diversity down into a cozy echo: Babel in drag. In fact, it could be argued that as diversity exponentializes, there should be more and more different styles of worship and various places for them, with a biblical Pentecost undergirding and nurturing each uniqueness and at peace with the whole.

The 2002 Winter Olympics is a prime example of false diversification in that the overwhelming ethos was Western commercialism and giantism. What few indigenous expressions there were came across more as tokens, even refutations, of the full interior dignity of what it means to be Bantu, Quechua, Romanian, or Tobacco Road American. To experience diversity by dipping into an attribute that mostly closely conforms to ours is simply assimilation modified by a few token accents.

Third, in going over the model, I could not quite locate the central theological handle. I confess to the possibility of being blind to it, and I await further help. I did run across phrases such as "we are depraved," "something is wrong," "reinstating Creator-referenced, God-focused expressions," "to engage worshipers primarily with the person and continuing works of God through Jesus Christ," "placing oneself inside the ongoing redemptive saga of God," and the like. But these are more like brief truisms searching for a theological whole.

Fourth, I could not avoid the overwhelming artifactual ethos in the numerous polymedia scenarios she proposed within the model. I found them less than radical in that they took me, strangely enough, back to the 1960s when virtually every sense, conviction, and passion could be illustrated in gesture, metaphor, sit-in, teach-in, walk-on, and street art. What was missing then seems missing in emerging worship: simplicity, directness, and spareness—and in directly theological terms, a Christocentric, Good News-atonement-repentance-pressing-on model, with the Word as the leading evangel. It is almost as if the imaginatively rich palette of things the worshiper has at continual disposal eventually turns into a vast sensory icon: sacraments about Sacrament and nonverbal homilies about Homily.

So I see the Word diffused, hidden amongst the various expressive media. But please understand: I am nowhere near saying that Morgenthaler has personally lost sight of the truth. Rather, I am asking the question from the other side of the issue: How does the seeker, the un-Christed one, the newly Christed one, the Word-deprived cultural cohort, find the stark, dividing-asunder force of truth in the plethora of symbols and metaphors? There is a lesson in full-fledged liturgical worship, with its multiplicity of languages (gestural, olfactory, visual, tactile, musical, color-and-vestment) ever humbling themselves and pointing to the Word, the homily, the prayers, the responses, the text-driven chant and song, the articles of faith, the creeds, and the rubrics. Hence, in this culture in which experiential narrative has preempted concept and proposition, in which language has become circularly relativized, and in which a musico-visual matrix turns out to be the communal glue, the last thing any worship model should do is to modify the centrality of the Word simply because culture does. All of this being said, I truly commend Morgenthaler for her deep concern for contemporary society, for her research into its many hurts, particularly the one that has come in the face of personal and societal brokenness, and her passion in trying to locate a model that walks alongside and embraces brokenness and disorientation.

Fifth, assuming the validity of the emerging model, this question arises: How would an average, well-trained worship leader be able to come up with the kind of variety from week to week without succumbing to a set of habits that could only be called "liturgically repetitive"? How many ways are there, even with large amounts of money, space, time, and an imagination-laden staff, to continually vary confession and absolution or the Apostles' Creed or the Eucharist? I can certainly see that quarterly, maybe monthly, liturgies could be created that would follow along the lines of emerging worship, but not weekly. In this case, the intervening weeks could set the stage in a variety of traditional Word-and-Sacrament liturgies that would guarantee a more centered approach to symbol, gesture, mime, dance, graffiti, butcher paper, and the like. The only other alternative would be to include artifactual work in a Word-and-Sacrament liturgy. But then we would be back to one of the kinds of tradition that Morgenthaler questions.

Finally, it was difficult for me to frame a response to this chapter in that Morgenthaler seems to find little good in any worship style other than the one she proposes. She leans toward caricature in criticizing all other models and friendly portraiture to defend hers. The result is a confusion of apples/oranges with right/wrong. Whereas apples and oranges make up a good fruit salad, right and wrong are simply incompatible. The current worship scene, to my way of thinking, is more an apples/ oranges affair than a right/wrong one. In spite of my concerns about each system in this ecclesiastical fruit salad, including the one(s) that I may personally prefer, I become apprehensive each time one ventures into right/wrong territory instead of apples/ oranges.

Despite the objections to other worship styles taken by Morgenthaler, God is obviously at work bringing countless people to the birth and countless more from milk to meat in every context imaginable, for it is his name that is at stake, not our style. It is the power of the gospel that is continually at stake as much as it is the province of the Holy Spirit to turn a Quaker silent meeting into holy polyphony or ignite a crackle-dry parish in Anywhere, USA into an unquenchable blaze. That the Spirit does not do more of this may be more directly bound to our lack of ceaseless, pestiferous intercessory prayer for lostness and disorientation than to our having missed out on the right worship style. So, with both professional respect and confessional brotherhood, I wish that Morgenthaler simply had built her own model, defending it front to back and allowing the wind of the Spirit to direct the right people to its use.

A CONTEMPORARY WORSHIP RESPONSE

Joe Horness

I have known Sally Morgenthaler for many years now, and whenever the opportunity has arisen, we have enjoyed great, fun-spirited discussions of what worship really looks like and what we dream the church could really be. Next time I see her, that discussion will pick up right where we left off, and the chapter Sally has written here will certainly become a topic in our next conversation. I am deeply moved and challenged by it on the one hand, while finding it troubling on the other.

I have just experienced a weekend of Good Friday and Easter services at our church, and my heart is overflowing. Our Good Friday service contained old hymns sung to new melodies over powerful video . . . contemporary choruses sung to cello and mandolin . . . a dark drama that cut through our defenses and exposed our brokenness . . . the Word and Communion . . . and time for reflection and prayer. Some of us were broken. Some of us declared that in this broken world, if ever there were a time to fully follow Jesus, this is it. Others understood for the first time the power of the cross to clean our sin-stained hearts and received Christ as Savior and Lord.

Our Easter services were equally powerful, but different altogether. People of all different ages and cultures experienced opening music that spilled over into a stage full of dancers, mostly junior high and high school students, exuberantly celebrating the risen Christ. Later came a drama that took an honest look at the differing perspectives our troubled world might have on Easter today. During the message, mustard seeds were passed in a bowl for each person to hold, personal props that would eventually enter into the theme of the message. And an artist painted on a huge canvas directly behind our pastor while he taught. Not until the final moments of the message did we realize he was painting a magnificent hand of Christ, splashed in red, reaching out to you and to me.

These services were creative, worshipful, Spirit-filled, and powerful. They were contemporary and outreach-oriented, but interactive and full of integrity. And for those with eyes to see, they were deeply influenced by the culture and creativity of those in our emerging generation.

Coming fresh from these services, and knowing similar stories from pastors I know and interact with from around the world, I cannot broadly label contemporary worship as the bland and powerless entity that Sally describes in her chapter.

Sally's discussion of the contemporary church neglects to acknowledge the tremendous strides that many of those churches have taken in the arts, in worship, in discipleship, in community, in relevant teaching, in technology, in reaching out to the poor, in becoming more diverse, in excellence, or most notably, in evangelism. Leaders initiated these changes out of a deep passion to love God and build his kingdom. Lack of knowledge or experience certainly invited some ministries to simply imitate outwardly what they did not understand inwardly, resulting in the ineffective copies that Sally refers to. But many others have moved from stuttering starts to become fully functioning authentic ministries that have a profound impact on their communities and on our world.

Sally continues by painting a cartoonish caricature of contemporary ministry. Using terms like "enforced-happy," "vaudevillian" style, "outfits," and "church logo," she accuses the contemporary church of being "stripped of personal journey" and "devoid of humble descent." Does this happen in the contemporary church? Of course it does. But her viewpoint seems shortsighted to me as I think about the faithful men and women I know who are leading churches around the world. She points her finger at "prototype" ministries and accuses them of ministering to "cultural profiles," not real people, although the entire contemporary church movement grew out of a passion for real people and real friends who desperately needed Jesus.

At churches that took the courageous step to introduce drama and media and drums and dance in the hope of creating transformational moments in the modern church, she levels the charge of uniformity. And Sally describes churches that have led the charge in turning their focus outward—to the lost, to the broken, and to those most in need of the transforming person of God—as bland and shallow, only without the prayer and the worship. Sally seems to forget that those who have struggled to build the contemporary church she portrays were those who pioneered the kind of church in which this emerging generation can now find its voice.

On the other hand, Sally paints an emotionally moving picture of the world we live in. She describes in living color the heart and needs and mind-set of the emerging generation. She passionately pleads for those of us who lead the contemporary church not to grow smugly satisfied, but to continue to lead our churches to reach the emergents. And with this plea I wholeheartedly agree. Her chapter has stirred me to a renewed commitment to understand, to listen, and to learn. My children are growing up in this generation. I have a deeply vested interest in seeing the church of tomorrow be powerfully relevant and meaningful, not just to me, but also to them and their friends. Sally has succeeded in raising my hunger for the church to be a place of mystery, variety, and new ways of experiencing God. If we will listen and be teachable, I believe that the worshipers of the emerging generation have much to teach us. Ultimately, I want to see God as he is making himself known to their generation. I want to know the "wild, untamable miscellany" of God that Sally describes, and I have a lot to learn. And they are the ones who must teach me.

Many contemporary churches are open to change. They got where they are because they were passionate about reaching real people. They were willing to brave opposition, to lose members, to make mistakes, and to try something new. That they might not have stayed right on the cutting edge of reaching this new generation is at least understandable if not acceptable. The fact that some churches expressed their newfound freedom or creativity less authentically or powerfully than others is certainly reality. But as this new generation emerges, what I think it will find in many contemporary churches is a willingness to listen and an openness to change. If you look at contemporary churches of today, you will find that many are taking Sally's challenges to heart. You'll see the fingerprints of the emerging generation already leaving their mark.

For the contemporary church to become all that God continues to want it to be, we have to learn from what the emergents have to say.

1. *They are teaching me to listen.* Listen to them about God, about our world, about their perceptions of people and the church. It is easy to dismiss them because their perceptions or thought processes are different from ours. But as Sally reminds us, their insights are important. Their ideas and views enrich our world. Listen to their music. Read their writers. Try out their ideas. Notice how they create! See the world through their eyes. Let them help us see God through their eyes.

2. *They challenge me to create space for emerging leaders.* At Willow Creek we are constantly trying to identify those who can lead us into the future. If the contemporary church is to stay relevant to the needs of our world as it continues to change, then we need to create space for young leaders to lead. Work at mentoring, partnering with, training, and supporting young artists, leaders, and influencers of the church. Empower them and step back.

3. *They are making me grow younger.* There was a time when the church in which I grew up was probably on the cutting edge. As those who led it grew older, however, the church grew older with them. As culture changed, the church did not. By the time I came along, the church had evolved into something that was no longer relevant to the world in which I was growing up. As those of us who have built contemporary ministries grow older, we are ironically in danger of making the same mistake. At our church we constantly work to add worship choruses that may be outside our normal comfort zone, to watch movies and read books that help us be students of the next generation, to be open to new ways of being creative in our services. The contemporary church must be willing to change the instrumentation on stage, to make room for young singers, actors, and worship leaders. We must strive to be more interactive, to raise the value of community and relationship, to create encounters with God that involve our whole person: passing a spike around during Communion, sticking Post-it notes on the windows, leaving our seats to go somewhere and pray. In short, we must constantly remind ourselves that to stay relevant and meaningful to people we really love and care about, we have to grow younger or our church will just grow old.

4. *They remind me to passionately pursue diversity.* Sally's assertion that "the incapability of the contemporary church to move from homogeneity to diversity is, frankly, its biggest hindrance" deeply concerns me. At Willow Creek we believe with all our hearts that God has called us to build a community of people that fully represents his desire for the kingdom of God. We are passionate about not sitting comfortably in the midst of the homogenous congregation Sally describes. We long for our church to be a place where people of every race and tribe and tongue and nation are welcome, where every person finds value and community, where those who are gifted to lead or teach can do so regardless of race, color, or gender. We are extremely intentional about raising up artists and leaders of diversity. We sing songs that reflect a variety of cultures and styles. If you walked into our service these days, you would find leaders on stage who are Hispanic, African-American, Asian, Caucasian, male, female, deaf, hearing, physically challenged, short, tall, young, and old. This is the community God has called us to be, and we are doing everything we can to make sure that it takes root and grows in our church. While some churches refuse to take these steps, it is not because they are "incapable of change." Theirs is another issue altogether. My prayer is that every church will passionately pursue what it means to be the community God has called it to be. It has to happen, and it can be done!

5. *They help me to continue to celebrate change.* Many of us thought that the change from hymns to choruses was a dramatic one. Having gone through it, we thought that the major changes in the church were behind us for a while. But as Sally points out, this next generation brings musical styles, creative ideas, and personal perspectives all their own. To invite them to the table—to include them in leadership, in influence, and in our futures together—is to invite change. But with it will come new horizons of creativity, new energy, new insights, new directions, new learnings, and most of all, new experiences of God.

The call to embrace the emerging generation in our church is a call to openness and creativity. It is an invitation to use all available means to understand and know our awesome God. We know that the church of the emerging generation, if we will learn from them, will only make our community in Christ a richer and fuller place.

A CHARISMATIC WORSHIP RESPONSE

Don Williams

Sally Morgenthaler writes a bright, intelligent, breezy, jour-nalistic analysis of contemporary, postmodern culture and a failed church. This sets up her case for new worship in the "emerging church." Her polemic is filled with sound-bite insights and acidic critique. She charges that Christian leaders in "entrepreneurial church land" have slept like Rip Van Winkles, only to awaken to a world they fail to recognize. The unchurched Harrys and Marys (of Willow Creek fame) are now worshiping at a New York street shrine. New praise songs sound alike as "distant sequels." Pastors are bored with their Sunday routine while building their services to the sermonic "punch line."

Morgenthaler's context for these bright jabs begins with the apparent parable of worship leader Kirk McPherson. His church life is frantic. His wife drinks heavily undercover. His thirteen-year-old daughter owes him six months rent on her cell phone and is late for her sleepover. His world is falling apart. A friend wants his unchurched neighbor to share a no-Jesus spiritual experience of healing on Sunday. "Nice story, but what would people think? This guy isn't a Christian." As Kirk eats fast-food Sushi served by two Latinos and an elderly Russian, he misses his predictable past. In his marriage pain, he avoids counseling, fearful of a judgmental church. So he rationalizes and stuffs it. Loveless abuse, the emotionally abandoned crowd at Starbucks, and two men in profane conflict surround him. Here is the post-modern world of dislocation, pain, hypocrisy, pluralism, ethnic diversity, abuse—and Kirk seems to be slowly dying in it, concluding, "Better to look good and let people have their illusions. It's the way ministry gets done."

With this setup, Morgenthaler stresses that emerging church worship begins with a clear, deep consciousness of personal and social brokenness. This then leads to what she calls "the gift of realignment." Postmodern worship is not about dark spaces, candles, and icons. Its core is found in Romans 1, the "realignment of the human heart." This will take place through focusing on God as Creator—getting off our needs and feelings and engaging with the "person and the continuing works of God through Jesus Christ." Transformation (the transformation of our brokenness) happens here. Emerging worship begins, not with a needs survey, but with God and our identity and destiny in him. Rather than developing religious consumers, we must develop worshipers who are seeking to act in God's story and ongoing activity.

When we enter the biblical story, God is a person, not just the author of principles about himself. Now we know "by narrative." Realignment is experiential more than mental. It is whole-person and whole-community immersion into the divine life. In the movement toward God, the self is seen clearly. But what forms might this take?

Certainly, emerging worship will be culturally current. This does not only mean PowerPoint, film clips, and situational drama, but also "gathering prayer ... John 1:1–5 recaptured in poetry and set to a video loop of a swirling galaxy." It means an ancient hymn in digital and electronic dress. It means worshipers sketching images on butcher-block paper and the Apostles' Creed with graffiti art.

Rather than hearing a sermon, we move from exhibit to exhibit, like the Stations of the Cross. This radical recontexting of the message may mean that the order of service is concurrent (several things happening at once), using visual displays, taped messages heard on headsets, charts and pointed questions about how a biblical figure felt (her example being Joseph in Egypt forgiving his brothers), and what we would do if we were he. Here proclamation is reduced to speculation, role-playing, or self-help therapy.

Like postmodern art, classic forms of worship need to be deconstructed and reassembled as something "unprecedented." This will display paradox and eclecticism. Corporate confession will be reconfigured, and Communion will "get a dramatic face-lift." Predictability is out. Diversity, tribalism, and "wild, untamable miscellany" are in. Here God will surprise us. (Is this Morgenthaler's hope or experience? She offers no supporting evidence.)

What are we to make of all of this? Morgenthaler's insights hit home. Most of us do live in a world that seems to be coming apart. Churches tend to minister backward (to the last generation) rather than forward. What seems new and innovative is actually dated and passé. Leaders are preoccupied with control issues, which results in hypocrisy. Yet incarnational theology demands that we respond to each cultural shift and dislocation. The end of the modern world (two hundred years of the Enlightenment) is such a dislocation, at least in the academy, the arts, and the media (which drive mass culture). Whether postmodernism is a passing fad or permanent cultural shift remains to be seen. Nevertheless, American society has radically changed. Fifty percent of its children today grow up in single-parent households, with the father basically absent. This has huge consequences for ministry: the need for parenting, family, belonging, authority, community, and dealing with child-abuse issues, addiction, and gang violence.

Morgenthaler's thesis that worship is "realignment" is attractive—especially because she keeps it God-centered. She identifies realignment with Romans 1, Paul's critique of idolatry and its consequences. Unfortunately, she does not develop this further. Romans 1 (and 2) offers Paul's diagnosis of our depravity. But this is simply the setup for the real realignment. As Karl Barth says, the wrath of God, the "no" of God against our sin in Romans 1, is the "next-to-last word." And the next-to-last word is for the sake of the last word, the "yes" of the gospel. Realignment comes first with the atoning work of Christ in Romans 3, the resulting new life in the Spirit in Romans 6–8, finding our place in God's story in Romans 9–11, and the resulting new community in Romans 12–16. Morgenthaler only hints at this, at best.

Her proposals for the deconstruction and reconstruction of worship sound radical. In fact, they were virtually all tried in the late 1960s and early 1970s as mainline churches felt the crush of the counterculture and the new winds of liturgical renewal. (The exception to this, of course, was the absence of our current electronic and digital wizardry.) Most of these experimental services passed away as the culture changed again. Their impermanence was due to shallow theology, a lack of any historic continuity, the difficulty of finding truly creative artists and leaders outside of major cultural centers, and the constant tendency of art toward the bizarre, always pushing boundaries. Means became ends, and what was memorable was not a fresh encounter with God, but the unique ride and excess of a particular Sunday. Morgenthaler's proposals, pulled from their postmodern setting, sound too familiar. And in fact, in past decades experimental worship services died a slow death.

Does Morgenthaler offer us a jolt, a wakeup call, or simply fascination with her critiques, fed into our own sense of dislocation and rebellion? Is she a prophet? She makes no claim here. She offers possibilities and suggestions rather than the thundering word of the Lord.

What about the dilemma of Kirk McPherson, worship leader? Indeed, his world is falling apart. Is his answer to be found in his realignment with Romans 1 and the deconstruction of old forms of worship? Will he find peace savoring a digital presentation of drum loops while meditating on flashes of disconnected images thrown on a screen? Will his answers come as he journeys around a set of stations, challenging him to think through what he would do if he were Joseph in Egypt?

Perhaps. But it is just as arguable that he will find peace by getting off his rat race, entering a great cathedral, and working through a set, ancient liturgy, giving him a strong sense of divine transcendence and grace. Or it is even more arguable that he will find peace by a fresh encounter with the Holy Spirit in free-flowing worship and honest, vital preaching, where the presence of God, manifest in prophetic words and healing prayer, breaks his fears, melts his hypocrisy, and fills his emptiness again with the power of God, wedding him to a loving, transparent community. I think Morgenthaler would agree: There are many tribes among this people called "Christian." As H. Richard Niebuhr showed us a generation ago in *The Social Sources of Denominationalism*, we carry our culture with us. Pluralism is the name of the game.

A BLENDED WORSHIP RESPONSE

Robert Webber

One of the many things I appreciate about Sally Morgen-thaler is her passion for relevance in the postmodern world. Her contribution to this book is no exception. If anything, it is her most finely crafted and well-tuned summary of our digital cultural situation and the need to return to biblically based worship.

Her clarion call to get beyond the need-oriented worship of the contemporary church is most welcome! Her proposal that contemporary worship is "'self-referencing'—focused on human perceptions, needs, feelings, and desires"—and her recognition that emerging worship experience begins in an entirely different place—"not with what people feel their needs to be, but with who God is, who they are, and who they were created to become"—shift the discussion from anthropology to theology. It puts back into focus a proper anthropology: God's revelation about the human condition and the need for forgiveness and reconciliation. The shift from "knowing-by-notion" to "knowing-by-narrative" also thankfully shifts the discussion from propositional theology to a recovery of God's story and how our stories get connected. These shifts provide a good foundation for the realignment called for by Morgenthaler.

In my estimation, this realignment cannot be critiqued, only affirmed and expressed in our worship making.

But it is here, in the worship service that Sally describes, where I have some question. I would like to be a participant in this recontextualized service surrounded by hushed tones, poetry, flashing images, singing with electronic kaleidoscopic, digital background, "drawn" prayer on large butcher-block paper taped to walls, children spray-painting truths of the Apostles' Creed on the walls, sensing God and experiencing God in community. Yes. I would love to be at this service. Once, maybe twice a year. But every Sunday? The burnout rate of the worship creators (yes, creators, not planners) would be excessively high, as would the burnout for the worshipers. Nobody could take this week after week after week.

Why not? It is too much like the world in which we live.

What we need in worship is not more of the culture in which we live. This only continues the failure of contemporary worship. Emerging churches need to avoid cultural captivity and resurrect the countercultural nature of the Christian faith and community.

The ancient church teaches us that the church sustains three relationships to culture all at once: It is part of it; it is an antithesis to it; it is called to transform it. These relationships are always held in tension with culture. And depending on the condition of culture, they change in intensity from place to place and time to time.

Without attempting to provide cultural analysis here, let me simply assert that the face of the church in the future is apt to look *less* like culture, not *more* like it. The shape of the church led by the emerging, younger evangelicals will look more countercultural than the contemporary church. The biblical values of community, relationship, authenticity, radical biblical discipleship, a Christian form of spirituality, the uniqueness of the Christian faith in the face of religious pluralism, the embrace of ethical absolutes—these are most likely to be the most distinguishing features of faith in the emerging church. And because of the new quest for roots, the emerging church will return to a more fully orbed embrace of the biblical narrative. My guess is that worship will become more biblical (Word and Table), simpler (not a show with all the cultural stuff), more authentic (real people doing real things like praying, giving testimony, responding to sermons, being participatory), much smaller (neighborhood churches), and quite eclectic in music and the arts.

We are already seeing the beginnings of this movement. It is more like the early church prior to the conversion of Constantine and the rise of Christendom. It will, of course, bear the marks of the culture in which we live. Probably none of the categories we use today—traditional, contemporary, blended—will work for the emerging church. I know that's what Sally has really said. So why she ended up with a digital show is beyond me. I do not think she is really there. But I will find out the next time I see her. Thanks, Sally, for pushing the envelope.

Chapter 6: Emerging Worship Notes

Proposal: Sally Morgenthaler

[1]From a 2002 telephone poll of 500 Internet users. Poll source: Pew Internet and American Life Project, Washington, DC. www.pewinternet.org

[2]William H. Frey, "Census 2000," *American Demographics*, 1 June 2001.

[3]From interview with author.

[4]William Langewiesche, "American Ground: Unbuilding the World Trade Center: Part Two: The Rush to Recover," *The Atlantic Monthly* (September 2002), 47Z.

[5]*A Statistical Report on the State of Religion in America: Index of Spiritual Indicators* (Nashville: W Publishing, 1996), 39.

CONCLUSION

Paul A. Basden

Insights into the mystery and majesty of worship, like the ones found in the preceding pages, make me realize again the profound truth uttered by the apostle Paul:

Oh, the depth of the riches of the wisdom and knowledge of God!

How unsearchable his judgments, and his paths beyond tracing out!

"Who has known the mind of the Lord? Or who has been his counselor?"

"Who has ever given to God, that God should repay him?"

For from him and through him and to him are all things.

To him be the glory forever! Amen (Romans 11:33–36).

The truth that grasps me, that will not release me, is this: God is past finding out, more powerful and holy and gracious than we can imagine, beyond our highest thoughts, deeper than our most intense emotions. Yet he calls us to worship him. Such is the challenge before us: We humans—mortal, flawed, fallen creatures that we are—offer our worship to God—the eternal, perfect, all-wise Creator and Lord. No wonder we approach worship a little differently from one another! Given our paltry perspectives, how could it be otherwise? When it comes to understanding how to worship God, the limiting and leveling factor facing every one of us is this: "Now we see but a poor reflection as in a mirror; then we shall see face to face. Now I know in part; then I shall know fully, even as I am fully known" (1 Corinthians 13:12).

Until we see face to face, our worship will always be partial. Until we know fully as we are fully known, our worship will always be incomplete. We may intend to worship God to the best of our ability as long as we have life on this earth, but we might as well embrace the fact that our approaches to this awesome task will differ. Hence there are several views of worship. We have highlighted six in this book.

Each of these views reveals vital truths about corporate Christian worship, and each raises critical questions about style and substance. Let us consider them one at a time.

FORMAL-LITURGICAL WORSHIP

Paul Zahl reminds us that worship should be vertical, biblical, and Godward. No element of worship should creep into a service without having to pass this one-question test: "Does it accurately reflect Bible truth about God, Christ, and humans?" But Zahl invites debate by equating "Bible-based verticality" with the formal-liturgical approach. When he suggests that services should be dignified, formal, and predictable, does that logically follow from his commitment to biblical, God-oriented worship? Or does he merely prefer the Anglican style because it is his heritage or it suits him best? While several Christian traditions historically have advocated and defended this approach as the biblical way to worship, we are living through a time when many Christians are finding bondage, not freedom, in liturgical forms. When they attend a formal-liturgical service and rise and sit and genuflect and say the creed, they sense that they are "strangers in a strange land." They may find the otherness of God in such a service, but they feel too out-of-place to sense his concern.

What is the future of formal-liturgical worship? Don Williams answers that its user-unfriendly bias means that its audience is graying and shrinking. Robert Webber counters that its emphasis on divine transcendence means that it is reaching the younger generation, who are desperately seeking more than a sound bite when it comes to God. As for me, I think formal-liturgical worship will have to adapt stylistically—not theologically—to our changing culture, or it may become nothing more than a historical relic.

TRADITIONAL HYMN-BASED WORSHIP

Harold Best claims that "we were created worshiping" and that whether we worship the one true God or any of a hundred false gods, we cannot not worship. That insight alone explains the appeal of contemporary seeker services, the passion of charismatic services, and the dignity of more formal approaches. Best then highlights an approach to worship that centers on the hymn, or "texted song," where biblical truth is expressed in musical form. He rightly values the theological richness of hymnody and disparages the paucity of depth in much contemporary worship music. His warnings should be heard and heeded by worshipers of every stripe.

But is hymnody a litmus test for wholesome worship? Can meaningful worship occur without hymns? Joe Horness and Don Williams are right to ask if eighteenth- and nineteenth-century poetry-in-song is automatically the best musical vehicle for carrying twenty-first-century Christians into the presence of God in worship. Best commends newer hymns by modern hymn writers, but he apparently has little use for praise choruses. I hope he remains open to the Holy Spirit's surprises. I think we are witnessing the gradual merger of contemporary choruses and modern hymns. If that process continues, new choruses and new hymns will eventually become virtually indistinguishable.

CONTEMPORARY WORSHIP

With contemporary worship seemingly taking over in church after church, Joe Horness cuts through the heated debate to explain its appeal and popularity: It speaks in a familiar tongue. It uses "the language of this generation to lead people into authentic expressions of worship and a genuine experience of the presence of God." Why should worship be in the language of the common people? The New Testament was originally written in *koine* (common) Greek. It tells the story of Jesus, who came to earth in the form of a common Jewish man. Nonetheless, contemporary worship leaders must avoid the trap of planning their services or gauging their effectiveness solely by pragmatic or popular standards.

Because contemporary worship is mostly defined by contemporary music, we should listen carefully to Paul Zahl's caution that such music easily passes from intimate feelings toward God to intimate feelings that have nothing to do with God—and may have a lot to do with our sinful nature. And Robert Webber is on target when he reveals that the performance side of contemporary worship tends to move us into the realm of works and out of the realm of grace. Excellence can go by another name—perfectionism—that denies grace altogether. Let contemporary church leaders beware: Performance-driven worship leads to a treadmill mentality where we think God rewards us for our hard work. And that means the death of worship in Spirit and in truth.

CHARISMATIC WORSHIP

Don Williams points out that worship without the Spirit is dead. The goal of charismatic worship is for "worshipers to experience some measure of the full life of the triune God, including the Holy Spirit." His reminder that "every revival births new music" places the emergence of new praise choruses in the "surprising works of God" category. It also breathes new hope into the future of worship songs.

The pervasive problem of charismatic worship, however, seems to be charismatic theology. It can all too easily "pole-vault over Calvary on the way to Pentecost" (Zahl) and ignore both the problem of and the solution to sin. The necessary conjoining of Spirit and Word is often ignored, resulting in too much "God told me to do this or that" (Best). Sally Morgenthaler's quip that "uninterpreted weird language is a problem" may make us smile, yet it reminds us that sign-oriented worship still has to battle a built-in bias to celebrate the Spirit's visible outward manifestations over the Spirit's quiet inner working. Charismatic worship will be more faithful to Scripture if it relinquishes control of the outcomes in worship, allows the Spirit to "blow wherever it pleases" (John 3:8), and rejoices in the Spirit's role as the Counselor who testifies about and points to Jesus—especially his victory through suffering.

BLENDED WORSHIP

Robert Webber does the church a true service when he reminds us that "worship is both divine and human." It is divine in that God's grace stands behind worship, motivates worship, and empowers worship. In that sense, worship is all about God. Yet it is also human in that we, the worshipers, must recognize his worthiness and give expression to that recognition in ways that are pleasing to him. There can be no worship that is solely God-centered as long as we humans are doing the worshiping.

But this is not the only paradox Webber espouses. He also commends worship that exists in tension—what he calls a synthesis of the liturgical and contemporary worship renewal movements of the twentieth century. What he describes (and what I have experienced in services he has designed and led) is "blended" only in the broadest sense of the word. If percentages were used, these services are twenty-five percent contemporary and seventy-five percent liturgical. The result? A doxological building that bears the distinct design of liturgical worship (lots of order and formality), with a few window treatments purchased at a nearby contemporary worship store (a couple of praise choruses). Blended worship that fully embraces both formal-liturgical and charismatic styles—in a one-hundred percent/one-hundred percent fashion—may be found in the recently formed Charismatic Episcopal Church, which unashamedly celebrates both Anglican liturgy and charismatic gifts. But I do not think Webber intends to go that far in his blend. If not, can his approach escape the fate of so many formal-liturgical churches—namely irrelevance, decline, and death?

EMERGING WORSHIP

Sally Morgenthaler uncovers the cultural manifestations of human sinfulness, especially the impact on those who have grown up in a post-Christendom, postmodern world. Her passion to reach out to this alienated generation calls all churches and leaders to realize that Christianity is one generation away from extinction. The question her chapter evokes is this: Does her approach to worship truly lead people to "engage . . . with the person and the continuing works of God through Jesus Christ"?

While Morgenthaler's theology is solid, her doxological proposals are more "iffy." Can, or should, a church employ every new cultural or artistic expression as a vehicle of worship? If so, does that not "prescribe an exhausting regimen of living absolutely in the moment" (Zahl)? More important, is there not a high probability that the clarity of the Word will get lost in the shuffle of moving "from exhibit to exhibit" (Williams)? Certainly that would not be Morgenthaler's goal—but it could become the result. Emerging worship, porous as it is toward postmodern culture, will risk its effectiveness if it uncritically adopts current art forms as vehicles of God's voice but fails to elevate the preached Word of God above them all.

"YES, BUT ..."

In reading these chapters, my mantra became "yes, but ..." (also known as "almost thou persuadest me"). I always found much that I agreed with, yet I sensed that only a portion of the truth came to light. My conclusion? The human worship of God is too profound to be captured in one particular approach. The reasons are many and have received lively discussion in the chapters and responses. These include:

Past versus Present—Which is more important: "The faith that was once for all entrusted to the saints" (Jude 3) or "He is not the God of the dead but of the living" (Matthew 22:32)? We value the past because so much revealed truth has been transmitted over so many years from previous generations to our own. Indeed, awareness of this is why Paul wrote, "For what I received I passed on to you" (1 Corinthians 15:3). Tradition is clearly important! But even as we stand on past truth, we also look for God to do new things in the present. He clearly states, "Forget the former things; do not dwell on the past. See, I am doing a new thing!" (Isaiah 43:18–19) Balancing the known value of the past with the promising value of the present is a major challenge for today's churches.

Bible versus Culture—Is there a way to exegete both Bible and culture so that worship is the beneficiary? Studying the Bible leads to certain conclusions about worship, such as the priority of prayer and praise and preaching. But Scripture never suggests specifically how we should do those things; we have freedom in the Spirit to decide the form of our doxology. Studying culture can provide insights into the forms that best communicate to those who seek to worship our God and understand our message. So here we have another paradox to explore.

Permitted versus Forbidden—Since the Bible does not regulate many, perhaps most, of the forms of worship, how do we know what is permitted and what is forbidden? As Jesus-followers we want the written Word of God to guide us in matters of faith and practice, and that includes worship. If we were under the old covenant, we would turn to the Pentateuch and find our outline for corporate worship there. But as children of the new covenant we must find our direction in the words of Jesus and the apostles—and they are strangely quiet on the details of worship. Wisdom suggests that we permit in worship anything that connects people to God in a vital way and that we forbid only what tarnishes God's reputation or violates Christ's love or glorifies human egos. This cannot be easily codified, but requires discernment and sensitivity to the Holy Spirit.

The answers to these questions will inform, probably even determine, one's worship.

THE FUTURE

The doxological spectrum is blessedly broad, with Christ-followers offering their multiform worship in a heavenly variety of types and styles. Thankfully, the six views offered in this volume point to the full-bodied richness of united worship that we will offer to the Lord on that final day. Then we shall gladly join the chorus of "every creature in heaven and on earth and under the earth and on the sea, and all that is in them," and sing with one voice and one heart:

"To him who sits on the throne and to the Lamb

be praise and honor and glory and power, for ever and ever!" (Revelation 5:13)

Amen. [Maranatha!] Come, Lord Jesus. (Revelation 22:20)

RECOMMENDED READING

BY CONTRIBUTORS

Paul F. M. Zahl

The Collects of Thomas Cranmer, co-editor. Grand Rapids: Eerdmans, 1998.

Harold M. Best

Music through the Eyes of Faith. New York: HarperCollins, 1993.

Unceasing Worship: Biblical Perspectives on Worship and the Arts. Downers Grove, IL: InterVarsity Press, 2003.

Don Williams

Bob Dylan, The Man, The Music, The Message. Grand Rapids: Revell, 1985.

The Psalms, 2 vols., The Communicator's Commentary. Nashville: Word, 1986, 1989.

Signs, Wonders, and the Kingdom of God. Ann Arbor: Servant, 1988.

Robert Webber

Blended Worship: Achieving Substance and Relevance in Worship. Peabody, MA: Hendrickson, 1994.

The Complete Library of Christian Worship, ed. Peabody, MA: Hendrickson, 1997.

> *The Biblical Foundations of Christian Worship*
> *Twenty Centuries of Christian Worship*
> *The Renewal of Sunday Worship*

Music and the Arts in Worship, Book 1
Music and the Arts in Worship, Book 2
The Services of the Christian Year
The Sacred Actions of Worship
The Ministries of Christian Worship

Liturgical Evangelism. New York: Morehouse, 1992.
Planning Blended Worship. Nashville: Abingdon, 1998.
Worship Is a Verb, 2d ed. Peabody, MA: Hendrickson, 1996.
Worship Old and New, rev. ed. Grand Rapids: Zondervan, 1994.

Sally Morgenthaler

Worship Evangelism: Inviting Unbelievers into the Presence of God, rev. ed. Grand Rapids: Zondervan, 1999.

Paul A. Basden

The Worship Maze: Finding a Style to fit Your Church. Downers Grove, IL: InterVarsity Press, 1999.

BY WORSHIP APPROACH

Formal-Liturgical

Dom Gregory Dix. *The Shape of the Liturgy.* New York: Continuum, 2000.
Robert G. Rayburn. *O Come, Let Us Worship.* Grand Rapids: Baker, 1980.
Frank Senn. *Christian Liturgy.* Minneapolis: Augsburg, 1997.
James F. White. *Introduction to Christian Worship,* 3d ed. Nashville: Abingdon, 2001.

Traditional Hymn-Based

Frank Segler. *Christian Worship: Its Theology and Practice.* Nashville: Broadman, 1967.

Contemporary Worship-Driven

John M. Frame. *Contemporary Worship Music: A Biblical Defense.* Phillipsburg, NJ: Presbyterian & Reformed, 1997.

Charismatic

LaMar Boschman. *A Heart of Worship*. Orlando, FL: Strang, 1994.

Jack Hayford. *Worship His Majesty*. Glendale Heights, CA: Gospel Light, 2000.

Matt Redman. *The Unquenchable Worshipper: Coming Back to the Heart of Worship*. Glendale Heights, CA: Gospel Light, 2001.

Other Books That Compare and Contrast Various Views of Worship

D. A. Carson, ed. *Worship by the Book*. Grand Rapids: Zondervan, 2002.

Barry Liesch. *People in the Presence of God: Models and Directions for Worship*. Grand Rapids: Zondervan, 1988.

Elmer Towns. *Putting an End to Worship Wars*. Nashville: Broadman & Holman, 1997.

ABOUT THE CONTRIBUTORS

Paul F. M. Zahl is dean of Cathedral Church of the Advent (Episcopal) in Birmingham, Alabama. His 1994 doctorate in systematic theology is from the University of Tübingen in Germany. He combines parish ministry with theological thinking. He has written seven books, including *The Protestant Face of Anglicanism* (Eerdmans, 1997) and *A Short Systematic Theology* (Eerdmans, 2000). He is a member of the Inter-Anglican Theology and Doctrine Commission. He and his wife, Mary, are the parents of three sons.

Harold M. Best is emeritus dean/professor of music of the Wheaton College Conservatory of Music, where he was dean from 1970 to 1997. He holds degrees from Nyack College, Claremont Graduate School, and Union Theological Seminary and has taught at Nyack College and Southern Baptist Theological Seminary. He is the author of *Music through the Eyes of Faith* (HarperSanFrancisco, 1993) and *Unceasing Worship* (InterVarsity, 2003) and composer of several published choral and organ works. He composes in a wide range of media and styles. He is active at the national level in matters of accreditation and is the author of many articles in the areas of curricular philosophy and cultural/multicultural contexts. He was vice president of the National Association of Schools of Music from 1991 to 1994 and president from 1994 to 1997.

Joe Horness has been on the staff of Willow Creek Community Church in South Barrington, Illinois, since 1981 and worship director for the past eight years. He leads worship weekly for the 6000 people who attend the two midweek services, and he leads and trains the other worship leaders on the staff. He has traveled with artists such as Darlene Zschech, Ron Kenoly,

Abraham Leborial, and Justo Almario and has written and recorded many well-known worship choruses, including "Everything I Am," "Awesome, Amazing," and "Still I Will Worship You." He and his wife, Becky, have two daughters, Torri and Abby.

Don Williams holds degrees from Princeton University, Princeton Theological Seminary, and Columbia University. He served as minister to students at the Hollywood Presbyterian Church and was intimately involved in the Jesus Movement in the late 1960s. He was the pastor of the Mount Soledad Presbyterian Church and founding pastor of the Coast Vineyard Christian Fellowship and has taught at Claremont McKenna College and Fuller Theological Seminary. He is the author of eleven books, including a two-volume commentary on the Psalms in the Word Communicator's Commentary series (1986); *Bob Dylan: The Man, the Music, the Message* (Revell, 1985); and *Signs and Wonders in the Kingdom of God* (Servant, 1989). Don is married to Kathryn Anne Williams and lives in La Jolla, California.

Robert Webber is the William R. and Geraldyn B. Myers Professor of Ministry at Northern Seminary in Lombard, Illinois, and president of the Institute of Worship Studies. He holds degrees from Reformed Episcopal Seminary, Covenant Theological Seminary, and Concordia Theological Seminary. For thirty-two years he was on the faculty at Wheaton College. Webber has written or edited more than forty books on worship, including the eight-volume work *The Complete Library of Christian Worship* (Nelson, 1994). His most recent books include *Ancient-Future Faith* (Baker, 1999), *Journey to Jesus* (Abingdon, 2001), *The Younger Evangelicals* (Baker, 2002), and *Ancient-Future Evangelism* (Baker, 2003).

Sally Morgenthaler is the founder of Sacramentis.com ("Reimagining Worship for a New Millennium") and president of *Digital Glass Videos: Meditative Mosaics for an Emerging Culture.* As a photographer, musician, and worship designer, Morgenthaler cut her teeth on missional worship ministry in the 1980s and 1990s. She is now adjunct professor of worship at both Denver Seminary and Covenant Bible College. She is the author of

Worship Evangelism: Inviting Unbelievers into the Presence of God (Zondervan, 1999). She also writes the worship and popular culture columns for *Worship Leader* and *Rev Magazines* as well as Group Publishing's *PreachingPlus*. Ms. Morgenthaler lives in her native state of Colorado close to her two children, Peder and Anna Claire.

Paul Basden has served as pastor of churches in Alabama and Texas. For a number of years he was pastor of Brookwood Baptist Church in Birmingham, where he was also adjunct professor of divinity at Beeson Divinity School, Samford University. Currently he is co-senior pastor of Preston Trail Community Church in Frisco, Texas. He is author of *The Worship Maze* (InterVarsity Press, 1999), editor of and contributor to *Has Our Theology Changed?* (Broadman, 1990), and co-editor of *The People of God* (Broadman, 1994). He holds degrees from Baylor University and Southwestern Baptist Theological Seminary (M.Div., Ph.D.). He and his wife, Denise, have two daughters, Kari and Kristen.

Paul E. Engle is associate publisher for editorial development and an executive editor at Zondervan. He graduated from Houghton College before receiving his M.Div. from Wheaton Graduate School and D.Min. from Westminster Theological Seminary, Philadelphia. His background includes twenty-two years serving as a pastor and adjunct seminary teacher. He is the author of eight books, including *Baker's Wedding Handbook, Baker's Funeral Handbook,* and *Baker's Worship Handbook.*

DISCUSSION AND REFLECTION QUESTIONS

CHAPTER 1: FORMAL-LITURGICAL WORSHIP

1. What attributes of God do you think are experienced in a formal-liturgical service?
2. How do you see Holy Communion—more as memorial or as magic? Does Paul Zahl's discussion help you understand this mystery better? How?
3. Zahl says, "For formal-liturgical worship, Western music will continue to be the central source and feeding." Do you agree or disagree? Why?
4. Zahl identifies and then responds to three common objections to this view of worship. Do his answers satisfy you? Why or why not?

CHAPTER 2: TRADITIONAL HYMN-BASED WORSHIP

1. Harold Best's analogy for worship is "continuous outpouring." How does this image shed light on our creation in the image of God?
2. Name two of your favorite hymns. Why do you like them so much? What biblical truth does each one teach?
3. Do you ever use a hymnal as a devotional tool? If not, why not start with the two hymns you named above and meditate on them this week?
4. Does looking down at a hymnal ever hinder your worship? What are some arguments for and against projecting the words of hymns on a screen in the sanctuary?

CHAPTER 3: CONTEMPORARY
MUSIC-DRIVEN WORSHIP

1. What is the difference between "living worship" and "dead worship"?
2. Name two of your favorite praise choruses. Why do you like them so much? What biblical truth does each one teach?
3. Do you think contemporary music-driven worship is too much like charismatic worship? Or not enough? Explain.
4. What would you tell someone who is concerned that contemporary music-driven worship stay current and contemporary without petrifying into dull routine?

CHAPTER 4: CHARISMATIC WORSHIP

1. What has charismatic worship discovered that other worship forms need?
2. What is there about charismatic worship that attracts you? What deters you?
3. Don Williams identifies and discusses three criticisms of charismatic worship. Do his responses satisfy you?
4. How is the Holy Spirit active in the worship services you participate in weekly?

CHAPTER 5: BLENDED WORSHIP

1. What do you appreciate most about liturgical worship? What do you appreciate most about contemporary worship?
2. What are some of the challenges in embracing both in one service?
3. What are the values of celebrating the Lord's Supper (Communion or Eucharist) weekly? Are there any drawbacks to weekly celebration? Why do you think many churches do not celebrate it weekly?
4. If true worship is Trinitarian, what roles do the Father, Son, and Spirit play at your church when you gather to worship?

CHAPTER 6: EMERGING WORSHIP

1. Do you have a close relative or friend who is under thirty? What would he or she think about this chapter? (If you are under thirty, what do *you* think of it?) Is it an accurate and fair reflection of what is happening in your locale?
2. What are the differences between "religious consumers" and "developing worshipers"?
3. Look at Sally Morgenthaler's worship proposals in this chapter. As you envision yourself worshiping God in these venues, does it seem natural or forced? Why?
4. What can you learn from emerging worship leaders about the world? About the church? About God? Is there anything in this chapter that could be applied in your church? How might people respond?

INDEX OF NAMES

SCRIPTURE INDEX

We want to hear from you. Please send your comments about this
book to us in care of zreview@zondervan.com. Thank you.

GRAND RAPIDS, MICHIGAN 49530 USA

WWW.ZONDERVAN.COM